STAND AND DELIVER

A DESIGN FOR SUCCESSFUL GOVERNMENT

STAND AND DELIVER

A DESIGN FOR SUCCESSFUL GOVERNMENT

Ed Straw

Treaty for Government

Published by Treaty for Government

www.treatyforgovernment.org

A CIP catalogue record for this book is available from the British Library.

ISBN 978-0-9929476-0-6

Book design and layout by Clare Brayshaw

Cover design by Tim Albin

Prepared and printed by:

York Publishing Services Ltd
64 Hallfield Road
Layerthorpe
York YO31 7ZQ

Tel: 01904 431213

Website: www.yps-publishing.co.uk

Ed Straw was born in 1949 and educated at Manchester University, Manchester Business School, Harvard Business School and Oxford University. He has seen government from every angle: as a citizen and consumer, adviser to several government ministers, chair of Demos and Relate, and a specialist on government task forces. He was a consultant on Thatcher's public sector reforms and then New Labour's, a policy moderniser during Neil Kinnock's leadership of the Labour Party, and he designed the organisational blueprint for the party under John Smith and Tony Blair.

He was also a global and UK board director for PwC, and his work has taken him to countries and governments around the world. An early training in civil engineering taught him structured analysis, and perhaps most importantly for this book, how to design things so they don't fall down.

Contents

PART 2 – WHY GOVERNMENTS FAIL

PART 3 – THE DESIGN FOR SUCCESSFUL GOVERNMENT

1

Context

It was snowing in London. The dinner to raise funds for playing fields had ended, and it had been a long day. Usually I would have walked into Bank station and be home thirty-five minutes later.

My feet dragged. The Central Line, which carries 500,000 people a day, was closed. Some weeks before, a train had derailed in a tunnel after its engine fell off (no one knew why), injuring thirty-two passengers. My route home that night was overground to Chingford where I came out of the station at 11 p.m., and with no buses operating or taxis for hire, I walked for an hour through the beautiful, snow-covered Epping Forest.

Three months after closing, the line fully reopened.

Being a problem-solver by occupation and inclination, my frustrated mind turned to this: how on earth could one of the world's most advanced cities manage to disrupt its essential transport infrastructure, the lives of so many, and its economic activity so foolishly, and with such little interest from those in power? Surely keeping the engine attached to the train is a key task for rail operators. Who was responsible, first for trains with detachable engines, and second for sorting them out when they went wrong? And where was the sense of urgency? To whom did this matter?

The answers were fuzzy. Responsibility for London Underground at that time – 2003 – lay with the Department for Transport, which is of course run by civil servants, who value the 'clever generalist' and the ability to 'master a brief'. Because they are clever in an academic sense, these generalists believe they are capable of almost any of the hundreds of diverse tasks found in every government. But no one there had any operational experience of commuter railways, or of running a large organisation like London Underground, or of attaching engines to trains. Neither had the ministers, who were unable to interrogate the rail management and challenge its decisions. In terms of public pressure, the chain of accountability was as strong as a cardboard bicycle lock. It wound its way from us, the users and voters, through to the national government and the election of a political party every four or five years, through its many priorities, on into a minister of the day with his or her agenda, onward to the civil servants and thence to London Underground. In other words, the next time the government might feel some heat over this issue was two years hence at the general election, by which time it would have been put to bed and politically forgotten. In effect, there was almost zero accountability of London Underground to the public.

In many modern countries, the metro is the responsibility of the city government run by executive mayors. These are politicians who, rather than having to work through unelected officials (who control most of what happens and are immune from public pressure), are elected to get things done — that is, to act in an executive capacity. The electors then know who to hold responsible. In local governments, non-functioning train lines become top priority very quickly. In national governments local issues are way down the pecking order.

When the Central Line was closed, London had recently elected its first executive mayor, Ken Livingstone. Here was another piece of the governmental jigsaw. Margaret Thatcher had abolished the Greater London Council in 1986. As it was expensive, grossly inefficient and irreformable — the culture lay thick in the walls — she was right to get rid of it. (During my brief time working there, we were well paid but had so little to do that some alleviated the boredom with afternoon trips to the cinema.) The problem was not that it was abolished, but that out of vindictiveness and revenge, Thatcher did not replace it with anything. (The UK system allows so much power to be exercised by the prime minister that she had become like an absolute monarch.) No city can function properly without sound local government, but that was London's fate until finally a new government did the right thing — in 2000 the Greater London Assembly came into existence, including its operational arm, Transport for London.

However, the government of Tony Blair — another of the 'absolute monarch' tendency — prevented the transfer of control of London Underground to the GLA until 2003, after itself signing controversial, flawed and ultimately failed private finance initiatives for track maintenance. Why they stopped the transfer was as much to do with political and personal jealousy as contracts – the new mayor had stood for office as an independent against the wishes of his party's hierarchy. Even worse, he was popular and competent. Once he got hold of the Underground it started to be managed more for its passengers than for the rail union's officials and drivers. (Much of my commuting life had been spent at Leytonstone station where the line divides, waiting for an Epping train as a disproportionate number were sent in the other direction to Hainault. I always presumed that the drivers lived that way; only recently did I discover that the rail union's boss, Bob Crow, was based in Hainault. Was it he I should have been thanking for consuming so much of my life at Leytonstone station?)

As an executive mayor, with both the power and the responsibility to appoint his civil servants, he brought in hardened and experienced metro managers from New York. The service improved as the executive mayor delivered what he had been elected to do. It still has a long way to go. If the government system around it is further developed – developments we will identify in this book – then it will get there. Otherwise it won't.

Totting this all up, the underlying reasons that led to the engine dropping off were: an unaccountable London Underground; civil servants without the experience or idea of how to run a large metro service, nor interest, nor organisational motivation; no feedback or monitoring of results by Parliament; prime ministers with too much power, and with psychological flaws; and no executive mayor in control. Two political parties, three prime ministers, five governments and a herd of transport ministers had between them created, or allowed the conditions for, something off the dumb scale. And none of them meant to.

There was no single cause, no headline howler. It was the system – the System of government to, in this case, run the trains – that was at fault. Contrary to what many in power would have us believe – that the system we have is essentially the only one possible, that foreigners may do things in other ways but they wouldn't work here (why?), that you mess with our age-old democracy at your peril (how large is their vested interest?), or whatever other rationale for feet-dragging is trotted out – there are all manner of ways to run governments and public services. The UK happens to have one way. The government system for running the Underground was changed. It now looks more like every other modern city's. Don't say it can't be done – it can; but not by using the thought processes usually employed by those within these government systems. A different perspective and discipline is needed across the board.

From Failure to Success

The chances are that sometimes, if not always, you are frustrated with the standard of government we endure. As weird decisions emerge from behind the tinted glass, you too might wonder why on earth we end up with so much semi-competence. Is good government just impossible? Is excellence a foolish dream? Are we the victims of vested interests preserving the status quo and thus the roles and egos of the current participants? These interests have come to dominate and skew, be they Wall Street, oligarchs, corporate boardrooms, Civil Services, legal professions, party political establishments, or news media. Soft corruption has become normalised both through the informal institutionalisation of these influences and through the job, pay, and pension protection of those in government.

Government really doesn't have to be this bad. We don't have to be overtaxed, underserved, annoyed by semi-competence, spun into resignation, and excluded from power. Informed and aware as never before, some are no longer willing to accept crap service, opaque decision-making, and this rather shoddy mixture of vested interests found in every government. Some people's standards are higher than those their governments give them.

This book is about a design for successful government, called a Treaty for Government. A treaty is a formally concluded and ratified agreement between countries or groups, usually covering peace, an alliance, commerce, or other relations. In the context of this book, it is an agreement between the people – us – and government. My motivation for thinking about the Treaty came from a combination of personal frustration and a belief in the equality of people, and my organisational nose which can tell that our system is crumbling. Sooner or later things this bad go bang. And when governments go bang, there is a lot of suffering all round. Similar conditions can be seen around us to those anthropologist Joseph Tainter finds as causes for the collapse of complex societies in past ages – more and more cost being absorbed by the complexities of government bureaucracy, the banking system, agricultural subsidies, and/ or construction booms: 'When the marginal cost of investment becomes noticeably too high, various segments increase passive or active resistance, or overtly attempt to break away.'[1] The list of today's segments is long – from the Scottish National Party and UKIP to Occupy and simply not voting.

The Treaty seeks to redistribute power and establish essential disciplines via tamper-proof rules, including rigorous feedback on every arm of government and all of its policies and decisions; a 'Resulture' for government by results rather than by procedure and spin; a consequent abandonment programme of redundant or broken legislation, regulation and policy; rigorous vetting of policy, both to get better decisions and to prevent preferential lobbying by the rich and powerful; a revitalised and energised House of Lords with authority and a positive job at last; the Civil Service split in two with the traditional arm sticking to the apolitical 'Northcote–Trevelyan' role it can perform and the 'new Civil Service' run by a new breed of executive ministers and staff who know how to do the necessary jobs; effective supervision and regulation of public sector organisations and of companies delivering for the public; and a new set of duties for all working in the public sector, including one of straight-talking.

The Treaty contains a fairness and intergenerational deal to establish fair pensions for everyone, fair taxation, fair welfare, and fair terms and conditions, and to constrain the transfer of costs to future generations for pensions, debt, and climate chaos. A Congress for the Future would be established. Corporate behaviour would be redirected through company law changes. The Treaty would re-establish real local government – very different from what we experience today; introduce the right to referendum; end our bipolar political party disorder and introduce proper competitive democracy between the parties; and level the funding playing field by limiting donations and providing base state funding.

---

1   Joseph A. Tainter, *The Collapse of Complex Societies* (Cambridge University Press, 1998)

Who am I to try to come up with such a treaty? Firstly, I'm not a politician, or civil servant, or lord. My background is thirty-five years of experience of organising to perform –whether in the public, private, or third sectors – from voluntary bodies with no paid staff, to global corporates with turnovers measured in billions and staff numbers in the tens of thousands. My formal education was at Manchester University, Harvard Business School, and Oxford University, alongside countless programmes with specialist trainers and academics – from stress management to creativity, from project management to short-interval scheduling, from the Hoffman process to design. My early life in civil engineering taught me structured analysis, and perhaps most importantly for this book, how to design things so they don't fall down. I've learnt by doing, by teaching, and by making mistakes. Learning is in my veins and I hope never to stop – after all, surely the purpose of life is to learn.

I've seen government from every angle. First, like everybody else I experienced and judged governments as a consumer and citizen. Then as trustee and chair of the relationship agency Relate, with government as a major funder and with the coincident objective to reduce family breakdown. As a founder of a government-established family institute. As a think-tank author developing new policies, from criminal justice to public engagement. As chair and trustee of Demos. As an adviser to several government ministers. As a specialist on government task forces. As a consultant advising on and implementing first Thatcher's public sector reforms, then New Labour's. As a policy and organisational 'moderniser' during Neil Kinnock's leadership of the Labour Party. As the designer of the organisational blueprint for the party under John Smith and Tony Blair. As European head of entertainment and media consulting where government's role in regulation came to the fore and where industrial policy or its absence could be observed. Working with company boards, not least to remove their collective cataracts obscuring their futures. As a global and UK board director acutely aware of the impact of governments on our business in the UK, US and EU. As a member of compensation committees seeking to rein in executive pay (and yes, they are universally overpaid). As an overseer of a merger and the design of a global firm. I knew over half of the Cabinet for more than a decade. And I have a brother who had four big governmental roles.

For some curious reason people assume that you must be party to your close relative's thinking and decisions, and that you share responsibility for their acts. Periodically I would be attacked at a meeting for no apparent reason. Only later did a psychologist explain that what they were really attacking was some recent decision or statement made by my brother. No need to take it personally – they just wanted to lash out. Him not being to hand, I was the next best thing.

In terms of knowing his mind, no top politician – especially one who survived in Cabinet for thirteen years – says any more to anyone than is absolutely necessary. Every word can be a hostage to fortune. Phone calls were clipped and formal. Both of us had to maintain firewalls as conflicts of interest could be levied against us. My knowledge of his specific actions was strictly limited. He did not read this book before publication and may disagree with every word; but as a dedicated observer of organisations and of people and their motivations, I had unusual insight into the pressures, obstacles, choices and working life of a heavyweight minister. It was invaluable, and with my personal and several professional lives coalescing, I had acquired an external view as a recipient and experiencer of governments, and from the inside trying to get something useful to happen. Putting this all together looked like an unusual combination of experiences with which to dissect government, why it fails, and more importantly how to make it succeed.

The Basis of This Book

To find answers takes an understanding of what a government says it is going to do and what it achieves. That all sounds quite simple, and expressed that way, it is. Yet life in government is extraordinarily multifaceted. What is going on, who is doing what to whom, and why? What motivates these people at the centre? At this point vast complexity and dysfunction come to the fore. To unravel the puzzle the analysis has to grasp the causes of policy, the causes of odd decisions, the causes of underperformance, the causes of good and bad leadership. The causes are, at times, almost as many and varied as the problems, and often stem from the psychology and motivation of those at the top. Mostly they are hidden from view.

The book uses analytic tools to assess government in a way that hopefully makes sense to people outside. The analysis holds a mirror to government for those that want to look (a challenge for some large and embedded egos). Government is an organisation – a very large one, but an organisation nevertheless. Organisational analysis shines a light in hidden corners, finds unexpected villains and fresh insights, and explains why government performs with such mediocrity. It is worse than you think.

Whenever something happens in any organisation, my first thought is why. Not the why on the surface but the hidden, organisational why. Why has one football club been consistently successful and one not? Why is this train late? Why have we run up so much debt? Why was the M25 built with a perpetual bottleneck at the A10 junction which wasn't removed until about twenty years later? Why is politician X trying to persuade me of Y?

Several types of analysis have been employed. In analysing policymaking, alongside my lifetime's experience in and around government, I examined fifteen policies from the mid-1980s to the 2010s as case studies. (Refer to the website www.treatyforgovernment.org for details.) I also examined the ways in which old ideologies drive policies. Just where do policies come from? (You may be surprised.) Delivery of government services occurs through many channels, and here I wanted to identify the causes of failure or poor performance. Another key area to look at is the feedback on what any organisation is doing.

The largest analysis, though, has been of 'root causes' – specifically of the organisational reasons why the New Labour government lost the 2010 election. Flipping my mind from internal moaning at the state of things to investigating with a purpose, there in front of me was an obvious analytical place to start – the political party that I had played a part in modernising and which had become electable again, that had been a long-standing administration with many very able and talented people in and around it, that started with quite a bang, had run into the sand. What went wrong? Well that's pretty clear, is it not? They had the wrong leader, somehow they had engineered the largest mass immigration in the country's history without meaning to, and their miracle economics turned out to be apocryphal. But there is more to these causes than simply a wrong decision somewhere. Why on earth would a political party go into an election with a leader it knew could not win? Why would a government pursue an immigration policy whose detrimental effects were becoming as apparent as its merits and which, on its own, was sufficiently unpopular to lose them the election? Why would a government of intelligent and motivated people (that started with such vision and impact) self-mutilate and display 'initiativitis' and not much else, finally losing to an Old Etonian? Why, by the end, were many of its activists so angry with their party that election campaigning felt false? Is all of this just the inevitable consequence of the political playing field or is losing an election wholly unnecessary? Should the new leader of the Labour Party just wait for the slings and arrows to wound the coalition and around the party's turn will come? Or is there more to successful politics than politicking? Is it just possible that government could be made to work better and be more than the mixture of people, policies, practice, chance, events, the media, and public perception interacting to a conclusion? What can organisational theory and practice tell us of how government could reform to improve its performance sufficiently that losing an election would be pure carelessness?

The 'why' questions kept rolling. As I interviewed more and more people, my question went beyond why Labour lost. The underlying issue was why had its failures so outrun its successes – a far more complicated but potentially fruitful quest. And, by that point, the coalition government of Conservatives and Liberal Democrats was accumulating its own roster of failures. And I could not help noticing that no government in the world appeared immune from failure.

It was quickly evident that thinking in the old ways was not going to provide the answers. Hundreds of politicians, civil servants, commentators, and academics are doing that all of the time. But the frame through which they view the system *is* the existing system. Their beliefs are that this system can be flexed here and there – chairs of select committees in the House of Commons can be elected by all MPs rather than being appointed by prime ministerial patronage, or hereditary peers in the Lords can be ended – but at heart the system has to remain. It is fixed, almost ordained. And, of course, all or most of these thinkers are in the system or dependent on it. It is impossible to see what is really going on from within.

Having spent a working lifetime with organisations of all shapes, sizes, and ownerships in many countries, and thirty years of working with and for and observing government from every angle, I started to look at government through an 'organisational lens' rather than from the usual perspectives of politics and their parties, of the positive and negative spin, of the dense bureaucracy, of legalese, of grand-sounding constitutional considerations, and of the 'this is far too clever for the public to consider' attitude that clouds so much of it. Within the world of government there is no awareness that an organisational lens will get to the answer.

Pursuing this line of sight some of what I found is obvious, some not. This book has emerged and become part analytic and part detective story – and a call to action.

Can an organisational perspective really come up with the answer? Well, this book provides mine – as objectively as I can. In reading it you will judge whether it is compelling. I think it is and that its conclusions and solutions are potentially profound for the way governments of all persuasions work and for the quality of government we receive. And in most countries. That's a big claim. I hope by the end you are convinced.

This is not a book about what governments should do to us, but about what we should do to governments, wherever in the world they are – a quite different journey.

Definitions

I've tried to write the book to be understandable by everyone, especially those without several degrees in organisational theory or political science. But we need some terms. So, what is meant by government, system of government, Civil Service, and the other elements of the machine?

Here the word 'system' means an organised collection of parts that are integrated in order to accomplish an overall goal. Our system of government contains several institutions and mechanisms to get things done, and to perform checks and balances on government powers. It uses information and debate. Accountability and incentives are vital components. Most significantly one part always affects another, and the whole is dependent on the functioning of each part and on their interaction.

The government is what we elect via political parties every few years to do all those things needed to run the country. This is called the 'executive' branch of the system. The legislature is the part with the power to pass laws – in the UK this is the Houses of Parliament.

The Civil Service can be split in two – essentially the central group of around 5,000 mainly in Whitehall in central London that administers the parliamentary, political and legislative processes and continues regardless of the party in power, the rest to be found in a considerable variety of public sector organisations (PSOs) doing things like tax collection, industry regulation, land registration. The Civil Service is not the government, although it often behaves as if it is (or as if it should be). Nominally it has no executive power. In practice it exercises much.

Power has to be spread. If all power is concentrated in the government then it is a dictatorship. In our system power is spread through laws that stipulate what governments may do, and the very separate branch of the judiciary to enforce them. The House of Lords exercises power by challenging proposed laws and sending them back to the MPs in the Commons for second thoughts. Power is further dispersed through semi-independent regulators with responsibilities to set interest rates or to determine whether a company has a monopoly, for example, because making these apolitical has been found to produce better decisions in the long run. Some bodies work best when they are political, and some when they are apolitical. This distinction is a running theme of the book.

Checks and balances are vital to good government. Select committees have powers of scrutiny to hold governments and their many arms to account, and to review decisions and see if they can be improved. Two heads are better than one. The Public Accounts Committee of the House of Commons regularly lambasts a public sector body for waste, inefficiency, or plain crassness. The drawback here is despite the public flagellations, little or nothing improves – these bodies are like memory foam, and after a brief flurry of press releases of news-speak, apology, or contradiction, they return to their old shape. This theme of continuous 'unreform' will also feature regularly in the book.

Underpinning these checks and balances is the National Audit Office (NAO) responsible for the accuracy of the accounts of all government bodies and for their value for money. The NAO is a product of Parliament and not the government of the day, and is independent – although also made of memory foam. A newish development has been the increasing independence of the Office for National Statistics to produce real and not massaged figures on government activities, from farm outputs to road casualties.

Finally there are what I call spreaders of best practice – bodies whose job it is to find out the best way of doing something, to publicise this, and to encourage all to do it that way. The now closed Audit Commission used to do this for all local councils, and had significant effect, despite limited powers of enforcement. The National Institute for Health and Care Excellence (NICE) is having greater impact as it scientifically assesses treatments for anything from diabetes to heart attacks to warts and all, and promotes application of this best practice by every member of medical staff. The establishment of NICE followed research in the US which found that it took seventeen years from the first use of a best practice to its near universal adoption. That's a lot of pain and death on the back of professional ignorance and ego.

People of many varieties work in the system. Their behaviour is as much determined by their particular employing organisation and its culture, as it is by the individual. Again this will be a continuing theme – how the system shapes the actions of the individual, and how we might like them reshaped.

If we then put all of that together – elections, their method, and political parties; the three branches of executive, legislature, and judiciary; the power-spreading, the checks and balances; the two-part Civil Service; the PSOs; and local government – then this is the System of government, and the subject of this book.

To set the scene further, we need to consider the context for the analysis – what is the place of politics and why it no longer works for us, how much can more or better democracy help, whether the proposed Treaty has an international reach that means it could apply to other countries, whether the degree of change it proposes is possible, and just what is this 'organisational lens'?

Will More Politics Fix It?

Having started aged six ferrying voting records from the polling station to a neighbour's front room that was temporarily the local party HQ, I had always believed in the importance of political parties. My emerging political awareness coincided with increasing depression as the landed-gentry Conservatives governed for thirteen years in the 1950s and 60s. This was followed by the relief and exhilaration of the socially reforming Labour government and the then ground-breaking laws now taken for granted, for universal and free contraception, the legalisation of homosexual acts (as they were somewhat clinically known), and equal pay. Politics worked.

My first direct experience of the democratic meeting the political was sharing a platform with the then prime minister, Harold Wilson, during the 1970 election. 'Students for a Labour Victory' had organised a rally in Central Hall, Manchester and as president of the Students Union I joined him on the platform. The Vietnam War was in full hideous swing and the US had started bombing Cambodia to cut the Vietcong supply lines. My speech focused on stopping the bombing – by any standard it was wrong, and was proved so to be many times over by future events. It felt like politics could do something. When we weren't rallying for social reforms, we were demonstrating against the South African rugby team's tour, for which Mandela publicly thanked us years later in Trafalgar Square. When we weren't talking to open up a speaker's corner in Piccadilly Gardens, we were delivering leaflets and putting crosses on ballot papers for local and national governments. It was more than just a bunch of naïve and idealistic students with few lectures to attend – although we were certainly that; mighty injustices prevailed in the world and they could and were changed. We still benefit today.

Sitting in the green room after the speeches, Wilson said that the Conservative leader, Edward Heath, was his secret election-winning asset – Heath was socially gauche, sailed a yacht, and single. However, Wilson's sure-footedness had deserted him and Heath won, and the decade of alternating Conservative and Labour commenced. The most significant political act was entry to Europe. What followed was eighteen years of Thatcher and Co., who proved to be about a third very right, a third the usual muddle, and a third destructively wrong. Is there a way of getting the right without the wrong, I wondered?

With election night in 1997 and the New Labour landslide, here it seemed was the new dawn without the old prejudices, with well thought-through policies, and a freshness I had never experienced. Much good happened. The 2001 election arrived with the certainty that the government would be re-elected, not least because of its triumphs, but also because the other lot were still living in the 1950s. But, disappointment was also around. With so much electoral and mood power, why had the really radical changes not been made? Where was the new democracy, proper proportional representation, the new legal system, the real public sector reform, the gripping of the Conservative's major privatisation mistakes in rail, water and electricity, executive mayors by the score, and the sorting of the hundreds of day-to-day problems? Discontent mounted, to the extent that come the 2010 election many Labour Party activists took to their armchairs waiting for the government to be put out of its misery.

Typically when in government, one party spends much of its time correcting the omissions and mistakes of the other, at the same time making a raft of its own, which are then there for the other party to correct once it gets back into power. And so on and on in an endless waltz – forward, side, back; forward, side, back. Crablike government. This is very expensive. And boring. In our minds we view the source of good government as the periodic competition between parties with the most-likely-to-do-better being elected and given the job. This contest for power should raise standards. Government should get better. But does this long-standing view stand up to apolitical scrutiny? Only if by chance a good minister happened to be appointed, and happened to last long enough, and happened to have a good bee in their bonnet, and happened to have some civil servants at hand who knew what they were doing, did any long-standing but not very visible problem get addressed, and even sorted. The longer a government stays in power the less it achieves and the more mistakes it makes. As citizens we sort of half expect this and are conditioned to disappointment, and are mightily relieved that we live in a democracy not in the callous dictatorships of the Arab and African states or the old totalitarian regimes of the Cold War, with no choice and the joys of informants, secret police, and fear. Undoubtedly, the UK government's performance lies in the temperate zones compared with these frozen wastes. But do governments have to be passable and only better than the non-democratic alternative? Is there a better way? Could they be judged not by peering downwards at dictatorships but upwards at what is possible? Surely the existing constitutions should not be merely a means to avoid oppression.

Whilst many stick with party voting, others have concluded that it makes little difference to real lives. They have taken another route, which is not to vote. This may appear irresponsible but it contains a significant truth: it is entirely rational with a system of government that fails with such regularity. Political parties seek to distinguish themselves by their policies – by what they say. But the discerning non-voter judges them by what they achieve, and governments spend much of their time achieving little, often at high cost. The non-voter has a point. The point is that governments and their oppositions are often not worth the candle of the voter's time and attention. Political parties and their media bedfellows make an awful lot of just how different they are in objectives and philosophy, how much better they are, how much more they listen to the citizens. But, stand back and observe how much has actually changed on the ground, how little your or my life has been affected by a new government – as distinct from the ups and downs of the global economy.

The ranks of non-voters have been consistently swelling. I grew up with the belief that voting was a civic duty. Australia, where not voting is illegal, seemed to me to have got it right. But then an entirely responsible, highly educated young colleague at work shocked me by commenting that she did not vote. Why? It makes no difference, came the reply. And is it not emotionally sound to avoid getting mixed up in this flawed world of hope and disappointment, of vision and frustration? It's rather like listening to the news late at night – people who do are more likely to be depressed. So don't. Gradually I came to terms with the non-voters. Maybe they are the only rational people amongst us.

Dissatisfaction with the political classes is often registered by protest voting. After all, believing the failures of government are down to the political classes is not unreasonable. Apart from riot or a letter to the editor, voting for another party is really the only manner in which a protest can be registered. So others have taken the middle way between voting and not, by supporting other parties – the Liberal Democrats, the BNP, the Greens, and most recently UKIP. This is called democracy. But in our system its effect is 80% diluted by first-past-the-post voting. The Lib Dems have managed to turn their support into noticeable parliamentary representation, but not the others. Protest votes are allowed but no significant power is taken from the two main parties. Our system places massive obstacles in the way of new entrants to the political marketplace with the consequence of major strands of public opinion being unrepresented. We are forced into the dismal choice of the Conservative/Labour duopoly – a market as rigged as electricity and banking. Any self-respecting competition authority in the world would rule it illegal.

But surely, you might say, the differences between the political parties matters most. 'I vote for the party that best represents my beliefs as to what society should look like.' Well, if that used to be the case, today it matters far less than how well a government functions. In a post mass–redistribution age, these differences are not what they were. Formerly, huge political differences existed – socialism versus capitalism, the mass of the have–nots versus the haves, social justice versus survival of the fittest or wealthiest. The purpose of one side was to transfer wealth and income from the established landowners, aristocracies and the advantaged to the disadvantaged and poor majority; and the purpose of the other side was to keep wealth in the hands of the elite. The same huge differences were true for the distribution of power and influence. So, too, were the differences in their preferred economic systems – free market capitalism on the one side and common ownership and control of the means of production on the other. The old heroic politics of left versus right, public versus private, either this or that, are no longer relevant to any modern purpose.

Today, each side has stolen some clothes from the other. One Labour Cabinet minister in the mid-2000s described the social democratic hegemony we are now in. This, in his mind, meant that they would go on in government for the foreseeable future. What happened, of course, was that the Conservative Party finally and belatedly migrated to the hegemony, the coalition was born and turned out in some ways more socially democratic than the previous government. Thus modern politics occurs in a relatively small space. It is no longer realistic for politicians to take refuge in their historic belief systems, be they the left in the sanctity of a welfare system based on giving, or the right in the sanctity of the free market. Post mass-redistribution, the political playing field has become compressed. The space where genuine political judgements and preferences are needed to make choices is quite small. Just as science has progressively reduced the ability of religions to command our observance, so experience and facts have eliminated much political territory.

I have come to recognise the flatulence of the 'four legs good, two legs bad' debates – more state or less state, more private sector or less, right wing or left wing, high tax or low tax, generous welfare or tight welfare. These arguments only damage my psychological health. In fact, as difference has reduced, political cross-dressing has taken off as the parties seek to appeal to electorates from less prejudiced or ideological positions: we find the Conservative Party emphasising offender rehabilitation, whilst Labour is stressing prison works; Conservatives for gay marriage, Labour for vetting and kettling; Conservatives for universal personal pensions, Labour laissez-faire; Conservatives reducing police numbers, Labour increasing them; Conservatives for localisation, Labour for centralisation. Who is left and who is right in all of this? Do we care? Or would we prefer something to actually change for the better? Surely the objective is the right state, right government, right tax, right welfare, right answers, and right actions.

Consider for one moment this list of current problems in need of fixing or at least improvement: unsustainable government debt; corporate reward for failure; increasing and spectacular wealth inequality and decreasing social mobility; widespread ineffective enforcement on behalf of the public versus businesses; misplaced and counter-productive welfare; a loophole tax system; a candy-floss, ethics-free news media; a rigged market in electricity; failed regulation of pension funds that still pay themselves highly whilst producing derisory returns for pensioners; high-cost public sectors unsatisfying to work in, whose services are dissatisfying to receive; decisions consistently bent to the lobby power of corporates and well away from public interests; reams of rules for the individual and too few for governments; corporate entrapment of consumers, from printer cartridges to phone contracts; rates of migration that add up for economists but not for the recipient peoples to adapt and absorb; self-serving banks with those in the US and UK having sent our money to the bizarre asset bubble of sub-prime mortgages, and those in continental Europe backing government bonds without hope and construction booms without demand; a single currency introduced with much commitment and many benefits, but without the rules and enforcement essential to making it work; climate chaos still warming the in-tray; a secondary-school system under permanent criticism; a health system under permanent reform; the serial errors of government procurement that are never cured – defence and IT most spectacularly; Britain's joke road junctions; and countless minor poor performances enshrined in the underground ticket hall and its queues at London Euston station.

These visible manifestations of failure cross the traditional political spectrum of left and right, of our party and theirs, of any attempt at moral distinction. Many are common across countries. Many are long-standing. What does that tell us? Certainly, that there is more to their solution than party politics. Indeed the main parties' objectives for each of these problems are often the same. In fact, the politics of most of these nonsenses is clear in that there is little. Does anyone *not* want to fix the banks? Or schools? Or the health system? Or social mobility? Or debt? Or taxes, the news media, government contracting, the pension funds, welfare, or the London Underground ticket hall? You could write the manifestos of most political parties in many countries now, and they would all be much the same. There is no massive philosophic triangulation to be gone through, just the complex task of implementation. Not what or whether, but *how*.

This 'implementation' or 'delivery' question leads us to another factor which compresses the distance between the parties even further. The parties rarely debate the 'how' of a policy or the best mechanics for making something operational, just the policy itself. The politicians do not see themselves as directly responsible for delivery, which is perceived as the remit of the civil servants and the many agency managements. Implementing pensions reform, for example – a political act if ever there was one – was never led by a minister for the whole of the 1997–2010 government. Delivery is political in that voters make judgements as to what has actually changed for them, and vote according to results, not promises; but politicians of all hues appear not to see this clearly, yapping on about the worth of their policies.

In practice, then, political differences are much smaller than they used to be. What has a far bigger impact is a government's ability to bring about beneficial change on the ground. This is a matter of organisation. The irony is that organisation of government does not register with most politicians as a force. Politicians see and use power, politicking, and the media as forces for change, but few grasp the importance nor have the understanding of how to use organisation to achieve beneficial change for the citizens and for the country – which is their job, after all.

But the political classes are only products of the system. This is a fundamental truth of organisational behaviour – we may think that what we do at work is entirely of our own volition, that right-minded staff and management will do the right thing. What is actually most powerful in channelling and controlling out behaviour is the culture, the role models, the rewards, the means to promotion and what is measured. In my life in organisations of all types from companies to charities to governments, I have usually trodden an independent path. This has given me integrity and support – and I've been branded a maverick, or sidelined, or evicted. On one occasion I was told I was too moral. Any organisational culture demands at least some FIFO – fit in or fuck off. Organisations control our behaviour, and organisations of government are no exception. Indeed with all that personal politicking around they are a prime example.

So in totting up how we seek traditionally to improve government through the process of periodically electing political parties, where have we got to? We have copious government failure that is not being solved by political party or leader competition, the two main parties here in perpetuity but with a steady decline in support – our bipolar political party disorder, protest and third-way voters on the rise but with very limited real power, non-voters becoming the majority and opting out, and the traditional political playing field shrinking to such an extent that parties are cross-dressing to find some distinctive space. Evidently party politics, as we know it, cannot provide consistently successful government in today's world. This is not looking hopeful. One might as well vote for a bearded comedian.

But what if you could do something about government? What if there is a reason why it makes so many mistakes? What if most often the reason it fails is not because of some ministerial halfwit but because of a system that makes halfwits of the competent and heads-in-the-sand of the visionaries? What if the system attracts the wrong kind of talent? What if the system is doomed to fail because it was never designed to succeed?

Let us move on and see if we can find a more productive arena than party politics. Will we find the answer to the problems of government through more democracy?

Will More Democracy Fix It?

Systems of government exist within a democratic context. Democracy is a form of political organisation in which all people exercise equal control over the matters that affect their interests. Equality and freedom have been identified as important characteristics of democracy since ancient times. These principles are reflected in all citizens being equal before the law and having equal access to power. For example, in a representative democracy every vote has equal weight, no restrictions can apply to anyone wanting to become a representative, and legitimised rights and liberties secure the freedom of its citizens, who are protected by a constitution.

What I have learnt is that what we think of as democracy is actually a) not either present or absent, but rather a case of fifty shades of democracy, b) easily abused, and c) vital to a good society but contains an unconsidered assumption that more *by itself* will produce successful government. With representative democracy, you and I are allowed power at election time but only to vote for a political party. Occasionally an individual without a party is elected – Ken Livingstone in his first stint as mayor of London, for instance – but for over 99% of the time we are voting a party into power.

Competition and democracy are close relatives. Competition matters as much in politics as it does for supermarkets – probably more. First-past-the-post systems – as in the UK and US – are much less responsive to public pressure than those with proportional representation. The two perpetual parties only have to convince enough people – 'enough' being often a very long way from a majority – that they are better than the other lot. We are restricted to the dismal choice between two parties – with a third playing some part once in a century. Standards are so much lower and the democracy allowed to us is even more limited. Bipolar politics also is designed to promote argument, not thought – and when has any problem really been solved through adversarial argument?

With PR, parties can go out of business – their support can fall so far as to be overtaken by new entrants. A wide range of parties can be voted for that best represent our interests. One of the great crosses of the two-party state is that when one of the parties is effectively unelectable, a one-party state is all that is left. It led Thatcher to excess and Blair to flogging dead horses. Orderly competition drives improvement in all things. Multi-party competition for government that allows new parties to become established and old parties to die is essential for successful government. Proportional voting produces this.

Under either system, however, once a government is elected, we get very little power between elections with just representative democracy. Writing to your MP or going along to a constituency surgery might succeed in getting a pothole repaired, but not the banks. For anything other than the minor, zero democracy exists via your 'representative' at Parliament. You and I only get any democratic look-in via protest – from blocking the M1 to a serious riot. Although it is a blunt instrument, it can work (witness the poll tax riots leading to its demise), but it is costly and risky, particularly with the unaccountable Metropolitan Police around – you can be killed. And over the last thirty years, successive governments have placed more and more restrictions on this aspect of democracy, squeezing public protest and free expression.

In short, once 'our' new government has been elected, you and I have no democracy until the next election. The threat of us not voting them in next time exists, so we cannot be entirely ignored, but we have the problem that many of us feel we have to vote for someone. And once in government, various interests capture all parties. Between elections, the places where power resides are the news media running their various agendas, good and bad, political and business; large companies and industries with expert preferential lobbyists and party funders, dealing with a political and Civil Service class mostly ignorant of their businesses but knowing their importance to the economy and their own dependency on them for policy advice; banking ditto; wealthy individual party funders; large PSOs (the central Civil Service or the police are as much a lobby group as the pension funds); and trade unions, if their party is in power. Small businesses get no more look in than you or I. Essentially large organisations and very wealthy individuals hold the power. Just to be clear, this is not democratic.

The House of Lords does mitigate some of the worst power- and wealth-grabs and ideological indulgences, but only a few. These built in 'checks and balances' are vital to good government. If any democracy is not carefully constituted to avoid an uneven distribution, then one branch of the system of rule could accumulate power, and thus become undemocratic. As Franklin Roosevelt put it in 1938, 'The first truth is that the liberty of a democracy is not safe if the people tolerate the growth of private power to a point where it becomes stronger than their democratic state itself. That, in its essence, is fascism — ownership of government by an individual, by a group, or by any other controlling private power.' The current US system of representative democracy has largely become captured by business and personal wealth through the funding of political parties and the culture of preferential lobbying. The will of the people gets a look-in only at election time. Democracy of a sort continues in the US because of its federal structure and the strong powers held at state and township levels, and because of its customs. People hold on to their personal freedom with a determination not seen elsewhere.

Professor Colin Crouch introduced the term 'post-democracy' to describe our experience of national governments and how democracy has become marginalised in much of the developed world. In his 2013 book *In the Name of the People*, Ivo Mosley relates how representative democracy has never really been democratic as it has always been prone to capture by elites. The late Irish scholar Peter Mair coined the phrase 'the hollowing of western democracy' in *Ruling the Void* to describe our experience of the EU as another form of government out of our control. At the local level in the UK, we have even less democracy – indeed practically none. You may have noticed. The same election system applies but the power is either held by national government through directions or by local officials. The political parties count for very little here. Only with elected executive mayors does some democracy reappear, and this can be potent.

Under direct (as opposed to representative) democracy, the following are available: referendums, citizens assemblies, and electing officials. In other words we retain power or retain the right to power between elections. This is a big difference. In the UK very occasionally a referendum is held – but only at the say-so of the government. Direct democracy only exists if we have the power to call one. Referendums can include whether a given law should be rejected. This effectively grants the electorate a veto on government legislation. Initiatives, usually put forward by the populace, force the consideration of laws or amendments without the consent of the elected officials, or even in opposition to the will of the officials. Recalls give people the right to remove elected officials from office before the end of their term.

Switzerland is probably the most democratic country in the world, and one of the most successful. Its high-class democracy is the result of forming a single country from twenty-six cantons with four official languages. Key to this integration has been retaining decision-making for the separate peoples in order that they have the confidence to be part of a single country, and avoid the tyranny of the majority and the suppression of minorities. Hence the federal structure where only that which cannot be done at the canton or commune level is done federally. At all levels, direct democracy is embedded. Four to five times a year Swiss citizens receive a ballot paper and briefing documents prepared by interested parties on the subject in question – for example to vote whether to budget for a 3.2 million Swiss franc investment subsidy for 2013–15 to participate in financing the construction of five 'park and ride' lots, or whether a new town hall should be built, or most recently whether to end the 'free movement of workers' agreement with the EU (they did). The vote is by ballot box, post, or secure server. The most direct form of democracy is where citizens come together to debate laws and expenditures and then vote with a show of hands – and in the past by a show of swords. Is this the past? Or the future?

It is interesting to observe governments today and their ambiguous attitude towards the Internet. This has opened up decision-making to public pressure through online petitions and open lobbies – new direct democracy. While notable successes have been scored – the

Ugandan government did not introduce the death penalty for being gay, for example – governments and MPs find the process a nuisance as it cuts through the way they usually take decisions, largely in private. Having got power, 'representative' governments find this new forum an affront to their freedom to indulge their need to exercise it without being watched over. Hence the regular attempts to coral this new vehicle for democracy. Recently this has even gone as far in the US and UK as declaring personal emails open to surveillance, on the grounds that the odd terrorist has been stopped this way. The same argument could apply to the post and could legitimise the bugging of every home, office and building – if they were, a few more unwitting terrorists would be caught (until, that is, they twigged and communicated via other means). Are our emails a private space or not? Most governments have a major power problem with the direct democracy of the Internet.

As well as representative and direct democracy, the menu also includes consensus, deliberation, and public engagement. 'Consensus' democracy is the application of consensus decision-making to the process of legislation. It is characterised by a decision-making structure that involves and takes into account as broad a range of opinions as possible, as opposed to systems where vote-winning majorities can potentially ignore minority opinions. Consensus democracy also features increased citizen participation, both in determining the political agenda and in decision-making itself. Developments in information and communication technology are potential facilitators of such systems. 'Deliberative' democracy is where public deliberation is central to decision-making. It adopts elements of both representative democracy and direct democracy and differs from traditional democratic theory in that deliberation, not voting, is the primary source of a law's legitimacy. By people learning about an issue and talking to each other, the best solution is reached. The still rare practice of 'engaging' the appropriate public in a specific decision, from flood defences to the future of the health service, takes this a step further by both taking on board information and attitudes from the public and, given that the decision incorporates public acceptance, the process can lead to speedier and easier implementation of the decision.

For the dessert course today we can go even further. Indeed this is the icing on the cake, should you ever get to taste it –

workplace democracy. Though the term 'democracy' is typically used in the context of a political state, the principles are applicable to private organisations and other groups also. Grand Central is a more democratic company to work for than Virgin Trains. Typically, GC staff have more control over their work lives and over decisions taken. The Labour Party's original purpose could be rewritten in terms of workplace democracy, which has improved enormously in the twentieth century. But still many public and private bodies operate through the organisational model of the machine – procedures, rules, centralised decisions, and IT systems used to limit individual decision. Some of this control is essential – toilets must be cleaned properly – but much is no better than gross ignorance of alternatives: there's no reason it's policy; and/or the lack of pressure to do any better.

(Few, if any, public sector bodies use the self-directed work teams common in automotive assembly. This practice of local self-organisation was introduced specifically to improve productivity – local groups of workers invariably know how to assemble the rear suspension better than management, and far better than some remotely-set predetermined procedure.)

Workplace democracy is not about flabby worker's co-ops taking every decision by committee and going bust in the process, but about decentralising decisions and choice as far as the overall functioning and performance of the organisation is maintained or enhanced. Operationally, the SAS is remarkably democratic: everyone speaks at the briefing before a mission because someone may have vital information, and because all will be better motivated through being heard. The colonel listens and takes the final decision.

Democracy is a huge area of study. Perhaps most famously Alexis de Tocqueville wanted to understand in the mid-1800s why it worked in the relatively new country of the US but not in the ancient country of his birth, France. In *Democracy in America* (1835), he wrote that US democracy was successful because of: '1. The peculiar and accidental situation in which Providence has placed the Americans. 2. The laws. 3. The manners and customs of the people.'

The first – Providence – is simply that 'God gave them the means of remaining equal and free, by placing them upon a boundless continent. General prosperity is favourable to the stability of all governments.' Furthermore, they had no neighbours and consequently no great wars or inroads or conquest to dread. (Latterly the intercontinental missiles of the Cold War and then terrorism on the doorstep have changed that to an extent, certainly in the mind.)

The laws are those establishing the way in which democracy should function. The federal form enables the union to combine the power of a great republic with the security of a small one. The township institutions limit the despotism of the majority and at the same time impart to the people a taste for freedom and the art of being free. The courts of justice serve to repress the excesses of democracy, and check and direct the impulses of the majority without stopping its activity.

By the 'customs' de Tocqueville means the habits of the heart – the various notions and opinions current among people and the mass of ideas that constitute their character of mind. 'Democracy has gradually penetrated into their customs, their opinions, and their forms of social intercourse; it is to be found in all the details of daily life as well as in the laws ... I should say that physical circumstances are less efficient than the laws, and the laws infinitely less so than the customs of the people' in maintaining democracy.

What might de Tocqueville have concluded on UK democracy today? He would find an island uninvaded for a thousand years, but with regular wars on the doorstep, and no living memory of the mass surveillance common in the rest of Europe – hence the lackadaisical public attitude to today's intrusions on privacy. Being an island the country learns less from others' ways of doing things than those connected by land, where a drive is all it takes to observe an alternative. Thus it tends to the insular. The island is densely populated bringing internal pressures over space, resources, and noise. There is far less understanding and determination about keeping government at bay from individual freedoms. And the people tend to be easily conned by the rich and powerful.

Essentially, in the way it is practised in most countries, by giving power to an elected elite for a set period, representative democracy is vastly better than its alternative of power inherited through monarchies or seized through *coups d'état*, but never be fooled that for as long as those 'representatives' have the power it is democratic; the albeit temporary tyranny of the majority sets in; and long-standing governments and institutions become self-serving. We won't get tortured (usually) and we can say what we like in public (usually), but power does get concentrated in the hands of the rich and influential, and between elections our interests will get little or no look-in. The section on cake capture below takes on this theme. And representative-based governments tend to spend a lot of time and money doing things to us – all for our own good, of course. Switzerland may be a long way away and have an unusual history, but the UK could learn much from the way it operates democracy.

All of this matters, not because some ancient Greeks say it is a good idea, but because in all of its forms, democracy matters to each of us. The UK is at the democracy-lite end of the scale – and getting liter by restricting free assembly and free expression. Many countries use democracy in all sorts of ways that are ignored or rubbished here. There are some very obvious holes to be filled. First past the post falls at the first hurdle on the test of every vote having equal weight. Only full proportional representation passes the 'equal weight' test. Too much power resides with the prime minister and too little outside. The Civil Service exercises considerable power but nowhere in any definition of democracy is a quasi-independent self-appointed unelected government administration legitimised. In a fully functioning democracy, an independent Civil Service does not exist. The system in the UK is largely representative democracy. Consensus, direct, and deliberative democracy have little place.

For as long as a dictator or a 'first past the post' prime minister with few checks and balances and a monopoly Civil Service delivers good decisions and good change, they will be accepted. Voting and participating can, after all, be chores. But, when the dictator or the deficient democracy delivers too many bad decisions and bad change, the answer is to eliminate the deficit. It is time for power cuts in Britain – of those who have too much of it.

For as long as I can recall, thoughtful groups have campaigned to improve democracy. More democracy is seen as the solution to the ills of government. Democracy is right. Democracy is a self-evident truth. Democracy is attractive. Democracy is essential to delivery. The demise of authority as an organising force in society is well documented – the alternative organising force is democracy. Fully functioning democracy should be at the heart of any vision for a country. At present it is not. Democracy is an essential end in itself, with which I profoundly agree, but is not my purpose. More democracy can produce far better government (as in Switzerland), but the wrong kind of extra democracy can produce bankruptcy (as in California). For all of its democratic virtues, the Swiss system of government still suffers from the faults we find in all countries. These we will expose later. If you think democracy, by itself, will solve the problems of government, it will not, so divest yourself of that mindset. We need to work through what's wrong and how to put it right before the place of enhanced democracy in successful government becomes apparent.

Just to be extra clear, none of what's wrong is the fault of Her Majesty the Queen. I will not be examining whether we should have a presidential system, a parliamentary republic, or our existing constitutional monarchy with a ceremonial monarch – the solution below applies to them all.

International Context

This book originates from study of the system of government in the UK, with other countries' governments informing the analysis and conclusions. My wider experience, research, and interviews suggest that many of the conclusions here are applicable to any country seeking better government. Government performance around the world is variable. Some of the problems differ markedly, but many are common. Certainly I have not come across a fully functioning government anywhere. Nor have I yet found a country with a constitution of government designed to achieve the best it can.

Lest national superiority should cloud that view, let us not forget that the biggest error of government thus far this century has come from the European Union in the shape of a rule-free euro. How anyone imagined that a single currency could work without enforceable national financial controls, or with the middle classes in some Mediterranean countries paying little income tax, is a mystery (I say all of this as a convinced European).

The EU used to provide better government than the UK. It was new, fresh, with lots of determined people committed to the European vision. No more. Now it is long in the tooth, personal objectives are locked into the continuance of the organisation rather than being aligned to the value of a common Europe, and bureaucracy, rules, failure and cost flow from it. Some are so disillusioned or xenophobic as to want to leave the EU. By the same logic they might want to leave the UK too. Rather than seeking a structural solution to the EU's failures by withdrawal, our Treaty for Government could be applied to it first. Get the government of the EU functioning successfully, then decide if you want independence. The same is true of Scotland, where far better government driven by the Treaty would provide so much more for its people than full independence. Without the Treaty, an independent Scotland would still have mediocre government.

Many countries find their governments dominated by business interests – the potential fate of all democracies according to the thinkers of ancient Greece. Having been relatively clean in this respect for years the EU has now been captured. The US has its constitutional strengths and some large holes. In explaining its very limited action on the banks, Barack Obama's administration has been described as a Wall Street government. Will the US government remain forever captured by big business at the public's expense? Or will this unholy alliance be somehow ruptured? With its apparent role model the Republican Party, Russia is dominated by a political and business oligarchy. Is this how this country will continue, forever Putinised as the price of stability, or will people demand something better?

Some governments find themselves willingly or unwillingly spending an awful lot of time in bed with their news media. Does this unnatural practice improve the quality of government, or the reverse? Can a press so entwined with the politicians it is nominally regulating be deemed 'free'? And can a press run by another group of the rich and powerful ever substitute for major weaknesses in the system of government?

Administrative corruption is rife in India, Italy, and Greece. Business corruption is common in Japan and China. The latter is a one-party state with market freedoms. How long will that last, once prosperity becomes the norm? Senior police corruption in London is a current affliction, alongside high vested interests in the central bureaucracy. For a country with a snobbish attitude to corruption in the rest of the world, acknowledgement of some home lies is yet to happen.

Elective dictatorships are in fashion – Hungary and Iraq are current examples – where weak constitutions have been changed or ignored to maintain a prime minister in office regardless of the wishes of the people.

The Arab Spring has seen the biggest stride for democracy since the demolition of the Berlin Wall – and Africa is heading in the same direction. Informed of life around the world through the mass communication of the Internet, and partially freed from their tribal and religious addictions, the populace is no longer willing to accept its dictated lot. But what kind of government will follow? How will it be designed? Will it be based on the flawed models currently in use? The British or Westminster model has been exported to many former colonies, and given its longevity is often perceived to be a good thing. As practised in Britain, it is not. Will new countries now adopt the design in this book and leave the modern *ancien régimes* for dust? Are the new leaders ambitious for their new countries or for their own power?

For all of the specific circumstances of each country, there is a generic problem of government. The specific experiences related in this book may or may not have relevance to your country. You will have to judge their applicability. Governments operate within different cultures, in countries with different histories. But there are commonalities to having a top-class government. The solutions proposed in this book provide the essential design. They could be used, too, to test the efficacy of a country's current system of government, and to design systems for new democracies emerging from dictatorships.

'Change' Context

At this point, you may be starting to believe that this book possibly has a point, but are we really serious about revolutionising the entire system of government? Can it be done? Surely the degree of change required by the Treaty is too big a bite. Won't it all peter out?

Clearly the forces against the Treaty will be many and various. All of the vested interests will try to convince you that nothing can be done – it's unsafe to change, our system is as good as it gets, fear of the unknown, and so on – and, of course, it's OK to have some fat cats even if they are unpleasant human beings. Will all of the beneficiaries of the existing shambles seek to undermine the proposed Treaty? Of course they will, with high-class spin, long words, quasi-academic gloss, held captive by their own beliefs, and by inserting poison pills into the Treaty. But actually we all recognise spin and dissembling by how it feels – just check your intuition; you don't have to buy it.

Media empires built on government deals and on their own politics will shout foul. Businesses and industries used to manipulating an uneducated government system will threaten. Dumb interviewers habitually exercising their apparent right to ask dumb questions as a way out of knowing the subject will ask dumb questions. Civil servants will predict the end of the world if they're not in charge of things. Think tanks run from desks will fear life on housing estates. And politicians hate constraints – after all, the task of a politician is to bend and morph on the winds of public opinion, and to blow them back.

But, let's reflect a little on our recent national history and whether we can change when we really want to. First, consider the fate of the British motor car industry in the 1970s: ancient machine tools, decrepit factories, outdated hierarchical organisation, amateur management untrained for its task and drawn from one demographic, trade unions on power trips and social-justice excuses, each side blaming the other and neither grasping that they were all in it together against global competition and low investment. The collective head was in the sand, suspicious of innovation and foreign methods, and failing, failing, failing to change as it had to if it wanted to survive. It went bust. It was revived, but only by takeovers by the very foreigners the national ego had not the humility to learn from – companies that had innovated, embarked on long learning journeys from practice around the world, led by example, and shown the courage and vision to flourish. Today, one of the world's leading car plants in terms of productivity is in Sunderland. British management in genuinely competitive industries is now up to world standards. The sight of inept self-satisfied British company management that I grew up with has gone. This has been a major transformation.

Our attitude to food has also undergone a sea change – from utilitarian to celebratory. Today we have world-class chefs and enjoy fine wines and cheeses far more than we used to. Gone are the days of cardboard sliced white bread ham sandwiches and instant coffee as the café standard. There is still some way to go before we reach the higher standards across the board, but food and cooking are now widely celebrated. This was unthinkable thirty years ago.

Relationship knowledge and education have gone from almost zero when I started out on this rocky road to as much as you can absorb. At the time of first working with the National Marriage Guidance Council in the 1980s, as Relate then was, even raising the subject of couple counselling at dinner parties evinced an uncomfortable silence. A teenager today may have watched all 256 episodes of *Friends* by the age of thirteen – a comprehensive relationship primer. Plus magazines, websites to interpret dreams, parenting reality TV programmes, social and emotional education, counselling, and simply a willingness to talk and enquire. It is not measured, but my observation puts the average degree of emotional literacy up tenfold from the 1970s. What a transformation.

I flag these big shifts to show just how far and quickly our country has improved some of its 'core competences' – management, food, relationships – and thus to stress that we can do this in parts of our society, indeed probably anywhere, once we make up our minds to. It's all a matter of will. Government is no exception.

And, there is already a track record of great change having been effected. UK government and its performance was revolutionised in the Second World War, as nothing was allowed to stand in the way of winning. Alas, once won, the forces of the status quo reasserted and inserted themselves. The UK system of government today is not so different in its performance and complacency to the extinct motorcar industry of the 1970s. The question is will we allow it to continue, or will it follow the example of the nation's successful transformations?

The Organisational Lens

Systems of government are usually debated and analysed from the perspectives of history and political philosophy. Changes are assessed on the basis of their fit with these powerful theories, from Plato onwards. This book comes from a very different place. It takes how government actually works and does not work, and analyses this through a lens of organisation and management theory and practice. This body of knowledge has been developed only in the second half of the twentieth century. It was not available to the drafters of the constitutions governments live by. It has reached its pinnacle with the advent of the world-class manufacturers – those that quickly deliver extraordinary products at low cost. We take them for granted now. Organisation theory has provided them, and extended its remit into public sector and not-for-profit bodies. Could government make the same progress to world-class standards with the application of similar theory and practice? What relevance has it to governments getting things done? Can developments in air-crash investigations improve the operation of public services like child protection, for example?

If we look at New Labour through this lens, we see that after 2005, the distinction in organisational terms between Tony Blair and Gordon Brown as prime ministers and leaders was zero. Both were the products of a very long period in a largely unaccountable organisation with weak opposition and ineffective competition. Both had disappeared into their central courts with almost zero disturbances from the outside world. Both were well into the phase of their survival being more important than competent government. Both felt the emotional pull of historic unpopularity. A purely political perspective sees Blair and Brown as very different people with their successes and failures being largely down to them as individuals. From an organisational perspective, this is not the case. In the second half, both were products of weak governance. Both performed poorly. Both for the same reason. Organisations determine our performance and behaviour far more than most of us realise.

One caveat at this stage. In the course of this book, many comparators are used to challenge conventional thinking and to illustrate. Some of these are from the market or private sector. Understandably, many public sector officials find it tiring and demeaning being admonished with the view 'the private sector is better, if only you did things that way all would be well'. Each of us has probably had as many bad experiences with private sector organisations as with public to know that these homilies are not true, and I for one have spent much of my working life deep in malfunctioning companies. But, markets do have one major advantage: competition, and its capacity to improve the quality, performance, and cost of products and services. The imperatives provided by consumers having real choice, and of companies going bust if they do not keep up, or of becoming rich if they win the competition, have enormous impact. We are all aware of sectors where this has not happened – banking is the obvious example, or electricity, gas and water supply – but this just proves the point, as in these markets proper competition and the discipline of bankruptcy do not exist. We can learn much from fairly regulated and effectively competing markets.

What is 'Organisation'?

An organisation is a social arrangement that pursues collective goals, controls its own performance, and has a boundary separating it from its environment. There are a variety of legal types of organisations, including: corporations, governments, non-governmental organisations, international organisations, armed forces, charities, not-for-profit bodies, political parties, partnerships, cooperatives, universities, hybrids operating in both the public and the private sector, simultaneously fulfilling public duties and developing commercial market activities.

'Organisation' as a subject is a big and expanding field. When I started, London Business School tended to the technocratic – finance and strategy were its forte. Manchester led on the people aspect and organisational behaviour and systems thinking. During my life the extent and sophistication of academic and applied research has grown enormously. Previous black holes that we tended to pass by have come into vision. The field ranges from business economics to motivation of the individual and group, from political theory to psychology, from managing charities to distribution, as well as the better known marketing, selling and accounting. As globalisation of business has proceeded, this body of knowledge has drawn from every continent, discerned what works and why, which has then been promulgated back around the globe. This body of work applies everywhere – World-class manufacturing is organised the same in Xanshiou, Sunderland and Philadelphia. I wonder if, from an organisational perspective, there is any reason why government should be different.

Let's have a look at some of this organisational theory and practice. Peter Drucker is considered by many to be the first significant management thinker. His work appears to have been used extensively by the Japanese to take the manufacturing lead in the 1970s. In 1969, he wrote an article 'The Sickness of Government'[2] which also appeared in his book *The Age of Discontinuity*. By this time Drucker had settled in the US but had lived till 1933 in Austria and had also spent ten years in the UK. His reference to government took in every form then in practice: right and left, communist and capitalist, democratic and dictatorial. He concluded that government was good at only two things: waging war and inflating the currency. The problems he described of non-performance in government are strikingly similar to today's. Here is some of the flavour:

> Modern government has become ungovernable. There is no government today that can still claim control of its bureaucracy and of its various agencies. Government agencies are all becoming autonomous, ends in themselves, and directed by their own desire for power, their own narrow vision rather than by national policy.

> Bureaucrats keep on doing what their procedures describe. Their tendency, as is only human, is to identify what is in the best interest of the agency with what is right, and what fits administrative convenience with effectiveness. As a result the Welfare State cannot set priorities. It cannot concentrate its tremendous resources – and therefore does not get anything done.

He outlined a solution of disaggregation, decentralisation, autonomous units under separate control in NGOs (including the private sector), public reporting on the results of programmes, and an abandonment programme for the failures. He saw the 'need for new political theory and probably very new constitutional law', needs which remain unfulfilled today. His proposals formed the basis of New Public Management (NPM) that dominated public

---

2   Drucker, Peter (1969) *The Sickness of Government*, The Public Interest

sector reform thinking in the 1980s and 1990s in the Anglophone countries and can now be found in many parts of the world. NPM is still going strong. Other schools have arisen, for example focusing on governance and public value, but have never had the same take-up. NPM has had its successes and failures (but do not lay the latter at the door of Drucker – the developers of NPM omitted some essential components of his original conception).

So what is NPM? No single prescription exists but, in practice, Christopher Pollitt and Geert Bouckaert in their monumental work *Public Management Reform: A Comparative Analysis – New Public Management* describe it thus: 'The new model was to be business. Management was the key skill. Markets and incentives were the key mechanisms.' It is privatisation, competitive contracting out, and disaggregation of large multi-purpose bodies into separate agencies at arm's length to government, performance measurement, attempts at performance-related pay, accruals accounting. NPM spawned other models. I have lost count of the diagrams attempting to represent the unified field theory of public sector reform developed in central government agencies like the prime minister's Strategy Unit and Delivery Unit in the UK, from international management consultants like McKinsey, from think tanks, and from academics. Some are worth reading and some so limited as to be aberrant.

If you read only one book to understand the principles of organisation and why they do what they do, to grasp the nature of leaders and of leadership, to see how organisations shape and limit their heads, and to see how organisations can produce and promote the wrong kind of leaders, it would be Norman Dixon's seminal 1976 work *On the Psychology of Military Incompetence*, which was subsequently incorporated into officer training at Sandhurst. Military incompetence refers to the failures of military organisations, whether through incompetent individuals or through a flawed institutional culture, and is the chronic inability to do a particular job or activity successfully. Incompetence can be found in any industry, field, or discipline. But incompetence in war is much more noticeable and has far greater significance – death and destruction. Administrative incompetence is the inability of an organisation as a whole to adapt to change and innovation, as well as the inability of an organisation to learn from past mistakes. This bureaucratic inefficiency is not caused by any one person, but by organisational culture as a whole.

Dixon finds that the most common cases of military incompetence can be attributable to a flawed organisational culture. Leaders take decisions within the context of this culture – if it is flawed then the decisions will be flawed, unless the leaders have both the authority and the skill to surmount it. Perhaps the most marked of these flawed military cultures is a conservative and traditionalist attitude, where innovative ideas or new technology are discarded or left untested. A tendency to believe that a problem can be solved by applying an earlier – failed – solution 'better', be that with more men, more firepower, or simply more élan, is common too. A strict hierarchical system often discourages the devolution of power to junior commanders, and can encourage micromanagement by senior officers. It is always interesting to vet one's own place of work for these characteristics. An institutional culture devoted to following orders without debate can help ensure that a bad or miscommunicated decision is implemented without being challenged or corrected. Strict hierarchies of command provide the opportunity for a single (wrong) decision by a leader to direct the work of thousands. You may have noticed that occurring occasionally in our governments.

Dixon goes on to postulate that it is the military organisation that contains the potential to create incompetent leadership or to promote incompetent persons to positions of great power and responsibility. He lists several characteristics and values that the military holds in high esteem and strives to achieve, as well as their negative consequences. Among these are:

- Uniformity, to the extent of oppressive conformity and the crushing of individual thoughts and the devaluation of initiative.

- Hierarchy and the importance of proper authority, to the extent of a fear to report bad news to superiors, the rejection of suggestions or corrections from the lower ranks, and hostility towards those of lower rank who initiate action without permission, however effective or necessary the action was.

- A love of regularity and regimentation, to the extent of leading to an inability to think outside of drill.

- The fact that ambitious and achievement-oriented officers are highly esteemed and respected in the military, so much so that self-serving and vainglorious officers are sometimes promoted to high leadership, with disastrous consequences.

Take time to reflect on which of these characteristics are prevalent in organisations of your experience.

I have picked out just two writers on organisation – Drucker and Dixon. There are many more, if you want to delve. Amongst those most influencing me have been Stafford Beer on systems thinking, Charles Handy on voluntary sector organisations, Max Nicholson's *The System: The Misgovernment of Modern Britain*, Michael Porter's *The Competitive Advantage of Nations*, Peter Senge and his identification of individual learning within any organisation as its key strength, Norman Strauss's theories of ethos and constitution as being the fundamental determinants of performance, and Chris Rose's *What Makes People Tick*. This body of work applies equally to the private, public, and not-for-profit sectors. There are important differences to take account of in any design, but much commonality.

How Organisations Improve

Businesses have to compete on organisational expertise and applied competence to remain competitive. Consequently, a vast international movement of knowledge has grown up to feed this demand – from specialist journals, quality newspapers, professional institutes, trade associations, universities, travelling gurus, books, software designers, industry conferences, benchmarking companies, data comparators, and management consultants. There remains much to uncover, as anyone working in an organisation of any kind will know, but today we can design organisations to work.

Let's look at this 'learning engine' in action. Why does one organisation perform so well and another is in terminal decline?

How is it that the modern miracle of a DVD player came to pass, for example? What was it about the company inventing it that meant it won the race and others did not? How were the subsequent standards wars fought? How can such massive amounts of hard precision components be made and assembled so cheaply and to such consistent standards? How can they be updated with such speed? And, amongst all of this triumph, why is the user interface so poor that at times one wishes for the simplicity of the four controls of a VCR? What happens next? Will we all be stuffed by next-generation technology and its incompatibility with what is on our shelves? And what has this to do with running a country?

Our understanding of why organisations do what they do has moved on enormously since the 1970s. The Japanese usurpation of western and particularly US industry, leading with motorcycles and cars, stimulated an explosion in research in the 1980s. Markets were becoming global, and the US had sat on its dominant organisational model since the innovations of Ford in the 1920s. The Japanese came with concepts of Total Quality Management, Just In Time Stocking, Integrated Supply Chains, Self-directed Work Teams, and Customer Focus. Unlike some oft-quoted management jargon, these concepts were tested and applied and have endured, to the point where if you don't do them you won't exist. Unless your manufacturing and distribution is world class, you are not in business tomorrow. Absolute conformity to design specifications in every part of manufacture is the basis. A notable characteristic of Japanese culture is conformity. Perhaps it is no surprise that the manufacturing revolution started here. Why can you get an astonishing piece of technology called a DVD player, almost 100% reliable, for £30? Because of all this organisational theory and practice and these learning engines.

Think of an old banger from the 1970s compared to a modern car that has been developed on the basis of designing out all of the old car's faults, of applying all of the new technology, all the competitive pressures that led one car company to copy success from others, all of the accumulated knowledge from all of the world's successful manufacturing companies to build in reliability, consistency, and quality. Massive informal collaboration stimulated by massive competition. All to our benefit. Now we don't expect our cars to break down. But governments still do. Progress in competitive markets has been exponential. By comparison, progress in systems of government has been almost non-existent.

Alignment and World-Class Government

Is it an attainable objective to say that unless a government is world class, it is not in business tomorrow (i.e. does not get re-elected)? What would a government look like that had made the leaps and bounds of DVD-player manufacturing? If you want much better government then the key is organisation theory. Much of this theory comes from companies operating in competitive markets precisely because to stay in business, forty years of organisational leapfrogging has occurred and produced that explosion in understanding as to how the staff, IT systems, processes, markets, regulations, culture, structure, strategy, and leadership work together to produce an Apple, or the former world leader in mobile phones (but now ailing) Nokia.

This is the point to bring in a rather complicated but vital theory, termed alignment. Let's start with a simple example. Students aged 16–18 years at a teacher friend's school receive what is termed Education Maintenance Allowance of £30 per week. To get the payments, the students have must have their attendance confirmed by the school. So, despite the school being in a tough area – my friend describes much of his task as crowd control – the students turn up for class. In organisational terms, the allowance and attendance are 'aligned' – both are pointing in the same direction. Alas, when it comes to homework, no such alignment exists. The payment is not conditional on submitting homework. The teacher struggles using all of the usual tactics to get the homework completed. The teacher is then criticised for this not happening, the students underperform. The teacher is demotivated. The organisation of the schooling starts to unravel. It would be simple to align the grant with the mechanisms for learning – including homework – and with the motivation of the teacher. Results would improve.

Another example is the buying of new weapons by the Ministry of Defence. In its Major Projects Report 2011 the NAO said: 'The Ministry of Defence has been hampered by a legacy of poor planning and performance on some past projects, and the resulting cuts and delays are not value for money. But it is welcome news that the Department has finally accepted that the financial position it is in is serious and is actively working towards balancing its books in the longer term.' The most notable recent case was eight Chinook HC3s ordered in 1995 as dedicated Special Forces helicopters. They were to cost £259 million and the forecast in-service date was November 1998. The findings of the NAO report were:

- When placing the order with Boeing, officials did not include in the contract access to security codes to test their airworthiness.

- In 2001 the helicopters were delivered and found not to comply with airworthiness standards. The MoD was told they could only be flown safely up to 500 feet from the ground on a clear, sunny day. They were put into store in hangars in Boscombe Down.

- In 2002 less sophisticated Mk2 Chinook helicopters were equipped for night vision flying instead – but the infrared computer screens partly obscured front and landing vision, making them less safe to fly. The cost of the upgrade was £32.3m.

- In 2004 the MoD decided on a high-level upgrade at a cost of £215m to get the aircraft airworthy by 2008. But it took much longer than anticipated to get the programme organised with the contractor and it became clear the helicopters would not fly until 2011.

- In 2007 the MoD cancelled the upgrade, at a cost of £17.25m, because it would take too long. It opted for a cheaper programme with a new night vision system, costing £53m. That cost later more than doubled to £112m, with a further unknown sum for night-vision equipment.

The MoD then said it would have one of the eight helicopters in operation by 2009 and the rest in 2010. In June 2008, the National Audit Office issued a scathing attack on the MoD's handling of the affair, stating that the whole programme was likely to cost £500 million by the time the helicopters entered service. On 6 July 2009 the first of the modified HC3s made its maiden test flight at Boscombe Down, eleven years after the date by which it was supposed to be in service.

The NAO reported in 2000 that the Ministry of Defence had changed the way that it organises and conducts procurement business 'following implementation of Smart Procurement, which is now sustained and reinforced under the new heading Smart Acquisition' (begging the question as to what existed before it became smart). It now has 'Gold Standards' for project control. New heads of defence procurement from the private sector were employed with a remit to fix it. With no authority over the staff, who were all part of the Civil Service and who therefore owed their allegiance and income to that, these solitary heads were largely neutered. In current advice to government the conclusion is that a single person cannot fix it and the need is to bring in 400 outsiders. There is even talk of privatising the entire empire – help! Privatising a monopoly is almost invariably a failure. And the clients – the armed services – would still be there and deficient in procurement and contract management.

Despite fifty years of trying, MoD procurement remains inept. It may have got better – although the Chinook experience is as bad as any – but the organisation as a whole is still not aligned with its purpose. Thus the strategy may say that it is going to improve and embrace best practice, but when the people who are meant to do this have neither the skills or the motivation to do so, it will not happen. As one infantryman transferred to procurement said, 'My job description was, day or night, over any terrain, close with the enemy and kill them. How does that qualify me to buy an aircraft carrier?' Or indeed what good is a 2:1 in PPE from Oxford?

We will see later how luxury terms and conditions prevent change and improvement. The MoD has all of these. No one has been sacked, demoted or even disciplined for the Chinook fiasco, or any of the many other poor performances. The top management can make as many speeches as they like heralding the new dawn but does any member of staff actually need to go through the pain and inconvenience of the changes required to turn the heralded changes into reality? No. The terms and conditions and cultural norms immunise them from that objective. Everyone is hanging on for the gold-plated pension. The top people may occasionally be publically admonished by the Public Accounts Committee, but upon return to their offices their scars are worn with pride – these are honourable people who have defended their organisations against the ignoble and headline-seeking politicians who have no idea of their world. And criticism usually provokes stubbornness. This is a donkey. Thus government and the taxpayer and Parliament are pushing in one direction, whilst MoD procurement sits fat and happy changing a bit but never fundamentally, its heels dug in. The organisation and its components of terms and conditions, of skills, of personal objectives, of skills acquisition, of learning, of accountability, of control, and of culture are not aligned with the objectives legitimately and correctly set by government.

This is the curse of the public sector in the UK, and many other countries beside. It explains why so much public sector reform has little or no effect, why productivity remained static whilst funding rose throughout the 2000s, and why the Coalition government will fail (indeed is failing as I write) with its reforms as much as the previous government did. MoD procurement is a serial failure of left and right, of Labour and Conservative, of politics, and of the Civil Service. They all know it's a major, ultra-expensive cock-up. They get elected and go into government, change this, change that, and it's still a failure fifty years later. Reforms that ignore alignment – and they all do, except by chance – are forever doomed. Conversely, if you want a government to succeed, then alignment has to be written into its job description (usually termed the constitution), and without wiggle room.

In this case study, we can also observe the rats in a maze at the NAO. One might have thought that after fifty years of adopting the same approach to improving defence procurement and failing, the NAO might do something other than investigate, write a scathing report, and set up a public ear-bashing by the Public Accounts Committee. They might have asked the question, why is our approach not working? After all, it has only been failing consistently for fifty years.

If rats are too strongly motivated in their original learning, they find it very difficult to change when the original path is no longer correct. Thus, in the classic laboratory experiment, rats in a maze learn the route to food. The route is repeated and repeated, and the original learning is reinforced. Then, the route is varied. But the rats still take the same learned path if food is found in that same position once in every ten attempts. Nine out of ten times, no food is found or consumed, but the original learning of the route was so successful in securing rewards that rats will persist with a 90% failure rate.

Organisations do this. Thus, in writing proposals for competitive contracts, consultancies will have found approaches that work. For the next proposal, rather than listening hard to the client, the same proposal formula will be used. It will often fail, but so long as it succeeds occasionally, it will be re-used every time.

The 1997–2010 government had much success with its early public sector reforms. But the programme ran out of steam and ended in the same cul-de-sac. It persisted with the same formula even when the reward (further improvement) only occurred say 10% of the time, and the failure rate stood nearer 90%. It is a comforting thought to know that these big logical–rational brains behave, at times, on a par with rats.

At this point an off-putting diagram appears.[3] The difference between this one and some others from organisational theory is that it works. It comes from two academics called Burke and Litwin, and is the model of alignment.

You can read up separately on it, but broadly how the organisation works in each box has to be aligned to how it works in every other box. When it comes to reform and therefore what is said in the mission and strategy box, each of the other boxes has to contain the changes that will deliver this reform – a point Norman Dixon made. Thus with MoD procurement, it is glaringly obvious that simply changing one person in the leadership box will produce almost nothing. With 400 new people in the senior roles a little more may happen. But how much is changing in the other boxes, how much can the 400 change in these other boxes, and by how much will the other boxes change the 400? Certainly little without control over recruitment, the terms and conditions, and

---

3   W. Warner Burke and George H. Litwin, 'A Causal Model of Organisation Performance and Change', *Journal of Management*, Vol. 18, No. 3, pp. 523–45 (SAGE Publications, 1992).

over the external environment that is substantially determined by the behaviour of the armed services.

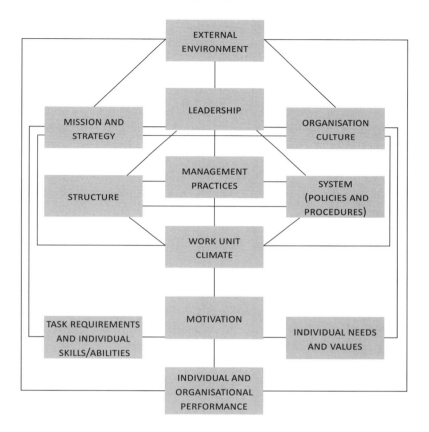

This particular misalignment of procurement and contract management is not just hidden in the offices of the MoD, but runs throughout the public sector. As well as providing services direct to the public, national and local government operates through many contractors. These range from trains, aircraft carriers, and road building, to council-tax collection, recycling, relationship counselling, professional advice, hip operations, congestion charges, and so on. A very considerable part of a successful public sector depends on selecting the right contractors and managing them well.

Much has been written about the problems of procurement in terms of the lengthy, time-consuming, and unfocussed selection processes, the excessive costs to bidders, and the common occurrence of government officials blaming all the ills upon the EU procurement directives. EU rules are often held up as the reason for doing something stupid in selecting the wrong supplier. The bureaucratic mind seeks only to follow procedure, as by doing so the back is perfectly covered. Judgement is avoided, and who would want to take the risk of making a judgement? Crass mistakes are made, and the EU fingered. Some in the public sector do aim to get the right contractor doing the right task at a competitive rate with the minimum process cost and time; but, in general, the public sector knows how to run procedures for competition, and not how to run a competition and most certainly not how to manage a contract.

The difference in procurement practice between the public and market sectors is stark. In the latter the right suppliers at the right cost are critical: without these the business or product would not survive. In the public sector, a procurement failure is not deemed business-critical and is usually blamed on the supplier. In the market sector, once a successful relationship is established, a supplier is retained: changing would be a big mistake, risking the business and throwing away a great deal of accumulated unwritten knowledge. The public sector has rules to change suppliers regularly (although the sensible managers here try to avoid them). Above all, in markets the whole of the chain of suppliers from raw materials to final assembly linking up through a series of companies to produce a high quality consumer durable like a smartphone, have a common interest in minimising the costs of procurement, which means the cost to the consumer is also minimised. Nowhere in the public sector does this imperative exist. Consequently procurement processes are not only not the lowest cost, they are hideously expensive. The overriding objective is to avoid any sense of impropriety – a legacy of the Poulson bribes of the 1970s in local government. The fact that today many other forces stop any corruption, and that vastly more money is wasted on the process and on poor contract management than any possible savings on corruption, does not register. And that secrecy is the essential growing medium for corruption, soft and hard. Of course, typically having very limited skills in the profession of procurement, and the organisation valuing bureaucracy, the procedural refuge is inevitable.

Rule one of procurement is that if the project fails it is the client's fault, not the contractors. Have you ever hired the wrong builder at home? Or been insufficiently explicit in what you want doing? Or not specified the standards of finish you want? Or driven the price down too much? Yes the builder may not have done a fair job, but whose fault is it in hiring the wrong company, in not thinking through the specification in advance, in changing it unnecessarily, applying the wrong pressure, conducting poor negotiations? Procurement failure is client failure.

A final point here is that the temptation is always to restructure the organisation to reform it – chop departments up and rename them, move social services to health, merge forestry with environment, etc. In every sector this is usually a waste of time and money – the usual analogy is deckchairs on the *Titanic*. Note in the Burke–Litwin model that structure is but one of twelve boxes. Solitary restructuring is for the uneducated – and for those looking to be seen to be doing something, when nothing is really changing.

I hope that this first contextualising chapter of the book has made clear that, in seeking to solve the problems of bad government, politics and political parties as we know them are a busted flush, democracy alone is not the answer, and the issues are not just for the British but run worldwide; that although the problems are huge, they are solvable and we can do it if we have the will; and that the means to the solution is organisation theory and practice, not political theory or another branch of academic government study. The same old thinking just gets you to the same old places.

In the rest of the book, Parts 1and 2 take us through what's wrong, and why. They are both a summary and a simplification. For example, the cause of the policy failure for telephony distribution is not simply 'the wrong people making policy', but I have used this to illustrate that particular fault. It is not possible to cover all of the nuances and complexities of every circumstance in a book whose purpose is to analyse the problem of the system of government and to produce a solution. The original notes and studies can be found on my website www.treatyforgovernment.org. If more detail is wanted on a particular example, then have a look there. As well as looking at root causes, examining why the last government to lose an election did so – and doing so not from a political but an organisational perspective – Part 2 also identifies the real villain of the piece, and is a useful introduction to the rationale for the Treaty in Chapter 7. Chapters 8 to 13 describe in some detail each of the components of the new system – feedback, policy, delivery, people, competitive democracy, and fair shares. The final chapter sets out what we can do to get the existing political parties to adopt the Treaty, and if they will not, looks at possible alternative of a new party. It is a call to arms. This big a change really can – and must – happen.

PART I
WHERE GOVERNMENTS FAIL

What's Wrong

The system of government has more wrong with it than you can possibly imagine. It groans under the weight of its own contradictions, but is shored up by the weight of opinion of its beneficiaries – from the adversarial industries of political parties, the news media and the law, to the senior Civil Service and some large public service organisations, to the banks, pension funds, corporates, and others who win more than their fair share of the cake through lobbying. This is not a system for you or me.

As you read through you may:

- Thrill to the way decisions are taken and policies made – a bodger's paradise where only a fraction of what is intended translates into beneficial change for us as citizens and consumers.

- Marvel at dodgy delivery – the means government uses to turn what it says into what actually happens (or most often doesn't happen).

- Wonder at governments flying blind without instruments, rarely knowing where they are, and with no systematic examination of whether policies have achieved their objectives.

- Rock to irrelevant ideologies, developed decades ago for societies long gone, but still able to get party activists on their feet stomping in the aisles.

- Catalogue the psychological flaws and ponder an insider/outsider's perspective on how the psychopathologies of power brought an end to one government's time in power.

- Gasp – if that's the right word – at the nineteen underlying reasons why one government lost an election and what this means for current and future governments.

Here is the truth about the inside workings of government, and why they fail so often – judged by our expectations and by their intentions. And why no one in government can do anything about it – and are often as frustrated as you and I. There are so many fault lines:

- Policy choices are bent to the most effective lobby – typically the one with the most money or influence, be it an industry, a profession, a company, or a PSO like the police – at our expense.

- Most policies/decisions do not produce the intended results. Often they generate waste on a grand scale, and at worst they exacerbate the problem that gave rise to them in the first place.

- We are locked into the enormously expensive cycle of one government correcting the mistakes and prejudices of its predecessor, only to make its own, followed by the next government repeating this ridiculous zigzag as the canoe of state careers from one bank to the other with near superhuman waste, all for the sake of political differentiation.

- We are living through an ideological hangover in a post-ideological age, a problem that is made worse in two-party systems.

- Usually policy failure becomes absorbed into the role of some institution or other, and no one has the time or expertise to call a halt.

- Politicians invariably suffer from economic-theory addiction, selected according to their personal psychopathologies, which ends in a bust of one sort or another. Economics bites the hand that feeds it.

- Real accountability of and effective means to improve the performance of most public sector organisations are largely absent, despite governments trying harder and harder. Performance varies – some is professional, some is truly inept, most is mediocre. Public sector productivity remains static. In desperation governments resort to blunt instrument 'reform'. The dominant method – New Public Management – has largely run out of road, but continues to be applied regardless. Proceduralism and managerialism are now rife and act as substitutes for any genuine outcome.

- The balance of power between the individual and government organisations is weighted very heavily in the latter's favour. There's a lot of noise in the relationship between government and the citizen. Complaint channels are difficult to use and mostly ineffective.

- As more and more delivery has been privatised or contracted out, the critical roles of effective regulation and professional contract management are performed to such low standards that much of the theoretical benefit of using the competitive private sector is forfeited.

- The political classes are selected mainly on their campaigning and political skills, when most of the job is about getting things to work – from schools to banks to energy markets.

- Civil servants are wholly unqualified for delivery and largely unqualified for policymaking, and operate in organisations that are not fit for their modern purposes.

- The feedback that would tell whether a policy, a law, a regulation, or a PSO is or is not working and how well or badly, is limited at best, usually totally absent, and always far too late. The subsequent mass politicisation of results is akin to leaving the scores of sports matches to the coaches to argue over. One consequence is that spin rules.

If governments frustrate you, you are absolutely right. It's a wonder that anything beneficial happens.

Parliament is not entirely blind to all of these flaws. Changes are made to the way things are run, invariably by new governments, but at the current rate we would be lucky to get decent government by the twenty-second century. Proposals get stuck because, for example, Civil Service reform means giving more power to the government and prime minister when too much is there already. Consequently, although absolutely essential, it is strongly resisted. House of Lords reform falls at the same hurdle – making it elected under the current arrangements simply means turning it into another prisoner of the bipolar political-party disorder.

The system of government limps on with its mixture of muddle, error, howlers, and the occasional success. Politicians rarely work out before getting into power that it's bust. Politicians arriving in their ministries are anxious to get on and 'change' things as soon as possible. Their horizons are short – their work lives are remarkably insecure. There's a manifesto to fulfil, news media baying for action (any action), and our expectations. So they try and often then have to fall back on spin to make it appear as if it worked. (If you've ever wondered why so much effort and time goes into spin then it is as much about convincing themselves that they are useful human beings as it is about convincing us that they are effective and in control.)

One answer to what's wrong is very simple: governments fail when they make the wrong decisions/policies, or the right decision/policy does not get put into practice. In the following pages I have attempted to convey the complex answer, here categorised under the four chapters: Policy Failure; Dodgy Delivery; People Failure; Feedback Failure. Inevitably these overlap, but I think you'll get the picture.

2

Policy Failure

Quality of government starts with the decisions it makes. Many of these come in the form of policies. Policy is broadly what a government proposes to do about something, as in energy policy, drug misuse policy, schools policy. It is a system of courses of action, regulatory measures, laws, and funding priorities intended to produce an outcome or result. Manifestos contain many policy proposals as the competing offers to the electorate. The need for further policies arises continually as events large and small occur.

We are going to use the vehicle of pensions to get to grips with why policies fail, and expand from there. You will find here ducked issues, gross unfairness, jealousy, zero political leadership, 'cake capture', interests so vested as to border on the corrupt, ideology driving the absurd pay of the pension fund managers and the disgraceful returns to pension fund investors, Civil Service ignorance, preferential lobbying, Enron accounting, trade unions on thoughtless power trips, inconvenient variables ignored, mass immigration, an expanding population, and no grasp of the criticality of engaging you and I and everyone on this most testing of issues. Welcome to the UK system of government, and to the dog's breakfast of pensions it has collectively served up for the last twenty-five years or so.

It all starts with longevity. Which is nice, as we get to live much longer than people around when pension systems were developed, and funding was based on living five years beyond the standard retirement age – broadly to seventy. Now the age to which one might expect to live is eighty-five – good. Except who is going to pay the pensions for this extra fifteen years?

This issue came to the fore in the late 1980s. Most pension schemes then were 'defined benefit', i.e. you got a proportion of your then salary, inflation-linked, on retirement. In the private sector and parts of the public sector these schemes were funded, i.e. the pensions are paid out of the money contributed by the employees and employers, plus the return on investments. But with longer lives, there was more to pay but no more contributions. The problem was being tackled in some of the private sector, simply by force of good accounting, arithmetic, and finite resources. Final salary schemes were scrapped, and 'money purchase' schemes adopted – which simply said that your pension would be the product of what has been saved by the time you retire. If you want more then save more. The responsibility is yours. There is no magic money growing on trees.

My company worked this one out in 1990 and we all got the bad news that defined benefits were going and the pension would be whatever we had put in. This was a real sickener, and we howled. The distant certainty of a secure and mildly comfortable existence in retirement was thrown in the air. Some of the risk in pension provision was transferred from the fund to the individual. Just as the shore is sighted, the tide pushes you out. Yet this is only the inevitable consequence of the huge advantage of a longer life. If ever there was a quid pro quo, this is it. Eventually we understood the simple maths, and starting saving more ourselves to cover our longer lives. If you think about it for a moment this is not unreasonable: we each receive the benefit of a longer life and are paying to fund that ourselves. Who else would, or can?

Various changes were made by government to facilitate this, but all the money had to go to the existing private sector pension funds, which were deemed big enough to be secure and of course the masters of finance in the City would do this vastly better than some tinpot public sector set-up. Except this is not true on three counts.

Firstly, the pension fund industry maintains its quite staggering share of the national cake at the expense of all those unfortunate enough to have their funds with them. In his 2010 report for the Royal Society for the Arts *Tomorrow's Investor: Building the Consensus for a People's Pension in Britain*, David Pitt-Watson discovered that if a typical Dutch person and a typical British person save the same amount for their pension, the Dutch person could expect a 50% higher income in retirement – that's an awful lot over fifteen years. The cause is the high cost and inefficiency of pension funds in the

UK. This represents the hard line of income redistribution from tomorrow's pensioners to today's pension fund managers – cake capture on a massive scale. Reducing income inequality starts here. The report sets out a 'pensions architecture' that would bring the UK in line with countries such as Holland and Denmark that enjoy the lowest levels of pensioner poverty in Europe. But regulators and civil servants make only tiny changes to the regime for pension funds.

Secondly, mutual pension funds have traditionally performed best untroubled by shareholder returns and overpaid managers, but these have been 'converted' by the missionaries from the investment banks bribing the management, and adopting the new religion – conversions promoted by the Conservatives' ideology. Once converted to a PLC, the fund's performance and thus the pensions of the individual bears no relation, except by chance, to the share price or to the pay of the fund managers. The latter can and do boom whilst the former languish. If ever there were a misaligned industry then this is it. However – and here is an investment tip – if your pension is invested with a privately owned pension fund then the owners' and managers' wealth and income increases in line with yours as an investor – classic alignment. Latterly, we must add here for balance, in the absence of good governance, remaining mutuals have been infected by managerialism – an organisational disease covered later.

Thirdly, the Universities Superannuation Scheme (USS) is one of the few sensible pension funds in the UK. It is self-funded and takes no government subsidy or tax, it is run to maximise long-term returns and minimise costs, it uses in-house fund managers, and has strong pensioner-focused governance. It still has sufficient self-generated funds to pay defined benefit pensions. Marvellous. It should be open to us all. At a stroke it would open up the market for private pensions. It should be also the model for all public sector pensions. But, of course, it is public sector and the Conservatives are in power.

Whilst the poor sods in private sector schemes were seeing their future incomes both necessarily reduced and squandered by the pension funds, the public sector was heading in the other direction. So long as salaries were limited by the anti-public sector Thatcherites, then the pension liability, whilst growing, was not

an immediately pressing financial tidal wave. But, both for fairness
and quality of staff, when Labour came in salaries went up, yet
the pension provision was not capped. Some of these schemes are
part-funded but others are not only unfunded, but gold-plated,
defined-benefit, and index-linked. Great news for your future
taxes and those of your children. Just think if you are not in one of
these schemes when you retire, out of your now much-diminished
pension, your taxes will be higher to pay for the civil servants'
blossoming pensions. The national jealousy quotient rose. Social
cohesion suffered.

Governments were ducking this issue like mad. A ducked issue
is one that a government avoids because either it fits into the too-
difficult box, or it offends a core constituency. The result is that
little or nothing is done, and the problem is left to fester until it is
too large to ignore. No politician wants to stand up and announce
the price of longevity. They all knew it, but announcing it would
be bad politics. Such was the accounting that, like companies
hiding liabilities through lax rules, governments could conceal the
growing and unsustainable public sector pension liability simply
by not having to record it. How convenient. Magic. At the end
of March 2010 the net value of future public sector pension
payments arising from past employment was £1.133 trillion, or
78.7% of GDP. Accounting is improving but still open to abuse.
When future committed liabilities are not accounted for, then the
decision to maintain or increase public sector employees' pensions
appears to have no cost.

The people in government with responsibility for unravelling
this accelerating Gordian knot were hardly equipped to do so. In
the thirteen years of New Labour, eight pension ministers came
and went, hardly having time to get to grips with the problem
before being shuffled off. They were appointed not for reasons of
expertise or performance, but to maintain the power of the prime
minister through patronage. (By and large, the nearer the prime
minister is to ejection, the higher the rate of reshuffle. This rate
is a sure sign it's time to go.) In any event, none of these eight
ministers had any great expertise in pensions, relying on a cadre
of civil servants who make it a matter of principle to stay in one
policy area for only three years or less. As the leading civil servant
of his time on pensions, one said that as his third year started it was

time to move on otherwise his career would get stuck. So bags of ignorance there. And, to ice the cake, why on earth would they want to rock other people's pension boat when their own might get caught up in reform (and theirs was the best of the lot)? Imagine then that you are the pensions minister, where will you go for advice?

At this point, whoopee, the door is held wide open to some preferential lobbying. There is some serious money at stake here. The pension fund managers are making a killing through all of this – they have captured a significant slice of the national cake – and understandably want to keep hold of it. They spend considerably on expert advice from economists and others to 'prove' that all is well with their service and that any change to open up the market would leave the poor pension investor prey to all sorts of new entrant knaves. It would be unsafe to allow these ignorant citizens to make choices over the destination of their money.

Each time pensioners try to escape from this cartel, they are rounded up and returned. Governments continue to protect the pension fund industry by requiring that to secure tax relief, private pension holders can only invest in these funds and not in other sources of return, thus maintaining their oligopoly and high costs. When SIPPs were set up in the mid-2000s, initially individuals were to be allowed to invest in property, art, wine and so on, but the industry soon found words to stop this – too risky, unsafe for the dodderers, etc. So the rules were changed to restrict investments to those provided by the financial markets. Once more the pension funds continued on their serene protected path, thanks to the government. The coalition recently introduced some form of universal pension provision – good, if twenty years late – but all the savings have to be invested with the same old fund suspects.

I term this 'sheepdog lobbying'. An industry has a monopoly hold over a government-provided franchise. Because it comes with sweeteners, usually tax relief, only the existing players are allowed in. The public sector is excluded because the private sector is as we all know 'better' at providing these sorts of services, and the private sector lobbies have largely killed off mutual provision. Competition outside the established players is limited or non-existent. The punters, i.e. you and me, get a poor service from this oligopoly. After some time, our representatives in Parliament take up our cause demanding wider provision and wider services. Government proposes policy reforms, whereupon the industry sends in its quiet but most powerful lobby to the Civil Service and ministers, neuters the proposals, and retains its franchise. The farmer (the pension fund industry) sends its sheepdogs (the civil servants) to round up the straying sheep (you and me) – and pop them back in pen.

So, as the New Labour government, what are you going to do? The same unpleasant issue existed in the public sector – retired employees here were not dying off any earlier than their private sector counterparts. But increasingly, Labour's last remaining significant constituency was the public sector, and its trade unions represented many of these workers. Reducing pensions would not be welcomed. Despite some minor planned changes, the issue was ducked. And grew.

Fortunately, along comes a well-regarded think tank, the IPPR, with whom I've worked. They are good, but alas this time they simply ran with a pro-immigration agenda based on analysis that essentially said we needed lots of working immigrants who would pay sufficient taxes to cover future public sector pensions. So was born the Chancellor's magic, and the virtuous circle of immigration, pensions, and benefits. Thus, an expanding population of motivated working migrants would pay for the growth in the ageing population, and its future pension cost. The displaced and unemployed local population unable to compete with educated motivated migrants would have good benefits also paid out of the higher tax revenues from the expanding GDP. The benefits needed to be sufficient to keep the socially excluded passive, and to absolve any issues of conscience from party activists. You can still find public sector workers supporting mass immigration precisely because they have bought the line (mistakenly) that this will fund their future pensions. A pension based on unsustainable immigration – not pretty.

Alas, the Chancellor's magic omitted all sorts of costs of mass immigration that we will come to later. The point here is that governments have an extraordinary capacity to ignore inconvenient variables. It considers this normal, and often does it without thinking. The inconvenient variable is simply left out of the equation. This has several benefits – first, the policy can be put into practice more quickly without time-consuming analysis; second, policy based on prejudices or values can proceed without evidence getting in the way; and third, it takes less brain space and energy. Usually, ignoring a variable leaves a policy ineffective. Societal change being what it is, many policies are ineffective, and delivery may be too. Noticing that the cause of policy failure is the ignored variable is obscured – except in the case of immigration, where the public noticed what the economists had ignored (and which the book will take further in the section on systems thinking).

This formula fell apart with the finance crash of 2008 forcing the issue of public sector expenditure cuts. Along comes the new coalition government that had had plenty of time in opposition and plenty of non-civil servant advice to, at last, grip the issue. Governments only do much of use fresh from courting us at election time and before they have been absorbed by the indulgency system.

Public sector pensions have been reduced, to the sound of the understandable howling to which I gave vent in 1990. Governments tend to be fifteen to twenty-five years behind the times. The decision was inevitable but the government did not do what is always necessary in circumstances of major change with losers all around, and engage people in first understanding the problem and second in finding solutions. Yes, these may have been much the same as the government had decided upon – although invariably improved – but the people affected felt done-to rather than regrettably accepting of the inevitable. This is a big change in expectations – no longer a secure income from sixty or sixty-five to death, but every likelihood of a longer working life and funding more of ones retirement oneself. Public engagement – which we will come to in some detail later – is not an option when such controversy is inevitable.

The government has also had a shot at introducing mandatory saving for pensions for all employees. Again essential, and I would only remark that sensible countries – Australia and Singapore, for example – have had such schemes in place for many years. However, ideology once more is playing its part in government failure, as all of this saving is to be channelled into – you guessed it – the hands of the overpaid and underperforming pension fund industry, because, of course, the private sector does it better. Actually, collective schemes perform better, run far from the City of London by anyone but the masters of finance unless privately owned. Over at the near worthless semi-public sector, without any of its management with a carefully spun PR profile nor earning millions, the USS is still providing defined benefit pensions all funded from the universities' and staff's contributions. If only I could put my pension pot into the USS. But I'm not allowed to. My pot is someone else's cake, remember.

Where have the regulators been all this time? Determined by governments ignorant of life in financial services, regulation has followed the hands-off approach, with no forethought or risk assessment, acting only on failure once a fund has been well and truly robbed, putting in place guarantees for the individual only once pensions have been lost. The pension funds write to one annually and describe the comparative riches to be paid on retirement. This is pure fantasy. Up until very recently, the rates of return used to calculate these were set at 7%, on the grounds this was the historic return from equities. Whilst this is about right if taken over a long enough period, after the fund managers have taken their cream the return delivered is both much less and for some derisory. The calculation rate has now been reduced by 2%. Which is some improvement. But, the accountable and accurate rate would be that actually returned by the fund to its savers over the last ten years. Statements would then be real and show up the actual abysmal returns. Instead, government allows the mythology of the industry and its consequent earnings to continue.

By way of reassurance, do remember that all of the people who have governed and run these appalling arrangements – civil servants, politicians, regulators, and pension fund managers – are on good to excellent pensions. Versailles, here we are.

So, there we have it. What a triumph. Once again, two political parties, five prime ministers, a congregation of pensions ministers, a drift of regulators, and a carousel of the 'clever generalists' of our Civil Service have all failed us. If the very obvious issue of pensions had been gripped when it became apparent twenty or thirty years ago, and first those affected – most people – had been engaged with the problem and its scale, the modelling done and published, efficient pension funds established, and a programme of slow change introduced to people's expectations of retirement, then today the conflict, disappointment, and cost of ducking it would be unnecessary.

We really do put up with an enormous amount of dross from government. Inconvenient variables are ignored, issues dealt with in isolation from those that they are bound to affect, policies for the field made at a desk far removed from their target, statistics misused or misunderstood, insufficient grasp of the human condition, dark lobbying, fashion, ideology, self-image, media frenzy, the wrong people making the policy – and you know a policy is never going to work when a tsar is appointed.

There are even more causes of poor policy than this. These are summarised below under the headings 'Cake capture and lobbying', 'Zigzag government', 'Ideological failure', 'Too much economic theory' and 'The wrong people making policy'.

Cake Capture and Lobbying

Cake is captured in all manner of ways. The senior Civil Service maintains its armlock over central government administrative posts, its job security, status, lack of public scrutiny, and cashmere terms and conditions through its union and lobby the humbly named First Division Association. This has as its head essentially a spin-doctor who spends his days oiling and greasing around Westminster, and fighting off any threat to their continued independent existence. Maintaining farming stability through subsidy has been vital to the country since the Second World War, but the system of subsidy has perverse consequences and often ends in the wrong places. Farming keeps its subsidies. A train company wins a franchise to run part of the national rail network, and there's the next licence to print money. The big banks keep their cake by the regulators preventing new entrants into the market. Even electricians now have their slice to defend with mandatory checks of circuits in rented properties. The trick is to get a monopoly one way or another and to defend it forever.

But this is a zero-sum game. Whenever some group or other gets a disproportionate slice of the cake, you and I are paying, through higher prices and fees, or higher taxes. At the margin, we might say OK, tackling this abuse is not worth the candle, but once this much of the national cake is being consumed unfairly, then the price adds up to a fair chunk of the household budget. It is demotivating, it lowers productivity, and it is time to get hold of the cake-capturers.

Let's see how to get and keep your slice of the cake. Preferential lobbying is all you need.

In explaining why industry lobbies tend to dominate policymaking, one former minister said the alternative to listening hard to the industry was 'daft academics and generalist civil servants.' Better the useful devil you know, albeit with a vested interest, than the ignorant devil, might be the rationale. At least the industry is real, is producing employment and economic activity, has genuine practical expertise, and has the discipline of a profit and loss account to face once the decisions are taken. By contrast, the academics and civil servants have never worked in the industry and face no disciplines on their proposals. If they turn out in application to be a foul-up, their penalty is short-term memory loss. They live and live by the next research project or the next post. Their advice and views are often counter-productive and deemed less useful than those of the industry, which naturally is seeking to serve its own ends. At least the companies continue, and government needs their investment and for them to at least go along with the policy to make it work, goes one former minister's rationale.

The success of lobbies depends on the industry ignorance of those politicians and civil servants making the policy. Into this void comes the lobbyist with independent reports from experts that make the best case for the industry – I've seen them and even written them. Arguments to counter any press comment or pressure group, or public dissatisfaction. Lobbying also depends on decisions being made behind very closed doors and without public scrutiny or vetting. Thus the reasoning for the decision can be easily spun. No long-term accountability for the decision exists – the ministers and civil servants will be long gone by the time the chickens come home to roost, and no systematic feedback on the results of a policy is collected. And, in some cases and countries, the industry may be funding your party or yourself. All of this means lobbies can make hay. At our expense.

In the US, the power of the organised lobby goes much further. New federal nutrition guidelines would have increased the amount of fruit and vegetables in school lunches. But after large 'food' companies spent $5.6 million lobbying against the rule, in November 2011 Congress decided that the tomato sauce on top of pizzas meant that the pizza could qualify as a vegetable. These pizzas are part of the food disaster, containing all the processed fats, sugar and salt to generate addiction and to feed obesity. They also reform the taste buds in the palate. This is mouth control. What next – the mind?

Whenever a liberalisation agenda raises its head, Mexican drug cartels are said to lobby Congress hard to maintain the hard line war on drugs. At first, this is surely oxymoronic – an illegal drug cartel opposing its legalisation. The point is that the business model of these cartels depends on drugs being illegal in the US. Without it, cocaine growing would be another part of agriculture, and processing and distribution another part of pharmaceuticals. The ultra high profits of the cartels would disappear and their methods would be no match for farmers and corporates. So lobby hard to keep them illegal. Lobbies are also used to increase border controls. The better the controls, the less drugs gets through, the higher the price.

Besides wondering whether legal 'school pizzas' are more or less harmful than illegal cannabis or cocaine, and besides our horror at the reality and impact of lobbying, there is a crucial point here. Next time you wonder why the government has taken that particular and seemingly odd decision, the chances are that it will be the product of an industry lobby. Political parties funded by business and rich individuals, almost zero feedback, decisions taken in private, limited independent expert scrutiny, a career-tenured generalist Civil Service, and first past the post makes for a government squarely in the hands of corporates, vested interests, and bureaucracies. Your interests / needs / preferences will take second place – if any place at all. Current proposals to keep a register of lobbyists will make little difference. The solution needs to be far more encompassing.

Next on our journey through the whys of policy failure, we find government has left the lobby to spend time in the river.

Zigzag Government

Have you ever canoed down a river and found that no matter how carefully you paddle, your path zigzags from one side to other? Repetitive course corrections are essential simply to avoid crashing into the bank, being beheaded by low-lying foliage, grounding on a mudbank, or disturbing an irate swan. River guides in the Rio Grande term a boat paddled by a couple 'the divorce canoe', such is its behaviour and the mutual assumption of blame – it's his/her fault.

In predominantly adversarial parliaments, zigzag government is the norm. Every time the ruling party changes so the ship of state shoots off to the other bank. Two-party states, as in the US and UK, with first past the post, build in this phenomenon. Look back over a long period and watch the country zigzag down the river. Progress is slow, wasteful, and frustrating.

In 1979, Liberal MP Richard Wainwright said: 'The five depressing days that have passed since this debate was adjourned have done nothing to make less miserable the unhappy political plight of the National Enterprise Board, which is caught in the fatal zigzag of British politics.' The National Enterprise Board was set up in 1974 partially as a vehicle to hold the bankrupt failures of British management (shipbuilding, steel, cars) and partially to invest in hi-tec companies unable to secure finance from a safety-first, self-serving City of London. The NEB was a success, alongside other research and development investment vehicles. But it was public sector, so the Conservatives scrapped it.

Bodies are opened and closed and transferred according to the 'four legs good, two legs bad' school of politics. The notion of assessing rationally the role and performance of government in industry, using evidence, never surfaced in the political debate over the NEB, the National Research Development Corporation, or the British Technology Group.

In the UK, zigzag government has resulted in many flawed decisions. The Conservatives usually favour grammar schools or now academies, Labour comprehensives. For at least fifty years, much political energy has gone into arguing which is right. The structure changes. Fag ends of old systems cling on. All the energy goes into proving which is better. Actually, around the world, examples of both systems can be found that work. But in some countries, there is consensus on the system, and the energy goes into making the system work. In the UK, the debate just rumbles on with the political criticism eternally demotivating the teachers and pupils, and, whichever the system, it underperforms. Transport has followed a similar course – Conservatives essentially favouring road building (private transport uses roads) and Labour railways. Rather than a balanced transport policy it lurches from bank to bank.

The zigzag occurs at every level. Within the NHS, the Conservative government in the 1990s introduced internal charges for operations to incorporate some discipline over costs. Labour abolished these charges on its arrival in 1997, only to conclude cost-consciousness mattered and reintroduced the 'internal market' in 2003. Labour believes in the arts as a force for education and for good in society; the Conservatives stick to markets and support for established or flagship arts. Labour believes in regional economic development; the Conservatives do not: it gets turned on and turned off. Labour introduces the Giro bank operating out of the Post Office (as in most other European countries); the Conservatives privatise it (to later become part of the banking crash).

The largest zigzag is over public expenditure and public services. Broadly, Labour puts it up (too much) and Conservatives put it down (too much). Inconsistent funding over decades is inefficient, as services are ramped up and then ramped down or closed, both at high cost. The current cuts have destroyed large chunks of voluntary sector expertise in a range of important skills and outcomes. Their absence will be felt. In time, the clear-up costs will be high. Then, the government will change and this expertise will be built up again, all at great cost. Thatcher would gladly have seen the end of the NHS and a US style health system in its place. Labour 'believes' in lots of public services, not least today because that they are its principle constituencies (and of its funders, the trade unions). Conservatives 'believe' markets know best and too big a state crowds out the private sector. Public sector pay, and in the long run the quality of the people working in it, at its peak is sublime and at its trough, ridiculous. The quality of teaching partially follows this zigzag.

In the World Economic Forum's competitiveness survey for 2010/11, the UK ranks thirty-third for the quality of its infrastructure alongside Slovenia and behind Tunisia – roads, railways, ports, air transport, telephones, energy. Infrastructure depends on government investment and market stimulation. Being sophisticated thinkers, the Conservative government of 1979–97 was of the 'public sector bad' school, and wilfully and woefully neglected publically funded infrastructure and pursued ideological privatisations of rail, electricity and water with inevitable failure – only madmen privatise whole monopolies – as well as failing to get effective competition up and running in telephony. Infrastructure is long term in the making and the decline. The UK's ranking today is one of Thatcher's enduring legacies.

Enter the next government, which being of the 'public sector good' school put right public spending, but spent too much on employing people and not enough on lasting projects. It overdid the spending too, so having rebounded from the riverbank, once more infrastructure investment is in decline. Further, Labour's de facto population policy of a 20% increase to 70 million demanded 20% extra infrastructure to stay still, let alone catch up. None of this happened – population increase and its enormous costs being another of the inconvenient variables in the public sector pension 'solution' of economic immigration.

The further irony here is that Labour's public expenditure excess gave the incoming Conservatives of the coalition every reason to cut: first the level simply could not be afforded and was being funded in part by debt, and waste was obvious. Cue the anti-public expenditurites. If you want to blame someone for today's cuts, Gordon Brown is your man.

Quite why the two parties have elevated these simplistic views to beliefs is not clear. The most likely answer is the psychological need to be right, a need that drives much of the political competition everywhere. In government this need is as productive as the divorce canoe.

Some people believe that conflict and an adversarial system, and thus zigzag, are good for government. After all, politics is arguably all about difference and disagreement. But there is a difference between disagreement manufactured by a two-party system (by these parties being the prisoners of their history, obliged to repeat its myths and legends) on the one hand, and, on the other, disagreement based on a mutual desire to get to the right answer; between the need to be right and the intent to learn.

Ideological Failure

This leads us into redundant ideologies – possibly the largest cause of policy failure. A political ideology is a certain ethical set of ideals or principles of a social movement or institution that explains how society should work, and offers some political and cultural blueprint for a certain social order. In a 'winner takes all' two-party system, nominally we experience the construction/ imposition of one ideology for a period, followed by another, quite different ideology. For a while, one ideology is deemed to be correct. Subsequently, for another while another ideology is apparently correct. Both main parties cling to their roots with an extraordinary tenacity, even when confronted with the obvious fact: the conditions in society giving rise to these ideologies have long gone. Yes, there remain some downtrodden and some benign rich, but too few on which to base a generalised party ideology. In the compressed political playing field of the modern world, how useful is ideology? Unlike many films that are best watched with your disbelief suspended, this chapter is best read with your beliefs suspended.

The Conservative Party is as much trapped by its ideology as Labour Party, but this section focuses on the way ideology shapes and limits Labour. The usual caveat pertains: a similar analysis of other parties and governments would lead to similar conclusions as to the worth of their ideologies.

New Labour was intent on being non-ideological. Tony Blair and the party leadership assembled a formidable team of thinkers, organisers, strategists and communicators. Many others existed more widely, bursting to apply some unprejudiced thinking to the nation's problems after the years of Thatcher's guts as policies. Some much-needed remedial government repaired and revitalised public services and redeployed some power via devolution, some proportional representation, the Freedom of Information Act, and the Human Rights Act. They were successful for a while. People understand that New Labour tried.

But ideology lurked and was smuggled into many decisions. So now we are back to where we were. The Labour Party in opposition is simply talking to itself. It is unable to hold an adult conversation on welfare, immigration, gender or population. It evangelises minorities. It remains a party of sectional interest – the trade unions. Bring me the head of a person in need. Ed Miliband, as the new leader of the Labour Party opened a speech with: 'The Webb–Fabian tradition was born of an era where the challenge for the left was meeting people's basic needs for health, housing, education and relief of poverty. That need will always remain.'

Now, will it? Or, perhaps more appositely, who will meet these needs? And who will those with these needs want to meet them? These quite simple Webb–Fabian phrases – and there are quite a few in the party's lexicon – are held as eternal truths. When stated, they sound good, provide some certainty in a messy world, and give a sense of worth to the listener. They are self-evident. But when voters wake up in the morning do they feel: 'I have a housing need which the state will meet'? Or, indeed, 'I can look to those nice people on the left to meet it'? That was the model in the Soviet Union, of course. All housing was provided and allocated by the state. Or, when they wake up, do they think about seeing what is available in the local paper, or housing association, or council, or hostel, or Internet? And about negotiating their way through estate agents, landlords, mortgage applications, solicitors, removals firms, and utilities companies?

The Webb–Fabian tradition is not connecting here with real lives and the way things, in this case housing, get done today. If this tradition is now restricted to only those at the bottom of the pile, to those in real need, then perhaps the tradition has a place. The theory surely still applies that the state is here to help those in need. The difficulty that arises is that need, incentive and motivation have interacted to produce a muddle. The provision of basic needs by the state has led to some being incentivised to not work – the difference in pay being small or negative; incentivised to have babies to secure housing and some sense of purpose – every child matters and the better they are brought up the better for everyone, except this child would not be here at all if it were not for the benefits regime; babies being born into 'freakonomics' households where the circumstances are such the child is much more likely to end up as a tax-negative citizen and involved in crime; and economic migrants going into 'care' to secure somewhere to live. One person's need can be another person's (or indeed the same person's) incentive.

The difficulty for today's party is that, again, it has a mental model of what to do based on life a very long time ago. Thus, need is tracked down and surfaced in some triumph. Indeed, those that locate new 'needies' are accorded some status. These are the true custodians of socialism. The mental model for responding to that need is to give something – most often money (but never called that, thus 'aid' or 'benefits' or 'grants'), or asylum or citizenship. Bits of conditionality have been tacked on here and there, but the core model is the direct relief of need. Think of an earthquake and the immediate aftermath. The need is absolute – water, food, shelter and medicine – and the relief model is immediately absolutely right.

However, *Shameless* lifestyles in modern Britain have no relation to lifestyles in Haiti after an earthquake. This is an extreme juxtaposition, but something has to shake the party out of its dusty mental models. The overseas-aid model has seen a significant proportion of the money going to facilitating corruption and maintaining poor governments, which has, at the least, set back a nation's development – the real key to solving mass poverty. Is aid 'socialism'? Is the 0.7% of GDP target based on real principle or the relief of conscience?

When faced with a Webb–Fabian basic need in today's world it may be a need, it may also be insured misfortune, uninsured misfortune, bad luck, laziness, the wrong incentives from the state, choice, stuck in a rut, or no ladder to climb out. These options may or may not be the fault of the individual. The point is that responding to them all with the 'giving' model does not work. Ideological welfare is as productive as ideological privatisation. So long as the comforting Webb–Fabian tradition is trotted out as an anchor for thinking, Labour will miss the point by a large slug of indiscriminate public expenditure.

The party is drawn to these debates around 'isms' and to their fathers and mothers – Webb, Hardie, Rousseau, Methodists, whoever. The various intellectual factions of the party spend a lot of time and energy in these ism debates, but any political party can only win a majority by representing a coalition of isms, and other interests besides. In order not to be found out, a long-term government has even more need to coalesce the isms if in practice it has been pursuing a sole ism, as Gordon Brown did and, in part,

David Cameron is. Supporting gay marriage is just a sound bite, alas. Sleight of hand will not hide the ism intent for more than a few years in government.

So both as a matter of principle, the party should represent and value a multi-ism society – and as a matter of winning, the party needs to find a way to cohere its isms. Of itself, an ism means nothing, except being shorthand for describing a vision of society – the sort of society we believe in. But it is presumptuous for a party to believe it can create a different society, as distinct from riding its changes. The 80s were the 80s were the 80s. Thatcher exploited and reinforced its values, but did not create them. Britain learnt from that experience, as electorates do, and social democracy took hold with a lot of help from New Labour. It went wrong when it tried to smuggle in its isms (and practised its psychological flaws).

Labour has forever championed minorities and non-discrimination. Its origin was as a mass party representing the disadvantaged and oppressed majority of workers and families. This concern for the downtrodden extended to many of those suffering disadvantage. The government took a strong lead in the cause of unacceptable discrimination against immigrants and ethnic minorities, women, disabled people, gays, and non-smokers. Great. But its unwavering focus on these minorities who were accorded almost official status by the leadership and protected from any comment or question by 'their appointment to HMG' left substantive groups out in the cold or actively discriminated against. For all of its moral high ground on discrimination, objects of acceptable discrimination emerged during the 1997–2010 government – smokers, fathers, the white working class, private pension holders, and men.

Equal opportunities and non-discrimination will always be cornerstones of any social democratic party. But, the party has to look at just where and how significant the lack of opportunities is, whether it merits priority in its objectives, and what it will do in practice to change it. At the same time, evangelising a minority can lead it to becoming a protected species, given special treatment, screened from any criticism or healthy satire so essential for a functioning community, aggressive in its sense of rights, over-provided for, and a 'golf club' to aspire to. I have observed angry cyclists, demanding benefit recipients, domineering women, never-used disabled facilities, and migrants taking the piss. Not being in a minority does not mean the rest of us are wrong.

Since mass enfranchisement, politics has been about representing one section of society to its advantage and to disadvantage another – broadly the have-nots and the haves or the other way round, the workers and the owners, women and men, immigrants and the indigenous, north and south. As society has become more equal and diverse, sectional interest politics has become less relevant. Elections can no longer be won on this basis. But the Labour party was founded by the trade unions and has always pursued sectional interests. What of the future?

Trade unions were invented to defend workers from appalling conditions and to limit high-handed management decisions – to gain a fair day's pay for a fair day's work. In those days, any improvement was right by any moral standard. That world has long gone – the working man and woman have far bigger enemies today than British management: global competition, indiscriminate immigration, dirty banking, and some union leaders themselves. But the trade union link via party funding, party membership, and sponsoring of MPs has trapped the party narrative in the archaic terms of worker's rights. The reality of today's trade unions is that they do delay trains, disrupt services, reduce the educational attainment and social mobility of schoolchildren through preventing the dismissal of poor teachers, and they maintain the privileged conditions of public sector employees vis-à-vis their private sector counterparts. I know what trade unions subtract, but today I am uncertain as to what they add.

Once any organisation is no longer clear why it is here, performance will suffer and decline is inevitable. The same is true for commercial organisations and for the public sector. Labour is now in the midst of an identity crisis – though the business of daily politics may put that to the back of one's mind. After all, it has won. People are no longer oppressed. Generally we are well off. So what does it do? Some have been interpreting this identity crisis in terms of New Labour being a good or bad thing, and whether it should continue or be dropped. Thus New Labour is identified as the source of the party's uncertainty, and a return to more traditional values would provide the solution; others seeing the applied brakes as the cause, and thicker and more widely spread New Labour being the solution.

Neither is the case. This particular debate takes place up a creak, in a canoe, without a paddle. The New Labour project was necessary to winning the election in 1997 and to its successes in government. Such was the poor image of 'Labour', the irrelevance of most of its policies to most people, and the completion of its original mission, in 1993 my advice to John Smith was to change the party's name. At that time this was a step too far for the party (but perhaps not for the country), and the term New Labour wasn't born until later under Tony Blair.

Whether the future now lies with new, old, only used once, nearly new, or middle-aged labour is not the point. Understanding where the country is and what people want and need provides the basis for re-election, not tribalism based on backward-looking self-justification, in hock to its history and to its ideology. This will never work. The big question is will it take twenty years to work this out, alongside several election losses, or does the collective courage exist to take the difficult decisions now?

I like much of the world we live in – friends, the food, the landscape, the humour, the comforts, technology, art, music, kindness, humanity, and the quite extraordinary explosion in new knowledge. I accept much in this world I am stuck with, although I do not care for it – capitalism, organisational life, mass consumerism. There are things I do not like much that we can change– inadequately accountable state and corporate organisations, bent banking, extremes of wealth and poverty, congestion, illiberty, third-rate government, totalitarian corporations, noise, climate chaos. The antidote to the isms could lie with one simple answer to the question 'What do you want from a government?', and the answer might be: 'Someone who will make our lives easier.' No philosophical triangulation. No heroics. Just something straight. 'Here is my life. I am not selfish and I would like you to make other people's lives easier too. But I am OK. I have no great disagreement with the society in which I live, and, anyway, the chances of turning it upside down are slim, and I have too much on to do that. So, oh political party, please understand my life and make it easier.'

Note the emphasis here is on the verb 'make', akin to the 'get on with doing a decent job' vision, which wants a party with reachable ambitions and greater achievement, not a party with lofty ambitions and limited achievement. When setting objectives, is it better to go for a medium objective with 80% achievement or a high objective with 20% achievement? This is the usual trade-off. To paraphrase Voltaire: 'The best is the enemy of the good.' The party should be aiming for and delivering the good, not the unattainable best.

Too Little Accounting and Too Much Economic Theory

First a brief word about the role of accounting. As the name implies, it is about accounting for how money has been spent. As such, all it attempts to do is converge on a set of numbers that comes as close to a true and fair numeric representation as is material. Provided you read and understand the caveats and definitions and these are straight, modern accounting does its job. Governments fail with it simply because they do not use it enough or properly. If your company's profits are not looking too good, a common practice is to visit the balance sheet, remove some of the assets there, and pop them into the profit-and-loss account. Or take the cost of a project out of the P&L account and capitalise it in the balance sheet. In Germany, making staff redundant is difficult under the law so the tendency is to inflate sales, not reduce costs. Magically, profits look better. This can go on for quite a while. You need to be a sharp reader of accounts to spot all the transfers. There are always technical arguments to support them, some legitimate, some borderline, and some so ridiculous that any auditor signing them off is not an auditor but a fool without ethics. The major corporate failures have invariably been accompanied by 'creative' or bent accounting, with Enron arguably the worst.

You may view accounting as boring. However, regularly it is one significant difference between good and bad government. In the recent crises, the countries that fared worst combined all three of these drivers: banks allowed to 'invest' in asset myths (supported by barmy accounting), large government debts (supported by no accounting at all), and an economically significant banking sector. The right accounting not only stops bad decisions, it can also promote good ones. Consider this example: a report in 2000 found that some 'socially excluded' families were costing in public services £250,000 a year, often with little noticeable improvement. The costs were from the combined benefits, housing, social services, justice system, health care, and other services. This astounded the authors and many others in government. Government accounting was not arranged so as to show how much the end products of policies – in this case support to the socially excluded – was costing. Given the choice, would you spend a quarter of a million pounds in one year on a single family for any reason? Could you not find better ways to deal with that family for a lot less money? But unless governments know what the objectives of their policies are costing – through better accounting – these questions will not force themselves to be asked.

As much as accounting is underdone in government, economics is overdone. Curious. Economics is far more ambitious. It attempts to model how an entire economy or sub-economy works. In its theories, it seeks to embrace every aspect of human and organisational behaviour that impacts the economy. Inevitably, the theories are simplifications, often gross. No matter, governments like them and overuse them.

Reagonomics, monetarism, government-inspired booms, post-neoclassical endogenous growth theory, Keynes, Hayek, Adam Smith – all are plied. Sensible souls, without the psychological need to be seen to be right, conclude that none of them has entirely stood the test of time so you cannot rely on any of them. Use them? Yes. Rely on them? No.

Worse than a political party adopting a theory is that they become traded. Our theory is better than yours. No, our theory is better than yours, vote for us. By and large the theory simply fits the character of the politician who bought it (such as Nigel Lawson's 'spend today', or the brainy magic of endogenous growth theory for Brown – the son of a preacher man, presumably brought up believing in miracles). Every personality type has an economic theory to fit. Most theories contain some truth; reducing their application to either/or rather than both accords one theory too much credence and eliminates the truth in the other.

Hayek and Keynes are often juxtaposed. Thus right-wingers support Hayek, and left-wingers Keynes. Hayek is the classic theoriser of markets being set free and Keynes of them being regulated. Hayek believed that creative destruction during recessions is essential to move an economy forward, as dead wood is chopped out. Keynes is the counter-cyclical smoother, particularly during a depression when government spending via debt is essential to restart an ailing economy.

In the 1980s, one of the many weaknesses identified in Western management thinking was either/or. In other words, the thinking that companies should either be centralised or decentralised, the front line tightly controlled or autonomous, collaborative with another company or competitive with that same company. Eastern thinking does not recognise false juxtapositions or divisions, and is content with the ambiguity of both positions being right, or possible, or simultaneously applicable. Centralised and decentralised. Controlled and autonomous. Competitive sometimes and collaborative sometimes. Keynes and Hayek. As we've already suggested, a first-past-the-post two-party political system is essentially an either/or arrangement, with all of its weaknesses.

Economics has of course made great strides since the writings of Adam Smith and Karl Marx. Huge volumes of data and computer power have enabled the theories to be tested against empirical observations. Where the theory matches the historical data it takes to the mainstream. Economics has much to inform and to aid us in decision-making. Modelling business economics using systems dynamics, cost–benefit analyses of a new rail link or approach to criminal justice, behavioural economics in understanding consumer's buying patterns – all these are vital tools to inform a decision. (*The Competitive Advantage of Nations* by Michael Porter – an engineer before he became an academic – is essential reading for all those forming governments, and for any government's industrial strategy.) But at a national or macro economic level, forever bear in mind that economists rarely get right more than once their forecasts of the current year's growth, let alone anything more useful. Economic theories have only improved because they have reduced the number of simplifying assumptions contained therein. They are still full of gross assumptions, not least about the motivations of you and me. Post-neoclassical endogenous growth theory means simply that its theory of growth has fewer assumptions than the neoclassical version. It is an improvement, but is still full of holes.

The founder and former head of Apple, Steve Jobs, has produced more economic growth than all of the world's economists laid end to end. Economics does an increasingly accurate job of explaining history. It brings to the fore some of the key judgement calls to be made in government, like the extent of flexible labour markets, the productivity of regulation, and the location of future growth (Cambridge not Middlesbrough). But never, never buy an economic theory (used or new) to run your country.

The Wrong People Making Policy

It is a statement of the very obvious that if people without the skills and experience relevant to the subject in question make the policy, only chance will get it right. It is obvious, but it is the norm in government that the unqualified are let loose on your life. Here, it is entirely acceptable that the materially ignorant and unaccountable concoct policies that, when put into practice, enter your front room dressed in rags.

Unbundling the Local Loop, a policy commencing in 1984 and still not quite completed thirty years later, is one example. In the early 80s, governments around the world were starting to look at breaking up state and private monopolies in telecoms and other industries. Technically it goes like this. In the UK, the then nationalised BT had all the telephone wires connecting all the houses, places of work and so on to a series of ascending exchanges, which could route calls from any one place to any other. To create a reasonably open market with all the benefits for consumers in price, innovation and services, and the benefits to national growth and international competitiveness, this network had to be opened up to all comers. Installing a parallel network would be prohibitively expensive.

Thatcher's Conservative had a very clear policy both to privatise BT and to open up competition. In other words, the political intent was crystal clear, the political leadership was strong, and neither of these could be used as excuses for subsequent failure. But, every year that BT could drag its heels and slow or resist unbundling meant it retained its monopoly, an easy life, and high profits. Its actions were entirely to be expected. In practice they created sufficient doubt about the risk to themselves and the network, produced accounting to show how (unrealistically) high the price should be for access by competitors, pleaded unavoidable delay in making small equipment changes to provide connectivity, and just filibustered on the document exchange. BT was never going to give this facility voluntarily to emerging competitors, and was never forced to by the regulator, the Office of Telecommunications – OFTEL – nor the government department, the Department for Trade and Industry, until it became a requirement of European Union policy for competition in the telecommunications sector in 2000.

The basis for rebutting the many obfuscating technical and industry arguments expertly promulgated by BT requires significant knowledge of the telecoms industry and specialist technical experience. Understanding the technology is key to inter connection to competitors' networks at the right price. Unfortunately OFTEL and the DTI had only economists and the classic dead generalists to make judgements. In the early days of new regulation in markets dominated by former state-owned monopolies, little was known in the UK (although much more was known in some other parts of the world, and ignored) about how to regulate. For this industry, somehow the economists got hold of it and regulation was perceived as a matter of the correct economic analysis and application.

If local loop unbundling, open-book accounting, and duct sharing had been implemented quickly, the UK market of telecoms providers would have been very different today. Because of the stiffer home competition driving efficiency and innovation, BT and others would have been much bigger players on a global scale. In the long run, BT has suffered from its protectionism. At the time, it successfully sought to preserve a very soft life in a very soft market with very high profits driving bonuses for some very large and deluded egos at the top. But its best long-term interest – as well as the government's, and yours and mine – was in proper competition. This is where an industrial policy starts.

Something similar happened with rail privatisation. Here, the lawyers had hold of it, and persuaded an unqualified Civil Service that the new industry should use legal contracts specially developed by a major law firm, which would 'run themselves'. In other words, these contracts were so clever that simply by signing and regulating them (the contracts, not the industry) the whole privatised rail service would run well. Thus, the first rail regulator appointed was a corporate lawyer!

The contracts did not run themselves. Nobody in the regulators' world had a clue as to how real businesses, real industries, and real railways worked. No one had the slightest idea that successful regulation starts with knowing how the companies being regulated work and are motivated; that it depends on knowing the accounting fudges and technological smokescreens available to them; and on using carrots for those playing ball with the notion of shared endeavour and responsibility to all stakeholders; and on wielding sticks for those pursuing a narrow corporate management agenda, at the right time applying plain muscle; and finishes with knowing who are the good companies and who the bad when the time for bidding for franchises comes round, regardless of the paper offer.

Handing the policymaking role to the wrong people is a significant cause of poor policies, in this case stifling competition at birth. This example, spanning nearly thirty years, shows how important these decisions are to the consumer, how much difference would be made, and how poor is the approach of government to industrial policy and to the regulation of privatised industries.

One could go on and on – not only the wrong people making the policy but doing so from the wrong place (i.e. analysing an issue from behind a desk, not from the point of view of the person it is supposed to be helping), or even somehow managing to make sure the right people are missing entirely from a policy (as with the total lack of representation of the consumer in the Digital Economies Act, for instance). Rereading this chapter so far, it is no surprise that so much of government is so hit and miss. In some ways this would not be so bad except that it makes for such a costly way to get not very far. Our system of government says you can have all the policies in the world without checking whether any of them will work. This is not the inevitability of the messy business of politics, nor of the demands of dealing with difficult people, nor of the compromises of making international deals. Government is difficult, but its policymaking needs much more than a makeover. It needs disciplining. To this we shall return. In the meantime we will look at a related source of government breakdown – delivery failure.

3

Dodgy Delivery

We all make judgements about any organisation we deal with, be they the supermarket, the bank, the telephone company, or the car manufacturer. They may be crude judgements – electors may not have statistics to prove the point – but many people can sense when an organisation is delivering something of use to them, and when it is not.

As ideology, prejudice, and sectional interest recede as bases for assessing governmental delivery, so reality comes to the fore. Voters look at what positive and negative change has actually happened with increasing accuracy. The surrounding knockabout of party political debate, of editorial prejudice and inaccuracy, dirty tricks, spin and smear, has surprisingly little impact unless one side or other neglects its defence completely.

For every IT investment that now works (like online vehicle tax discs, albeit at high cost), there is another that has not (like identity cards or NHS patient records). For every world-class innovative cultural facility like the Science Museum, there are poorly filled and designed art galleries. For all the academies, inspections, behaviour-modification programmes, teaching assistants, and GCSE emphasis in schools, up to 20% of pupils emerge functionally innumerate and illiterate. Planning ranges from micro control of every window catch in a listed building under careful restoration by its domestic owner, to procedures and a dumb judiciary being used against itself to secure flagrant breaches of planning consent by hard-nosed developers. For every well-managed car park, there are some with machines to record the last three letters of your registration plate to prevent the communal act of passing on one's ticket to a fellow citizen – machines oversold on erroneous savings and bought by the bureaucratic and uncommercial mind. You could add your own catalogue of success and failure, of the many lotteries experienced alongside that of the postcode, of achievement and waste, of attempted fairness and of random application.

In the last forty years, all sorts of remedies have been offered to improve public services and for the more reliable delivery of government programmes. Some have worked, some have not, and some have run out of steam. Despite the 1997–2010 government funding public services properly, paying their staff properly and bringing talent into them, and all of its non-stop reform programmes, it did not change much at all in the way I experienced public services, nor their productivity, which remained stubbornly static.[4] Usually the ambitions are appropriate – better schools, wider health service, effective regulation, less bureaucracy, higher productivity – but few politicians know or have worked out beforehand how to deliver their objectives, and fewer still come equipped with the people to do it. Even with the most experienced and expert delivery staff and leaders, government is a tricky business. Being aware of this, in 1997 I proposed a unit both to vet the implementability of each policy and to guide getting it done. It would have made some difference in some cases, but in the event it was never set up (although in the same vein, but with a different remit, the prime minister's Delivery Unit did come into being in 2001).[5] By the time a government leaves office, our expectations of the public sector have marched on as we experience what is possible from other sectors and from other countries. It is change on the ground which governments are paid for and voted on, not erudite seminars in Downing Street.

---

4   The Final Report of the Commission on 2020 Public Services concluded thus on public sector productivity: the difficulties of precise measurements of productivity in public services are widely acknowledged. However, data from the ONS suggests that level of outputs has failed to keep pace with the rate of spending increases, particularly since 2002. Nothing suggests the coalition will be having any better luck.

5   The pinnacle for effective implementation probably came after the 2001 election with the establishment of the prime minister's Delivery Unit and before Tony Blair became a load more than a leader around 2003. This unit and the focus and pressure it created, certainly had effect. Once its founder and sponsor had gone, it lost impact. An exceptional unit like that can work with much muscle for a period, but unless its behaviour and values become institutionalised within the wider organisation, it will wither in authority, which it did, and which is what happens if you rely on individuals rather than the System to get things done.

ITEM RESERVED:
Name : Gilbert, Jennifer

Hold until: 12 Nov 2014

Branch : Aylesbury Lending Library
Date : 28/10/2014 Time: 12:03

Item : 152245796
Stand And Deliver : A Design For Succ

Brw No : XXXXX5225

Notes :

Library enquiries: 0845 230 3232
www.buckscc.gov.uk/libraries

So governments fail. Progress is made, but far less than intended. Why does so much of the reform not work? Even if the policy is the right policy developed by the right people, why does it so often struggle to be delivered effectively? At heart, governments either attack the wrong problem or try the wrong solution. Or both. Broadly this is how central government seeks to run public sector bodies now. It uses much directing and mandating from the centre; derivative and opaque funding; various performance-management frameworks run by the woefully inexperienced; performance indicators, some of which are inappropriate and many of which are fiddled; closed-door arrangements between the sponsoring department and the PSO – provided each keeps the other sweet, then little changes; extensive procedures; managerialism which entails much of the wrong kind of management; and luxurious and obstructive terms and conditions. It is both an ineffective approach and one that demotivates. It brings underperformance and stress.

Let's dig deeper for these unrecognised faults. Here is part of an email from an army corporal with a decade of experience including serious action in Northern Ireland and Iraq:

> The army recruits had an invalidation, where they are asked if they are bullied etc. A civil servant conducts this. It is his full-time job and he has his own office. He did a 3D flowchart that showed the other platoon's recruits had lodged more complaints than we had lodged against us. This was a problem and we were urged to encourage the recruits to make complaints about us. Two did this about me because I had pointed out how dangerous it is to run in front of someone who is shooting live bullets.

> We also have to fill out a discipline folder whenever we give a verbal rebuke to a recruit or give them press-ups. They then have to sign the book to acknowledge that they have received the said press-ups. We are only allowed to give them 3 x 10 press-ups within a forty-minute period. This is all in our very handy pocket-sized instructors' handbook that we are obliged to carry at all times. As management scrutinises this weekly, any errors are dealt with severely. To avoid extra shit people don't give out press-ups, so recruits are not disciplined.

There is also a non-freezing cold injuries noticeboard. When the weather is forecast for the week to fall below a certain temperature, everybody outside has to wear gloves or face disciplinary action. This doesn't take into account that I and many others' hands are not actually cold.

We also employ a civil servant as the unit security officer, who has no military or police background. This seems bizarre, as everyone in the military is actually a fully qualified armed security guard as part of basic training. I am an arms and ammunition security manager, as are many others.

We also have a facility called the dismounted close combat trainer. This is a big indoor range that operates lasers, in order to train safely before using live rounds. Every instructor is fully qualified to set up, operate, and close down this system. It is Windows-based. There are two of these systems within our camp. But each one has a full-time civilian responsible for doing these tasks, who has done exactly the same course as the army instructors. There is a big sign saying that under no circumstances are instructors (who are all in the army) to set up or close down the system themselves. The bloke was an hour late one morning so I set the thing up myself as we had recruits waiting to use it. He told me that he was going to have me disciplined and that I didn't know how to use it even though it was up and running. To justify these two full-time jobs they publish a weekly newsletter.

I also had a Body Mass Indicator test. This said that I was obese. Quite clearly I am not and I am one of the fittest blokes in my unit. So I had to go and see a doctor in order for him to say that I was not obese. He obviously said that I was in excellent health and that the BMI doesn't take big people into account. However just to be sure, I had to see a doctor once a week in order to 'update the system' until the doctor got fed up and had to speak to the senior medical officer to stop this. It only took four months!

I really could go on and on, this is just based on my experience at this training establishment.

Policing the British army in Germany was another story. Until October 2009, a service policeman had to ask for permission to arrest an officer. To arrest someone we had to hand write about six pages of A4 paper. We were not allowed to type them, as there was one individual case of two service policemen cutting and pasting their statements. So to stop this everyone has to handwrite. So, when you are already working thirteen-hour shifts for seventy-two hours a week, the solution is don't arrest anyone. Can you blame us? During one incident in Iraq I shot two people and all I had to do was write half a paragraph, and that was only in order to get some more ammunition. So it's not in proportion.

We have Ofsted come in so we are all CRB-checked. Mine took six months, but that is OK as I signed a waiver stating before that I had no convictions. But I could have been a sex offender, who would know, so what is the point?

Seven months after transferring, I had a workplace induction. I had to have a gym induction for half an hour even though I had had a membership card for six months and been using it about five times a week. Because of this day of induction and notice of it only the day before, I missed a deadline for some reports that I had planned to do that day and got a bollocking. During this induction, I was introduced to the unit security officer during his ninety-minute lecture on security, the health and safety man during his twenty-minute manual handling 'course', and to the 'chaplain' during his sixty-minute lecture. Funnily enough all are civilians and all were telling me stuff that I have been trained in more than once and am very proficient in.

I always get told, 'Oh it's in the system' or 'It got lost in the system' or 'The policy says …'. I would like to meet the system and the policy. Do any actual people have any input into it or does it even exist? What is it? I think the best analogy is Skynet from *Terminator*.

By the way, I think that you are wrong, the Civil Service obviously works flawlessly. People like these have performed a valuable public service for years, leaving a legacy of efficient and cost-effective measures and procedures, easing the burden on the public sector as much as possible. It is quite right that they should retire early on five- and six-figure pensions paid by the taxpayer.

All of this extraordinary waste, plus the demotivation of the only person delivering actual outcomes (the soldier, the rest are overheads) stems from a number of unrecognised faults in the system of public sector delivery. Let's see what these are.

The Age of Proceduralism

Procedure and process have become the main output of significant chunks of the public sector. These take precedence over the results or outcomes that we, the public, are paying for. Plenty of private sector bodies have too much procedure too, but at least there are clear consequences in losing profits, becoming uncompetitive, or going bust. In the public sector, many staff see their jobs as delivering procedure.

A good example is the Criminal Records Bureau (now renamed the Disclosure and Barring Service – that's sorted that then). Here is an excerpt from its annual report: 'We processed 4.3 million applications; bringing our total to more than 27 million since our inception. We met several of our targets, including accuracy, timeliness of Standard CRB checks and complaints. We enhanced our processes for Enhanced CRB checks, which enabled us to exceed our target in the last quarter of the year, bringing our overall performance in just below our target of 90% in 28 days and significantly reducing work in progress at police forces. I anticipate that these enhancements will continue to have a positive impact on performance and we will be able to hold our current position moving forward.'

What a triumph. No mention of why it was set up (in the wake of the Soham murders of two children,) nor of its results or outcome performance (child-molesting reduced, etc.) Just keep churning the handle. This a recurring theme in why governments fail – a pubic sector believing its purpose is to be doing procedures rather than producing results for citizens. This ineffective sledgehammer cost £132 million in 2011, plus all the costs to others, estimated by one report to be £220 million over eight years to the third sector.

At City University in London, the induction of new lecturers included a forty-point checklist within which the head of department showed the new staff member where the toilets are. The checklist included three columns for who is responsible for each action, by when, and the box to be ticked when completed. Such procedures may seem annoying but harmless; but checklists like this cost you and I money to produce, distribute and implement, and they demotivate staff. And the HR folks now employed to prepare procedures will be in search of further aspects of university life to reduce to paper.

In the early 1980s, my firm recognised that some of what we did needed codifying, and some clever people came up with the Assignment Management File, which set out in 250 steps everything one needed to do to manage a project well. This was both brilliant and useless. No one will read a file that large, nor seek to put 250 steps into practice for every project. This would consume the entire budget for the actual content of the project. Several years later, a few of us sat down and worked out the critical steps for any project. It turned out there are nine. We produced one piece of paper with the nine keys for assignment management. This worked.

Government is currently rooted in 1980s management thinking in its approach to project management where it has Prince 2, a high-volume, checklist-based, mandatory procedure with lots of procedure training. Repetitive IT project failure is testimony to its uselessness. Top-class project management stems from top-class project managers taking decisions and making judgements and applying pressure in the right places, and from what is called goal-directed project management − broadly, work out the sequential goals and plan and manage what needs to happen to get to each, using such tools as are useful.

Emphasis on procedure takes attention away from the point of the unit or department. Following procedure provides no guarantee either that something adverse will *not* happen or that the right thing *will* happen. The greater the volume of procedure, the less it will be followed.

So, what drives this age of proceduralism? The most obvious and understandable cause is as a defence against public failure. When something adverse happens – like losing discs with personal information stored on them, or the death of a child on a danger list – heads are demanded, and the best (and often the only) defence is 'We followed procedure.' In other words, management establishes a procedure for dealing with children at risk, say. Its intent is to minimise risk in an inherently high-risk situation. A child dies. A media witch-hunt starts with the top and then up and down the chain. Anyone found potentially negligent cannot use his or her professional judgement as a defence but has to rely on providing evidence that procedure was followed.

Proceduralism's origins and perpetuation actually go much deeper than this, into: avoidance of personal responsibility; a belief that a procedure will enable the generalist civil servant to fulfil any role: and exercising management's control needs.

Following the procedure developed and mandated by the employer socialises responsibility, even though the organisation as a whole has failed. This matters little to the individual employee. Organisational failure has few consequences in the public sector. HMRC suffered not at all from its enormous loss of individuals' data 2007. Its head was moved sideways to ameliorate the news media.

Procedure is a safe and often powerful haven for the bureaucrat with no appetite or aptitude for delivery. The Civil Service is a process factory. Some procedure undoubtedly is beneficial. But procedure instead of outcome is often the government approach. The standard practice of the Civil Service is to hide behind procedure, and to use procedure throughout. Thus the job of the civil servant becomes solely to follow procedure and in doing so never to be responsible for any outcome or result. The procedure is all. It is also a perceived means to enable the generalist to pick up any of the central management professional disciplines, be it finance, procurement, human resources, or whatever, as they believe (wrongly) that all of these functions are reducible to a process in the hands of a clever person. Measuring performance in terms of procedure is more comfortable than outcome. Outcome makes people realise how little has been achieved.

As ever, typically the people at the top of any public sector body will have high control needs and they will be under some improvement pressure. Procedures provide control over individuals – just look at our soldier.

Process and procedure can be very useful, as when some forms have been thought through as to which pieces of information matters, whether fraud detection can be designed in, and the whole put on one of those (too few) websites which are a joy to use. But a belief in it as a substitute for education, specialism, judgement, experience, learning and motivation is nonsense. We are back to the unaligned versus the aligned.

Managerialism

This is a close relative of proceduralism. It is a two-type sin and first came to the fore in business studies in the mid-1990s; Robert R. Locke described it as: 'What occurs when a special group, called management, ensconces itself systemically in organisations and deprives owners and employees of decision-making power (including the distribution of emoluments) – and justifies the takeover on the grounds of the group's education and exclusive possession of the codified bodies of knowledge and know-how necessary to the efficient running of organisations.'[6] Whilst drawn from corporates, local government would recognise this form of managerialism as its paid officials have come to dominate elected councillors, as would the owners of the public sector, i.e. you and me – the Civil Service is a master of it.

The second type looks like this: managerialism is the belief that organisations have more similarities than differences, and thus the performance of all can be optimised by the application of generic management skills and theory. To a practitioner of managerialism, there is little difference in the skills required to run a college, an advertising agency, or an oil rig. Experience and skills pertinent to an organisation's core business are considered secondary.

---

6   'Managerialism and the Demise of the Big Three', *Real-World Economics Review* 51 (2009). This form of managerialism lies at the root of the excessive pay culture, now also much in evidence in the public sector.

Generic management skills and theory undoubtedly do have a place but, in the public sector, they can take on a life of their own, unfettered by the disciplines of competition and profits. 'New managerialism' is emerging as a dominant force in British higher education, according to a 2001 study into how universities are run, conducted by a team led by Rosemary Deem, professor of education at Bristol University. The wrong management does this sort of thing:

> The research found that manager–academics' lives tended to revolve around long hours packed with meetings, mountains of paperwork and email and the search for additional resources. Research was marginalised and there was little time for reflection. The absence of proper reward structures and the lack of adequate administrative support for heads of departments and deans contributed to workloads. Only one third of the sample had received any formal management training.

The soldier and the academic are suffering from the wrong kind of management – the diminution of the doers, the people that actually deliver something to you and me. My generic definition of managerialism is 'the difference between the management an organisation needs to be successful and that which it gets'. Managerialism has come to be another enemy of success. I wonder if we could develop a test to spot when organisations have become infected by types one and two managerialism. It is a disease.

Terminal Terms and Conditions

These are next in contributing to our soldier's frustrations. They apply throughout the public sector. Although the coalition government has made some changes, they remain largely intact in their deleterious effects. How so? Surely, better pensions, flexi hours and so on are a good thing, a sign of a liberal society, and an aspiration for all? Well, I used to think so, but that view does not stand up to a look inside.

Every employee wants improved terms and conditions – longer holidays, more maternity / paternity leave, flexible working, better pension, and so on. Every sensible employer provides good terms to attract and to motivate employees. Employees who work long hours too often, or have too few holidays, are less productive. The problem in the public sector is that the terms have become so good that performance is being affected. Luxury terms and conditions are killing outcomes and ethos, and are unfair and unequal.

The most obvious place where this happens is at a time of reductions in funding for a public sector body. Because redundancies are so costly and the process so time-consuming, the last place for cuts to fall is on the in-house staff. The first place is on all the external spend – communications, consultants, and grants to the third sector; this is easy, you just stop it.

In the recent cuts many charities have closed or reduced in size. Terms for staff here are what can be afforded by a small body without any expectation of permanence not the luxuries of the public sector like top-hat pensions, flexitime, and long holidays and maternity pay. Staff are relatively easy to make redundant. If their terms are too generous, the charity will become insolvent and thus be without any money for redundancy. So the unequal terms and conditions means that these small, committed, innovative organisations working at the front line of results with hard-to-affect groups, like teenage pregnancies, are scrapped, whilst the procedure-bound bureaucracies continue intact. The reason for using the third sector is to get away from the procedures and to access the drive and innovation that many social problems take to solve or to ameliorate. At a stroke, unequal terms cut off this channel. Markets have the great benefit of suppliers coming and going as they find better answers to the problems and needs of consumers. Innovation in product, service and organisation flourishes. To an extent, government is able to replicate this process of development through using third-sector organisations, but not when the terms and conditions concentrate supply in itself.

Essentially the closer you are to the source of funding – central government – the better your terms and the least likely you are to be made redundant. The further away you are from the funding the worse your terms and the more likely you are to be made redundant. The first group is the senior civil servants in London and the last group is third-sector workers throughout the country. But this latter group are closest and most responsive to the customers, the citizens, and the taxpayers – the objects of the expenditure. The former are most distant from them. Besides its impact on performance, it is an issue for the equality bodies.

The most deleterious effect of luxury terms is the process for discipline and removal due to underperformance. It does happen, but staff expectations are for this not to. Disciplinary offences are, of course, not following procedure, use of un-pc language, not following equal opportunities policy, but rarely not achieving a result or outcome. The experience in the NHS perhaps sums up this cosseted atmosphere best, or worst. After concern about rising rates of infection leading to deaths, a National Audit Office report of 2004 had to draw attention to hand washing as vital to limiting infections, and even published charts on how to do it properly. Louis Pasteur had worked this out in the nineteenth century, with his remarkable breakthroughs in the causes and preventions of diseases. Somehow, staff became so sloppy in their care that this centuries-old practice (fitting into the 'bleeding obvious' category) was demoted in importance. Indeed, a friend recalls addressing medical staff in the 1990s on this exact problem and being hissed off the platform for suggesting anything so unnecessary and time-consuming. How many died from their complacency and arrogance over the next decade? More recently, the NAO has even observed that in hospitals where purchases of soap have gone up, rates of infection have gone down. Astonishing! Luxury conditions have destroyed the ethos of care, it seems. Now, it would be entirely wrong to turn back the clock to nineteenth-century employment when, for example, train drivers late for work were simply sacked, but there is a point of accountability to be struck somewhere before the point where NHS staff not washing their hands still receive a full pension. No doctor, nurse, or consultant has been sacked or even disciplined for not washing his or her hands between patients. And yet this kills people.

Such is the comparative value of a Civil Service pension and of many in the public sector that staff are locked in. In today's world, pensions of this value are unreachable outside the Civil Service and the very top of corporates and banks. Anyone over forty leaving the service is mad, financially. But staff now cannot move out when some will want to for all the good reasons for changing a job – to broaden, to change career, to develop personally – and many should do because they either never did do well or they have become tired in that work life.

Most obviously, this lock-in is seen with some teachers who have worked long and hard in challenging circumstances. Anyone would get worn down, and the time should come to transfer to an advisory or training role or to another job altogether. But the final-salary pension is there as a yoke to be lugged around for another term until the pension has reached an acceptable level. This is wrong for the teacher, the pupils, and the economy.

The terms and conditions of the public sector, far from being the nirvana of employment envisioned by every fair-thinking person, have come to crystallise inequality, envy, and unfairness in society; to insulate from reasonable demands for performance; to lock in staff with the pension who need to move on; and to underpin the high-cost, low-result public services we endure. The terms and conditions reward stasis – pensions are maximised by length of service which reinforces the existing ways and limits external influences arising from employee movement; pruning or regrowing dead wood occurs too little; pay rises stem from increments more than performance; recruitment emphasises compliance with equal opportunities; the rights of staff are greater than the rights of citizens/consumers.

Accountability

On a bank holiday Saturday, driving north on the Fort William road to the Corran ferry for the Morvern peninsula, a long queue loomed. Traffic lights for roadworks could be seen in the distance. The delay amounted to forty minutes. Passing through the single lane, the absence of any work was obvious, along with a small section only of the closed lane occupied with machinery and excavations. Forethought by the contractor would have cut the delay to ten minutes. But, to whom should I direct my point? Would they be interested? Would that point filter through to those controlling the work on the ground? Would they respond with due concern for road travellers and minimise delays? My annoyance and point drifted into the 'impossible' box, and we enjoyed the ferry and the prospect of dinner.

My need on that day was to speak to the site manager direct, make my point, and get the cones moved there and then. This could be termed hard-wired accountability: you press a button and the flap moves. The accountability to the public that actually operates in most of the public sector would have planes crashing every day – it takes so long, is so unreliable, and rarely has any effect.

The internal excuse mechanisms absolve any conscience – 'signal failure', 'overhead power lines down', 'passenger action', 'safety device malfunction', etc. In mechanical matters, there are actually very few real acts of God. The root causes may be in not maintaining the signals or points properly, drivers being late for work and no cover arrangements, turning a regular drama into a crisis (this is particularly the case for clearing up after road crashes), poor procurement of safety equipment, management stimulating poor motivation, clients inept at contract management, and so on. But the causers of these causes never come face to face with their victims. The staff need to feel the experience of the passenger. Employees are both insulated too much from customers and prevented from talking to them. The organisation puts up a front of corporate speak.

We can see these unrecognised effects – proceduralism, managerialism, terminal terms and conditions, absent accountability – in play with our soldier's story. Let us now go wider and find others in the delivery category, and start with a really contentious one.

The Wrong Model

The National Health Service was a great innovation, a world leader for public service, unique, for a while the envy of the world, an all-round success against its predecessors, and, for many, it still produces the outcomes wanted. It copes with rising demand, to an extent, and with some difficult patients. But the results of our NHS show us slipping down the league tables of mortality and morbidity. Many people have personal stories of mistakes small and large, of unresponsiveness, of being treated as a unit of throughput rather than as a human being. Consequently, it has been on an endless programme of reform since the Thatcher days, accelerating under New Labour, and continuing with the coalition. The permanent revolution in the NHS has echoes of Mao Tse-tung and his cultural revolution in China. Thirty years of continuous reform should send the alarm signals that no matter how hard governments try, the model is not producing the all-round health care people want. In terms of organisational theory, a quarter of a century of making limited progress, despite repetitive and costly reorganisations, indicates that the problem is the model, not the internal structure; and that it is time for a new one.

The NHS is rigid, far too large ever to be managed successfully, and unfair. The attempted national patient records system, eventually abandoned after spending billions, sums up why it does not work: it simply cannot be done at this scale. My local surgery has a records system that works. This is the scale to model from.

High levels of satisfaction with their systems are found in France, Italy and Denmark. Would these models not be worth considering here? They cost more, but then higher quality does. Given the option, would the public be willing to increase funding to get a model that gives them better health care? Is it fair that in countries with demand management that is more responsive to individual needs, new drugs and treatments are given and, in the UK, not? Is it fair that other models serve their patients with much greater consideration than typically is experienced in the UK?

This is not a discussion that is possible in our adversarial political system. Labour is wedded to one of its great inventions and is unable to countenance the prospect of the end of its useful life. Having as a principle the continuation of the National Health Service is easy. But, as a matter of principle, is the continuation of the NHS of higher order than its results? The Conservatives have too often wanted to remove this large lump of the state to be trusted with any change of model. The two big parties lock horns over its reform but never join hands to consider its successor. So we are stuck with an institution that will never catch up with better functioning models despite how hard anyone tries. The solution to this deadlock lies in the sort of public engagement Canada experienced when its health service model came under challenge in the 1990s, and which we will look at later.

Unenforced Enforcement

Unenforced enforcement for the comparatively powerful is a theme running through much of the public sector. It is a major cause of the endless difference between theory and practice, policy and delivery. The small people feel the brunt of the system which the powerful know how to play. Laws to stop a few bad people end up penalising good people and the bad people get free rein.

The Menai Straits is a good example of this. The sea between the North Wales coast and the island of Anglesey is rich in sea life, in mussels, and is a Mecca for canoeing, yachting, and fishing. In the 2000s, the Countryside Council for Wales raised the prospect of designating the Straits as a Special Area for Conservation to look after the extraordinary reefs. The use of the Straits would have been formalised and regulated. In a public engagement the various users could see the value in this and its environmental importance. A plan of fair shared-use was developed. But some of the users then reacted strongly to the designation being enacted. Why, when agreement was apparently there? It finally emerged that none of the public had any faith that the public authorities would enforce the designation. Thus the public would all play ball but the nasty people – like some of the commercial mussel fisheries – would ignore it. So the good people would be controlled and the nasties not. The designation would in practice be worthless.

We see a similar theme in planning – the little people get controlled, the big ones get away with it. Buying and renovating a listed building would seem to merit support from conservationists (otherwise the building will fall down) and housing authorities (another unit of accommodation brought into use). But the conservation officer in the local authority may and often does insist not on just good and realistic adherence to the original design but on irrelevant, costly, and unweatherproof practice for the sake of origin. Balance is absent in the enforcement process. And the private individual is stuck with it. By contrast, the hard-nosed developer in Southwark, planning an 'aparthotel' in a conservation area, knows how to play the system. Planning permission granted in 2006 required the precise type of bricks and glazing to be approved by the Council's planners. Notional attempts were made to do this, but then in 2008 the developer went ahead with cheap cladding and glazing which would not have looked out of place in an Albanian housing estate. All parties agreed both that planning permission had been broken and that the building looked awful. The story then for the next four years was one of repeated shuffling between the developer, Council Enforcement, and the Planning Appeals Inspectorate. At the end of the day there was no enforcement, and the building stayed as it was.

Part way through this game, I made a complaint to the council. This looked as if it might have legs and stir some countervailing force to the developer and the bureaucracy. The complaints department was polite and diligent and after twenty months let me know my complaint had not been upheld. Their point was that all procedures had been followed. My point – that zero result had been achieved – was foreign to their mindset. The total cost over five years of following procedure by the council and the appeals division of the Planning Inspectorate was considerable, and unquantified, and a waste.

Legislation without enforcement is akin to capitalism without bankruptcy and Christianity without hell. Government and Parliament quite happily pass legislation without even thinking as to whether and how it will be or can be enforced. Governments spend much time enacting toothless tigers. Parliaments should be required to vet all legislation for its enforceability. If it cannot be enforced with the people or companies it is aimed at, then there is no point – indeed there is only added cost and tax or debt in passing it.

Unregulated Regulators

Industry regulators are a fixture in government. There is not a way round them that I can see whilst remaining a civilised society or even a functioning planet, and as more is privatised the number of regulators has increased, but regulators underperform or fail with regularity across many industries – trains, electricity, water, banking, pensions, I could go on. This represents a major source of delivery failure.

In 1954, J. K. Galbraith wrote that 'regulatory bodies, like the people who comprise them, have a marked life cycle. In youth they are vigorous, aggressive, evangelistic, and even intolerant. Later they mellow, and in old age – after a matter of ten or fifteen years – they become, with some exceptions, either an arm of the industry they are regulating or senile.'[7] In effect the performance of regulators is left to government ministers with or without knowledge or prejudice; to civil servants often captured by the industry they are supposed to be regulating; to the regulators themselves a (mixed bunch); plus some media comment sometimes, and some Select Committee comment sometimes. This is all a bit random and not rigorous at all for something so vital. Why are we suffering from unregulated regulators? Someone has to grip them, so that they grip their industries.

Many in government presume that once something is privatised or contracted out, the task of delivering it has (thankfully) gone and the problem is solved. Competition, the market, and the efficiency of the private sector will now provide. This is a pile of naïve nonsense that has often led to higher costs and diminished service. The effective use of the private sector requires high standards of ongoing regulation and of contract management – standards rarely to be seen. Services cannot just be tossed over the wall and torpor resumed. Using the private sector without employing top-quality public sector contract management and regulators is as intelligent as attempting to switch on a light without connecting it to an electricity supply. Both are essential to the objective.

The Law of Derivative Funding

The greater the distance between the pound collected and the pound spent on public services, the less effectively will it be used. Money changing hands has a powerful effect on the consumer, giving an immediate sense of the worth of the transaction. Credit cards distance this equilibrium. In today's public sector, the distance is such that the degree to which the transaction is 'felt' is almost zero. It might as well be your savings in the bank that has found its tortuous and largely unaccountable way through many trades, several financial instruments, and a series of domiciles before coming to rest in a sub-prime mortgage in the American Midwest. Your public pound may be via income tax, National Insurance, VAT,

---

7   The life cycle of the European Commission has followed a similar pattern.

airport tax, road tax, parking fines, or leisure tax. It may have been collected by an agency of national government, local government, a contractor, county police forces, international airlines, telephone companies, builders, or shops. It then finds its way largely into central government, which uses incremental budgeting to allocate it to public sector bodies, to local authorities, to tied programmes, to grants, to contracts. Rather as Mervyn King said of the banking system, 'of all the models one could pick we have the worst', so too with the banking system for public services. Do you have any sense of the worth of your taxes? How well they are being used? What they are being spent on? In practice, special pleading by the funded bodies has most effect – as with, for example, police numbers – and the pleading might as well be by derivatives salesmen, for all its rationale and value to the public.

As with derivatives, the more organisations through which the money passes, the greater the cost of transmission. Your pound of airport tax will pass through up to six separate public bodies before it is used. Each is running up cost just to handle the money. Your money eventually finds its way to central government and to the Treasury, which shares something else in common with the financial markets: it is a passive shareholder. It has no incentive to be otherwise, so it takes the simple and untesting route. Each year all of the many public spending bodies submit their case for a bigger budget than last year. The only exception to this is when usual business is interrupted by cuts or a set-piece efficiency review, when more can change. As a rule, bodies making a better case than others will get a bigger increase. The making of the case typically bears no relation to performance. The officials at the Treasury get off on this: as one commented whilst working there: 'You can just feel the power.'

Opacity in the funding chain is another contribution to failure in this section. In many respects the approach of the Environment Agency to improving its efficiency and reducing its cost as a response to the Gershon efficiency review in 2003–4 sums up what is wrong here. The agency was set a target to save £25 million per annum. At the time, this meant real savings, and one of the turnaround specialists experienced with the health foundation trusts was called in. He identified relatively easily the required savings from overheads and the agency felt real pressure to deliver these. Just at that time, major floods had occurred and the agency, quite rightly, applied for extra funding for defences. The moment this came through from DEFRA and the Treasury, the pressure was off and the interest in real efficiency savings by management evaporated. Such was the opacity with which the agency operated, and the multitude of government funding sources, that it was able to disguise funding for flood defences as efficiency savings. Some might say this should be illegal. At the very minimum, it should be transparent.

Local Government

I look at this in depth later, but the key point here is that, with a few exceptions, the UK does not have local government, and locally delivered services will always be needed in many spheres. How so, you might say – I thought we had councils all over the place?

Here are some definitions and remits of local government: an administrative body for a small geographic area, such as a city, town, county, or state, a local government will typically only have control over its specific geographical region, and cannot pass or enforce laws that will affect a wider area. It can elect politicians, enact taxes, and do many other things that a national government would do, just on a smaller scale. Local government is authority over a small locale by the people living there rather than state or federal government, typically through locally elected politicians.

The twin tests of local government are the control of a local area by people who live there or their elected politicians. So, we do not have local government in Britain. We have bodies called local authorities, but not local government. About 75% of local authority funding comes from central government, much of it specified as to what it is to be spent on; local tax raising is capped by central government, with much of how it runs defined by legislation, regulation or guidance – it has become a cipher passing on central government's requirements to the local citizens; 95% of local decision-making is exercised by the paid officials; and elected councillors are left with about 5% of power. Only the fifteen local authorities in England with executive mayors exercise some local government. For most of us, real local government does not exist.

The previous government proposed regional assemblies, in part to fill this gap, but the first on offer in North-East England was rejected in a referendum. In the main, this seemed not an objection to local power but a rejection of further institutions of government. Yet more second- and third-rate government was not a cure for centralisation.

Real local government as experienced around the world is a very different kettle of fish to that in the UK. Ours fails for many of the same reasons cited in this chapter – lack of accountability to us, managerialism, proceduralism, terminal terms and conditions, and so on. It does not have to be this way – but at present it is a major source of government failure.

Delivery of government services occurs through many and varied channels. The causes of failure or poor performance vary widely too. Some are cross-cutting and some specific. We've looked at inept procurement and management of contracts, the age of proceduralism, epidemic infections of both type 1 and type 2 managerialism, terminal terms and conditions, unaccountability to us throughout and asymmetric accountability, the wrong model, unenforced enforcement, unregulated regulators, the law of derivative public sector funding, and the absence of real local government. To these can be added (again see www. treatyforgovernment.org for the analysis) an acceptable muddle in the flood-defence capital programme, overstructured mechanisms for change like the UK Council on Child Internet Safety, the lack of public engagement, the bureaucratic mind, no cost consciousness, and living off a glorious past (e.g. the BBC). It's a surprise anything worthwhile happens – and it does – after digesting this lot. But if I were trying to get there, I wouldn't be starting from here. All of the accepted conventional solutions applied by governments in the UK and by many countries throughout the world have not, and will not, solve these problems. Before we can design a solution that can work, we must look at the next source of failure – the people in the system.

4

People Failure

It is easy to blame the people in the system and to attribute base motives. My experience is that most in the political world arrive with good intent. You might disagree with their policies, but they want to improve our society. Most are honest. Most have talent. Some are exceptional. Politics is an essential and difficult profession. But, once they arrive in government, the problems start. Whilst the remit of government has expanded enormously the type of people becoming politicians and their experiences and skills has not. How many ministers have deep experience of organisation and delivery? This is where the coalition government's welfare reforms have come unstuck. Policy tick, delivery cross.

So who are these people and what motivates them? Are these the people of our dreams of balanced mind and sound judgement, possessed of clear vision, committed to our good as citizens, able to operationalise their objectives swiftly and without the unexpected? Or something else? Let's look at the politicians, the activists, the civil servants, PSO managers, and members of the House of Lords.

Politicians

In 1998, a probably deliberate leak put the phrase 'psychologically flawed' into circulation. Its subject was Gordon Brown.

This, however, is a core competence in the candidate specification for anyone at the top. 'Flawed' is a loaded word. And one person's 'flaws' are often the source of great strengths. As Alan Bennett said of Philip Larkin's famous line 'They fuck you up, your mum and dad': 'He should be bloody glad they fucked him up otherwise he'd have nothing to write about.' One way and another, our 'flaws' contribute to the essence of who we are. Typically, people who get to the top of most large organisations (including governments and political parties) are the people who need the power most. In my own organisation a wise people-specialist concluded that many of the partners could do the job of senior partner and chairman, but the person who spent most time working towards it, who put everything else secondary to his pursuit of it, who jumped every hurdle and shook every hand, was the one who most needed it. These are the people with high control needs, often very carefully disguised before achieving the desired office, but given full rein once there. Or as much rein as the governance allows.

Whatever the psychological source of high control needs – and there are many – they lead to the sort of driven people who will first get stuck into local politics, then spend many years seeking a seat, will experience convoluted selection procedures, and will live their lives as MPs partly in their constituencies, partly in the House of Commons and partly in some sort of home in London. Where their partners and families reside varies. Back-bench time must be spent finding patronage to secure a shadow or junior ministerial job. Gerald Kaufman was renowned for always being elected to the shadow Cabinet through picking up second and third preferences because he was well known to every MP. His tactic was to know their every birthday and those of their children. Out of his file each week came the prompt to write a card. Into his poll came lower preference votes for 'Gerald the friendly bloke'.

This is but one example of personal politicking – building relationships, persuading people, case-making, telling people what they want to hear, developing a following, gaining the support of the kingmakers. To become leader, much more is required. The more natural talent you have at the job at hand, so much the better.

Tony Blair was a consummate politician who had a strong empathy for the country to judge the right response. A few months into being prime minister at Lady Diana's funeral, her brother Earl Spencer unreeled his attack first on the media and then on the royal family. As the applause trickled in from the public outside, it was taken up inside the abbey and into the nave and the sanctuary where the royal family was sat near the coffin (with me sitting behind). Opposite them sat a prime minister conscious both of their gaze and of the television pictures and later interview. His face took on that apparently non-committal demeanour whilst his eyes masked multiple calculations that concluded with him clapping too, but with his hands under the pew. This is but one example of a politician at his peak in action, and the extraordinary judgements we required of him. He was clapping to public order, but minimising offence to the Queen.

So here is someone who is adept at the right appearances for the public, but always bear in mind that the primary psychological motivation of senior ministers is personal power. This has nothing to do with the needs of the country, the party, the right decision in particular circumstances, or anything external to themselves. This is about personal power. Proportional representation is objectionable as it dilutes the opportunity to exercise personal power. It is difficult enough climbing the slippery pole of one's own party only to have to share power. Why would you do that? A one-party state would be a better place to be a minister, where democracy and the views of the people are excluded from the 'How do I get and exercise power?' equation. Power-driven politicians would be psychologically happier in the former East German government under communism. Decisions would not need to be tested with the media, be open to rebuttal by the public, be subject to parliamentary scrutiny however weak, nor in sum be tested at a plebiscite every four or five years. Only the single-party pole would have to be climbed and the politics at the top kept safe to maintain all those levers of control in your hands. Heaven!

On 5 May 2006, a year after the third election win and a day after very poor local election results, Tony Blair sought to exert his authority and to fend off his inevitable departure, with a Cabinet reshuffle and some high-profile sackings. Short of ditching Gordon Brown, which would have proved to be the right move for the government and the country as well as for himself, he chose the minister least likely to be sacked (Jack Straw), in order to set an example, in true public-school style. The message was clear. Here was a minister who had performed well in the role for five years, who had stuck by Blair in his unpopular war in Iraq, and who had strong PLP support: 'If I can sack him I can sack anyone' was the unstated message that rang loud and clear to all those considering putting their heads above the parapet.

The psychological needs of those at the top explain the rise of the social authoritarian tendency in the government. These are people who like nothing more than telling others not just what to do but how to behave, and have the scale of ego to believe they are right in so doing. The notable transformation from assertion to aggression by some on the front bench tells a similar story.

H. L. Mencken wrote: 'All government, of course, is against liberty.' This quote took me by surprise when I first saw it. We elect progressive governments to extend not curtail liberty. In part, elections are fought and won on which party wants more freedom and which less. Surely, not all governments oppose liberty. But, those personal power and control needs are always present, no matter how left, right or centre the politician and the manifesto. Governments only extend democracy in their early years, as did the 1997–2010 government with devolution. Thereafter, it was all the other way – corralling the Internet, Big Brother watching you with CCTV and speed cameras, stalling on PR, local government enlisted into domestic service, social authoritarianism, kettling, and vetting, vetting, vetting.

Cult of the Leader

Quite often a 'leadership debate' starts as we attribute the cause of poor government to their leaders. Change the leader – preferably to the one you like – and all will be well, or at least better than it was. This was confirmed by one former top adviser in No. 10, who told me 'It's all about the leader', i.e. if the leader is good, successful government follows, and vice versa. Leaders do matter, but outstanding leadership is rare. Successful organisations are built on successful organising, not on waiting for an outstanding leader. Tony Blair was a very successful leader, for a time. Blair eventually became a poor leader because the rest of the organisation of government was poor.

With a constitution tipped more in the direction of the leaders, leaving them with considerable freedom of action and too few checks and balances (as in Britain now), success will depend to a considerable degree on the quality of the leader both as a decision-maker and motivator, and as someone able to hang on to sufficient humility to continue to have a real sense of service to the people, to acknowledge his or her own imperfections, and to be motivated primarily by running a good government and not by maintaining personal power.

In the history of the world, no records have been found of the existence of such a paragon of virtue. Perhaps the closest to this ideal was Nelson Mandela who, with an overwhelming electoral majority and massive personal support, could have gone the way of his successors in behaving autocratically and corruptly. He did not, and performed a magnificent job in establishing the new South Africa. But he was the exception to the rule which his successors have so unpleasantly confirmed: the more unchecked power is given to one person in office, in the medium term the more autocratic will be their behaviour. Dictators are allowed, not born, in the sense that a weak constitution allows a leader to become dictatorial.

The reality of organisational behaviour is that if you or I or anyone becomes the chief executive, prime minister, head of state, pope, club chairman, head teacher, or vicar, and the governance is inadequate, then gradually you or I will become more autocratic, will become more instructive, will move on and out those with different views to our own, will expect obedience, will take less and less interest in the outside world, will withdraw into a small court of advisers, will accumulate wealth, and will want to stay in office as an end in itself. When we are talking about the jobs at the very top, I repeat: it is only those that need that power the most who will make the sacrifices necessary to get there. We all want great leaders, but they are few and far between. And be careful what you wish for: anyone who has climbed that slippery pole needs controlling and directing. In weak constitutions or errant cultures, great leaders will only remain great for about five years, succumbing then to their innate autocracy letting out their mistakes unchecked. Even the wisest leaders have only so many right decisions in them. Organisations are there both to bring out the best in leaders and to control their excesses.

One of the world's consistently more content and successful countries (which of course has its own faults and problems) is Switzerland. A federal council of seven, with an annually rotating president, runs their government. There is no dominant prime minister or president. We have fixed in our minds this cult of the leader. It does not stand up to examination, except in extreme times.

People Like Us

One of the biggest obstacles to organisational change is the 'people like us' problem, where power resides with certain classes or types. This is prevalent in politics. It arises where those in leadership and managerial roles confuse performance with appearance. Thus, people with similar manners, behaviour, recreational habits, or appearance are subconsciously assessed to be good in their jobs, and those without to be average or poor. Classically, many organisational climbers have taken up golf, that being the game played by top executives. Or drink after hours. Or join the Reform Club. Or go to Oxford University. Or are repressively supportive of all management decisions. Choose you own distinguishing badge.

We all do it. But, no matter how much the appearance fills us with confidence, performance is not correlated. Performance always takes some independent and objective measure. Looking down from the top is no place to gauge that. Outside, across, peer, citizen, customer, pupil, user, this is where a reasonable measure of performance can be obtained and power allocated accordingly.

The present system is reliant on the people in government to get it right. In the absence of governments designed to succeed, most of what happens is left to party politics and to personal politicking. This then depends on the psychopathologies of the politicians. These are far from dependable. I have spent too much of my life watching people at the top of large organisations with their heads in the sand, not to know when another set are finding every reason to stay there. Is our system of government here to compensate for the psychological flaws of its incumbents, whose psychopathologies affect their decision-making – or for us? And what of the people surrounding our politicians?

Cadres of Political Activists

The backgrounds of the core group around the centres of the main parties are narrow. For Labour they include local councillors, public sector employees, academics, trade unions, and the pure professionals straight out of university whose only experience is of politics as it is. Other than the legal profession, a privileged and peculiar world with a high opinion of itself, few who form the core mind of the Labour Party have significant other experience – industry, commerce, engineering, self-employment, private sector pensions. It shows. Either the party has to broaden its activist base to balance its public sector bias or its activists have to embark on a crash course in understanding this other half of society.

And what else can be said about existing activists? Our motivations to get up in the morning are many and varied. Understanding the consequences of these motivations can redefine our politics. These motivations can be substantive blocks to change as they are unstated and taken as read. Do activists need to feel they are better people in order then to govern well? Does the sense of cause help? Is being a progressive essential? Do activists reject anything their opponents have acquired from them?

Hands up! Labour activists want to and do feel superior as human beings to members of the Conservative Party. They feel they have a better moral code, they feel they want to treat their fellow man better, they feel the flatter, fairer society is better in principle than the harsher world of the Tories. Just as some have the psychological need to please, or the need to agree, or the need for attention, Labour activists have the need to feel morally superior. (Meantime Conservatives are feeling superior too, but from a different psychological standpoint.)

Channelled in the right direction, this psychological need or motivation for Labour activists has undoubtedly had its benefits for the world. Yet now that we are all playing in much the same field, it leads to some unfortunate ends. First, a vast amount of intellectual energy goes into proving that the Tories are still immoral and Labour is still the wholesome party. Second, too little energy (none at all from most of the policy wonks) goes into the difficult and apparently amoral aspects of government, of doing it all better.

Huge numbers of words are sent running around Europe trying to locate the moral high ground for the left, when everyone is already there – social justice has won, and campaigning for it stems from the ideological hangover we touched on earlier in the book. There are plenty of issues to be dealt with. The dividing line is who will deal with them more effectively, with the most benefit, and with the fewest unintended outcomes. The banks need sorting? A treatise on the future for the left in Europe will not do it. Nor will fighting for 'causes' that no longer require anyone to fight on their behalf. Nor will moral superiority, whether justified or not. The issue is, what will?

This leads us to look at the term progressive (and its antonym, regressive), which is a term activists use when talking to each other, and which has also entered the arena of the policy wonk in recent years. Some acts and some people are now deemed progressive and thus a good thing, and some regressive. This seems to be an attempt to establish clear water between the good folks of Labour and the bad coalition, at a time when knowing who the goodies and baddies are has become confused by the social authoritarians at New Labour and the sepia liberals in the Conservative Party. The former distinguishing terms no longer work, particularly when the coalition government has a more liberal criminal justice policy than the New Labour government, which removed liberty from its objectives.

I want to be progressive, but how much this helps to produce good government is not clear. Although activists use the word amongst themselves, it is publicly confusing, as it makes the party look amnesiac. It would be an act of contrition owning up to the sins of the past and thereby showing the candour the electorate will need to witness in order to restore their faith. Former and potential decision-makers would learn how not to repeat mistakes, particularly in how policy is made. This is salutary and necessary (first on the list would be debt and spend economics), and it might also help in the way policies are put into effect by civil servants.

Civil Servants

My work on the reform of the Civil Service had been published in 2004 and reported quite widely; a heavyweight permanent secretary had been sent to mark me indicating they were taking it seriously; the director of the senior Civil Service lobby group had gone round Westminster spinning against me, so evidently I was scoring; the director of Demos and I had met the head of the Civil Service, Andrew Turnbull, at his request, who talked at us for an hour saying how difficult their job was and all was really OK; I had met Tony Blair's chief of staff, Jonathan Powell, to make the case for substantive reform; and now came the answer in *The Professionalisation and Specialisation of the Civil Service*. At last, having just about come to terms with employing qualified accountants only forty years after the Fulton Commission had proposed it, the Civil Service was to embark on what every other organisation in the world has found: as more and more becomes known, you have to specialise more and more narrowly. I presented a chart showing the relationship between specialisation and education in various professions and how behind was the Civil Service. The prospect loomed of actually having a senior civil servant who knew how to do a particular job!

But it never happened. The ideal of the clever generalist who can turn his or her hand to anything lives on. The conceit is quite extraordinary. It was this same dismissal of the power of professional education, the right experience, and personal development that led UK management to fail so resoundingly post-war right up to the 1970s when global competition killed off this particular self-satisfied collection of inadequates – a cultural legacy of that part of our landowning aristocracy that dismissed professionalism, of course.

Psychological flaws are not limited to the political class in government. People populate the Civil Service typically with high security needs, seeking the lifetime permanence of job and pension, as well as the power and status on offer that their own personalities might find difficult to secure in any other walk of life. They are protected by procedure and written communication from decisions with personal risk that elsewhere would entail judgement and relationships. Their egos believe too strongly in their intellectual powers.

So much has been written about the failures of the Civil Service there is little need here to repeat it. All you need to know is that it is mostly out of its depth, operating way beyond its competency reach, a major cause of policy and delivery failure, far too self-satisfied ever to search for effective answers from outside its rooms, and replete with its distinctive psychological flaws. In common with the supermarket trolley, some servants work and some do not, and the service has a mind of its own. As one very senior civil servant of the time said, action only follows if the minister knows his mind and the Civil Service machine agrees with it. So much for democracy. If the 'service' wants to obstruct, it will. The notion that the UK has an impartial Civil Service ready to do the minister's bidding is bordering on a bad joke. Departments always have a view as to what should be done. The senior Civil Service has a poor track record in achieving change in society and in running the many delivery arms of government. Developing policy is accorded the highest value, and where promotion is earned, delivery is not. Thus, even when the Civil Service agrees with what the government wants, the chances of effective action, although improved, remain low.

The question then for us is why has there been so little change?[8] The answers are many and various.

In the latest attempt to get hold of them, the House of Lords resisted any attempt to have civil servants being controlled and employed by ministers as this would give more power to the government of the day, and in the UK system the executive already has far too much. Thus the Civil Service retains its bad power in order to prevent more going to the government.

As we have seen, politicians are not selected for their delivery skills. When discussing with him how he would run a future government and get things to happen, John Smith said 'the Civil Service will do that'. A clever and delightful man without a delivery clue. Thus, most politicians and all of Parliament have little confidence to take on direct responsibility for all of the roles performed by the Civil Service. It's convenient and reassuring, particularly to new governments and ministers, to have these confident people to take care of this troublesome task.

'They'll get you back' was the response of one minister to my questioning why the service had not been reformed. In other words, if you as an individual minister take up the issue, they may spin against you − basing it either on something that you have done, or something that you have not done (e.g. Plebgate) − and your career will likely be over. The Civil Service leaks and spins as much as anyone.

Few politicians before they get into office realise just how bad the Civil Service is. After all, they have been busy blaming the

---

8   The coalition government is also trying hard at reform, for example with the Civil Service Redundancy Act capping redundancy payments (the maximum is now twenty-one months' pay – which is still a cashmere reward and grossly unequal in society. And in other ways the fundamentals stay the same.)

other political party for all the ills – there's no mileage in allocating it on faceless bureaucrats. Of course, the government might take up the issue, but imagine you have come into office with a large programme and high expectations on you. The suggestion that before any effective power can be exercised (even if it turns out to be largely apocryphal), an incompetent, uncontrollable, and devious senior Civil Service should be reformed root and branch is not what a new government wants to hear. As I put it to the shadow chancellor before the 2005 election, the notion that writing much of their manifesto was a waste of time as the senior Civil Service would and could not deliver it, is not welcome. The game must go on. Hindsight politicians know all of this, but those new to office ignore it. Civil Service reform should always be a day-one issue – it is costing us a fortune in wrong decisions, poor delivery, and continuing cake capture.

But it remains independent, and largely unreformed despite all of the reports, the memoirs of regret, and the needs of the country. The reason behind this obvious nonsense is that no one (previously including me) has proposed change within the context of whole-system reform. Thus we do need to remove its power, but not give it straight to the executive. This conundrum will be unravelled through the Treaty.

Public Sector Managers

The next group determining success and failure in government are the many managers of all the public sector organisations. We have already reviewed the affect of their terms and conditions on performance, and of their limited effective accountability. Operational staff and management want a quiet life, untroubled by questioning their service.

Here is another way in which the road to success is obstructed.

Long ago I lost count of the number of schools, NGOs, local authorities, and public sector bodies whose performance was blighted by the head teacher, chief executive, or whatever title the top manager had. Primary schools waiting for the head to retire before obvious and necessary changes could be made; meantime the pupils take second place. National sports bodies making no difference to their sport whilst the administration keeps itself in office. Government agencies seriously underperforming under a civil servant needing a job. Third sector bodies well funded by government to make some impact in the family world pursuing an easier course in the corridors of Whitehall and an 'honour' for the top person. Councils stuck with an old-fashioned unreformable and unreforming chief executive whilst the local public have no choice but to put up with the level of service they get.

Underperforming top managers are notoriously difficult to shift and a widespread contribution to government failure. Boards of governors or trustees or elected representatives whose job it is to shift them fail their customers, users, and citizens with frequency. The causes are common. The head/CEO will often spend more time managing upwards than downwards, and be careful both to cultivate personal relations with board members and to manage their impressions of performance. Negative numbers are spun away. The board may neither see, nor know how to see, real performance. Many boards do not really understand their job: sometimes getting over-involved (but usually under-involved), meeting at most once a month and often once a quarter, not specifying the information they want to examine the organisation and instead accepting the gift-wrapped head's report as a balanced and objective assessment. In many instances it is the chief executive who, in practice, recruits board members and will have been careful to bring in friends and supporters. Only the best CEOs go for people of quality and independence who they do not know and whose job is to challenge.

Also, heads are people, with families, home lives and futures. No one enjoys damaging that by getting rid of someone. The process for making change at the top is typically arduous involving first a board member being willing to be bad-mannered enough to suggest it, second views being collected from people more inclined to give the benefit of the doubt (how will I look the head in the eye if this attempt at change fails, and do I go then?), and third the terms and conditions lying in wait with both the potential for an unfair dismissal claim and a large bill. By and large it really is so much easier not to do it. So another reason poor-performing heads and CEOs stay on is because of the difficulties of removing them.

House of Lords

Finally (and briefly) in this chapter on people are the members of the Upper House. Before hereditary peers were removed in 1999 the House never had the legitimacy to challenge the Commons and the government effectively. Now it is largely comprised of individuals appointed after distinguished careers. It reflects how people vote more proportionally than does the Commons, and is a 'no overall control' chamber with 200 independents or crossbenchers. It has inflicted numerous defeats on the Blair, Brown and Cameron governments. The Lords has gained legitimacy and authority, and brings more of an apolitical mind to legislation than the party obedience in the Commons allows.

It has set up various mechanisms to make it work better, including an Appointments Commission with strict selection criteria, handling strategies for bills, and even some limited post-legislation review. Of course, there is far more to governing well than passing laws; but the Lords is certainly contributing to less bad government. I wonder if it could go much farther? And what this would take? We will see later.

The point about all of these people failures (and successes) is this. Just as with changing the rules for the Lords, it is the system of organisation that makes the people perform as they do. It is the system that attracts the right or the wrong kind of people. It is the system that gets the best or the worst out of them. Yes, we can criticise the people. But if we want them to change, then we have to change the system.

Before we do, we must examine the largest hole in all systems of government – feedback of results.

5

Feedback Failure

Imagine that you are a keen gardener, run a sports team, or watch television. You garden, but you never look at it in bloom. You coach the team, but never find out the final scores. You watch a drama, but always contrive to miss the ending. Odd? Extremely. Now, let us switch to what government does with its version of the garden, or the sports team, or the TV programme.

Government and its many agencies have endless checks on the equivalent of the sharpness of your spade and whether you have applied the correct fertiliser (correct at least so far as today's 'experts' are concerned, although tomorrow's might say different); whether your team holds the hockey stick in the prescribed manner; whether the drama has the 'correct' narrative arc. But how good your garden looks, how often your team wins, or whether you enjoyed the television drama they will never know. Today's politics lives in a mythical future of description: 'This is the world we intend to create, our garden will look like this, our team will win the league, our play will be exciting.' Political party manifestos are akin to science fiction – directionally correct in that you might like the future they paint, but whether it is possible to get there is unknown, and even if they do then mostly not in our lifetime. This is cooking with an approved list of ingredients, but never eating the result, and hence never knowing if the recipe is any good.

Our analysis here of where governments fail starts at the end of the telescope furthest from government and closest to us – that is what happens as a result of all these people, decisions, and operations, and whether and how this is fed back to government in order that it knows what is happening as a result of all of its usually frenetic activity. This chapter is not about what parties say they are going to do, nor about the part in the middle when they are in government and actually do things like pass new laws, bring in new regulations, establish new bodies, or change performance targets or the national curriculum; this chapter is about what happens as a result of all of this activity and cost. This is the 'bottom line', the outcome for the citizen and consumer of the fine talk, the manifestos, the policies, and the ministerial decisions. This is not how many people have been caught speeding but whether the number of road casualties has reduced, stayed the same, or increased generally and in a specific location. This is not about getting laws on the statute books, but finding out what has happened as a result of the application of the law, how much is it costing, and what is occurring as a result that we did not expect.

Does It Work?

Amongst the most significant policy developments in recent years in the US has been the establishment of the vast new Department of Homeland Security. Despite its political importance and cost, it has had no assessment to test whether it has made any difference (other than to add to public expenditure) compared with the arrangements before its advent. The US Congress continues to extend its long record of launching reorganisations for symbolic reasons and then quickly losing interest in the operational consequences.

Is there now a fair market in landlines and broadband, as intended by the 1984 Telecoms Act? Or, more than a quarter of a century later, does the owner of the infrastructure (BT) still retain an unfair advantage – an advantage for one company to the disadvantage of all consumers? If the latter, why did this policy fail? Or if it worked, why did it take a quarter of a century to succeed? Has the Litter Act of 1990 reduced littering? How much does this law cost to run? Are children any safer with the Safeguarding Authority? How many deaths has the 1997 Firearms Act prevented? What is the outcome of winter fuel payments? What has changed this year as a result of the existence of the Environment Agency? What is the result of all that money spent on the many parts of the criminal justice system? For each health and safety regulation, has the number of people injured or killed reduced, stayed the same, or gone up? How do we know if a regulator is being successful?

The answers to many of these and similar questions are unknown. Government has some data on where it is going in some aspects of the health service, for example, and for school examination results. Some evaluations of policies are undertaken. The Office for National Statistics is producing more information of value and accuracy. The Freedom of Information Act has been used to produce previously unknown results. Research projects of sufficient depth and quality do come up with important outcomes, as with Manchester University's on rail privatisation and its costs. But in the main government hasn't a clue. Or it pursues 'policy-based evidence', as doctored results are known, where facts and analysis are collared to support the answer first thought of.

Get into the detail of a government department and you will see how little they know of outcomes, of where something is actually going, of performance, of whether and how a piece of legislation is having the desired effect, of the actual impact of a new or old regulation, of the actual energy saved as a result of the actual installation of roof insulation according to its rules, of where the benefit traps are and of their deterrent effects, of the morale of staff in all its agencies, of the actual returns for savers with pension funds. The discipline imposed by dealing with reality is absent. This feedback hole allows for all sorts of spin (and now its grizzly usurper, smear), disinformation, proceduralism, managerialism, ducked issues, ignorance, media frenzy, corridor deals with business, personal power politicking, job protection, over salarying, and degraded and zero outcomes.

In economic transactions people experience the results of their decisions directly − if they buy a defective product, they soon discover their mistake − but in the case of political decisions there is no such feedback mechanism, and as a result politicians lose touch with reality and behave irresponsibly. Joseph Schumpeter wrote that 'Thus the typical citizen drops down to a lower level of mental performance as soon as he enters the political field. He argues and analyses in a way which he would readily recognise as infantile within the sphere of his real interests. He becomes a primitive again.'[9]

In the early 2000s, the Department of Constitutional Affairs (now the Ministry of Justice) undertook some innovative work with my firm in looking at some services through the eyes of the consumer

---

9   *Capitalism, Socialism and Democracy* (1942).

– domestic violence, relationship breakdown, debt, and community justice. At the time and by way of example, the statistics showed 300,000 bicycles stolen each year and 900 people found guilty of stealing bicycles – less than 1% end-to-end service performance. Imagine schools educating less than 1% of their pupils successfully or less than 1% of trains arriving on time. This was (and is) dire.

The purpose of the work was to find more effective ways of dealing with these problems. The justice systems seek to achieve outcomes through sentencing. Historically, justice has been the underlying purpose, but now deterrence and prevention through rehabilitation are as important, if not more so. You would therefore expect the justice systems to be measuring how effective the various sentences are in achieving these ends. Thus, what happened to the teenager sentenced to fifty hours' community service for possessing a modest amount of cannabis? Did he re-offend? Or not? What of the career criminal imprisoned for theft? Did she re-offend? Or not? For which types of criminal is prison the right sentence and for which types is it not?

The justice systems do not know. Sentences are dispensed for various offences to people in various life stages without any knowledge of how and with whom and in what circumstances and whether they have worked in the past. This is akin to doctors prescribing various treatments without knowing whether they work, for whom and in what circumstances. This would hardly inspire confidence. You would be right to enter the surgery with caution and trepidation, as right as those who criticise and experience the randomness of the justice systems. These systems and their ministers do have some broad research on sentences, but it is sweeping and by definition non-specific. It does what it has done for the past 150 years since the advent of magistrates' courts. Magistrates and judges try to find the right sentence for the individual in front of them using their experience, but on the basis of no evidence of sentence effectiveness. Sometimes they simply indulge their prejudices. It is highly ironic that a system based absolutely on the existence of evidence in order to prove guilt should have no evidence for its efficacy.

This is by far the most glaring example of a public service flying blind, but it is common. They know not where they are. They are in flight but not in vision.

Unguided Legislation

Governments have large legislative programmes, and no programme to ascertain whether the legislation has had the intended effect. Government hits the snooker ball with the intention of it going in the pocket, but its attention will have switched to the next ball or the next table before the ball does or does not drop. To legislate, a complicated process has to be followed. Once it has become law, no process is required to see if and how well it is working.

Governments work almost exclusively like this in every sphere to a greater or lesser degree. There are at least some checks and balances leading up to the point of decision, but then nothing once the decision is pushed out to become operational. This is odd, not least since for so much of government, the proof is in the pudding.

Astonishingly, legislation in the UK has no explicit purpose. A particular Act does not state what it is intended to achieve, nor what it might cost the state, nor its objects (who could be you or me or a business or charity). Parliament spews out new laws at a great rate with insufficient scrutiny, no purpose, and no costing. Once passed, government has a sense of achievement for pushing the bill through Parliament – a triumph is declared. Little interest is then shown as to whether and how the law has achieved beneficial effect on the ground.

For example, how much critical personal data has the Data Protection Act protected? How much critical personal data has been published in defiance of this Act? And what is its operational cost, to compliant and low-risk organisations and to the public? My observations are that public bodies lose data without sanction; that secret services and newspapers can get access to any personal data including police files, medical records, and bank statements; and that meanwhile compliant organisations like large accounting firms and charities have extensive and costly safeguards to prevent completely non-critical data being collected or held. 'The Treasury this week blamed poor data from Equitable Life for the failure to track down eligible policy holders, but in July 2011 it destroyed the details and addresses of 353,000 policyholders provided by the Equitable Members Action Group on data protection grounds.'[10] Remind me of the point of the Data Protection Act?

---

10   *Investors Chronicle*, 17 October 2013.

Systematic feedback should be as much part of a parliament's life as is passing the laws in the first place. Without it the country becomes silted up with ineffective legislation. Laws, regulations, instructions and guidance lie around clogging up the enforcement agencies, whilst respect for the law reduces and society loses sight of the vital laws. This is the concept of legislative devaluation: the more legislation there is, the less value each law has. The law in your pocket is not worth what it was in the 1960s.

Legislation and regulation are two of the biggest cost drivers of public expenditure. Running laws and regulations is expensive. Running ineffective laws and regulations is pure waste – for government, for organisations on the end of them, and for individuals adversely affected.

High Costs and Taxes of Zero Feedback

In 2005 the Better Regulation Task Force recommended that the UK should adopt the Standard Cost Model developed in the Netherlands and use it to measure the baseline of the administrative burden of regulations. A project was established in the Cabinet Office, budgets agreed and accountants hired to collect the data. Mostly, government departments resented 'their' regulations being vetted for cost and for effectiveness. They were (and are) used to operating these aspects of government without any check. But the project ground on. In the Netherlands this baseline data was then used to reduce unnecessary burdens, from filling in employment returns to logging websites on companies and individuals. What happened in the UK? A minister declared victory at some point and moved swiftly on to the next initiative. But if large, small and sole businesses were asked whether their administrative burdens been reduced, what would they say? Have their compliance costs been reduced in line with good practice around Europe?

Devon County Council came up with a good idea to bolster trading standards, by recruiting volunteers to spot violations on the high street and report them back to their officers for investigation and enforcement. In practice the scheme was a flop – the volunteers were often elderly busybodies with prejudices to exercise. But the scheme was the baby of an influential manager within the department and 'only' consumed half a post each year. It took ten years before it was closed. The council had zero feedback on this and most other policies. The cost of zero feedback was about £200,000 for this one policy for one council. Imagine the cost of all nugatory policies and programmes across all local authorities.

The theme continues with the many minor poor experiences we all have with government agencies. Here is an example of a not uncommon response that came up when I was interviewing people about this issue:

> I have received two separate tax calculations from two separate Inland Revenue offices, one from Leicester and one from Bradford. I received one tax demand of £7,338 and one for 20p. Even if I tried my absolute hardest, I don't think I could be as shit at my job as these 'servants'. Who the hell are they serving? They are there to be efficient and save the taxpayers money; all they seem to do is overcomplicate things and waste as much public money as possible.

Now that's what I call feedback, which the tax authorities should receive and would benefit from receiving. It puts performance pressure into their system. But how is it given? And who gets it? And what happens when they do? How does this failure get corrected? And prevented? And how do I find out what action was taken? Who is responsible for this? Who wants to be? Inevitably at present there will simply be some tortuous, time-consuming and opaque complaints procedure, which will usually find nothing, and nothing will change.

In the current set-up some external feedback occurs from the anecdotal, to good press work, to tabloid excess, to long-term campaigns, to sectional interest, and to lobbying. Such feedback is vital to the health of any democracy, but it is limited and partial, and the time lag on this feedback is huge – many years will have passed before these external mechanisms gain traction, if ever. The same applies to most programmes, policies, initiatives, agencies, departments, indeed anything and everything done by or for the state: the feedback so essential to knowing where you are going and whether you have got there does not exist. Of course, flying blind avoids accountability, a recurring theme in government and the public sector. If you do not know where you are then how can you be judged as to your progress? Even better, if you do not even know where you were intending to go, then no one can say you have not got there. Flying blind is not a recipe for successful or efficient government. Yet that is the norm. We exist because we exist. We do what we think or believe needs doing but we know only by exception if it is working, and whether it was worth doing after all.

Undisciplined Government

The inadequacies of every system in the world have meant that governments are not forced to observe and to learn from the outcomes of their actions. Governments become primarily motivated by the 24-hour news agenda, announceables, initiativitis, and the personal preferences of Cabinet ministers. They stop listening to and seeking to understand the public. The countervailing force to the comfort blanket of photo shoots is to face the actual outcomes of new legislation, regulation, instruction to local authorities, adverts, changed benefits and altered taxes. But this is not institutionalised at any place in our constitution – we institutionalise organisations, but not the fundamentals for making institutions work. Governments are allowed to change more or less anything without any duty of assessment as to its benefit or otherwise in practice. The mechanisms for accountability that could act as some sort of effective feedback are very limited. Without feedback, we get free-for-all, not government.

Politically mature governments would acknowledge that change is complex, that finding out whether something is actually working is more useful than spinning, shouting, and statistical deviancy in a short-term attempt to 'prove' that it is. But governments do not want to know that they have got it wrong. And political egos would rather not know.

Peter Drucker understood this long ago: 'We need something much more urgently: the clear definition of the results a policy is expected to produce, and the ruthless examination of results against these expectations. This, in turn, demands that we spell out in considerable detail what results are expected rather than content ourselves with promises and manifestos.' Ruthless clarity about the results being achieved would make for irresistible cases for change, where necessary. Unclear results are an opportunity for corporate speak, spin, obfuscation, and disingenuity as the more desirable alternatives internally to clarity.

Silos Endure

A further consequence of zero feedback is silos – agencies and departments working in isolation without joining up to provide an outcome or result for an individual or a society. Despite many years of ministerial speeches, government bodies feel no obligation to do anything other than pursue their narrow duty or remit, despite coordination between bodies being essential to minimising costs and to solving many social problems. However, a consequent problem is that coordination has become another end in itself with repetitive meetings of many people to discuss the issue – the cost of coordination and administration now typically exceeds the money spent on treating the original problem. Rigorous feedback would demand straightforward coordination and the end of silos.

To return to the judicial example from earlier in the chapter, the team at the Department of Constitutional Affairs developed and proposed a simple, cheap system to gather information for individual offenders and the outcome of sentences. The senior civil servants rejected it as the cost would be borne by their department (as the Court Service) while the benefit would go to the Home Office in the shape of the Prison Service. So long as there are departments of state, joined-up government will remain a slogan. These silos were put together under the Ministry of Justice, but the system of monitoring outcomes remained forgotten, on the shelf. (In 2010, the incoming coalition minister produced an excellent business plan emphasising rehabilitation. It remains to be seen whether his party's prejudices, the silos, the incompetence of the Civil Service, or the process rigidities of the legal profession will allow the country to use feedback to inform and develop its response to crime and to criminals.)

By contrast the private sector has the impetus of competition and price to remove silo behaviour. This drives conduct and performance. Extensive supply chains stretching around the world are built across companies. These are instantly coordinated electronically to produce an end product faster, cheaper, and better than the competition. Theirs is a combined interest to reduce costs throughout the supply chain, including the costs of procurement. In the absence of feedback, no such imperative exists for public sector bodies, who never see the results, and have no pressure to optimise the end cost to the consumer.

Lobbies Flourish

A further unfortunate consequence of flying blind is that it leaves government decision-making wide open to lobbies and powerful vested interests. It goes like this: if the results expected from policies were explicit and they were subject to ruthless examination against expectations, then the scope for bending decisions to favour a particular industry or company or sectional interest would face the discipline of exposure. Where feedback is absent or filtered through smoke and mirrors, decisions can be bent any which way. Typically they go to the most persistent, with the best or best-spun information, the access to enlist elected representatives, or the ability plausibly to threaten dire consequences (which will never be measured, of course). This is the land of the professional lobbyist, affordable only by businesses and others with deep pockets.

The absence of feedback also allows the news media to pursue its campaigns regardless of their actual future outcomes. 'Something must be done' in response to a tragedy (such as a child accident case), which leads politically to anything being done in order to stop the story. The 'anything' may or may not lead to a useful and beneficial result (or may indeed be positively unhelpful). But no one will ever know. So newspapers pursue their editors' or proprietors' views, heedless of any consequences. Self-righteousness, psychopathology, good idea, or malign beliefs can be expressed without any comeback. But of course there *are* consequences, and the press has raised nugatory public expenditure by an untold amount through its campaigns, expenditure with no benefit (beyond immediately feeding the beast of press triumphalism – a very high price to pay for short-term supremacy therapy for those running the stories).

Of course, zero feedback allows each of us to pursue the answer we first thought of, indulge our prejudices, and fire off opinions. One person's heroic act of welfare can be another's sponger's delight. And vice versa. Aid for the starving or free money for corrupt dictators. We would all do better to find out what actually happened. In my experience, sometimes my views turn out to be right, and sometimes wrong.

Undoubtedly feedback failure is the biggest underlying cause of government failure. In response to this and all the other failures catalogued in this Part you might say to governments and politicians, well, just 'do better'– better policy/decision-making, better delivery, better people, better feedback, better leaders. But in organisations, admonition does not work. The question is, what will *make* them do better? To find that answer we need to trace the origins of failure right back to their root causes. Having looked at the areas in which government fails, the following chapters address *why* it fails, why it is never properly put right, and how to produce sustained success, and even world-class government.

PART 2
WHY GOVERNMENTS FAIL

6

When My Lights Went On:
New Labour 1997–2010

'Root cause analysis' is the means by which we get to the core of the problems in the preceding chapters. Only through applying this technique can solutions be found that will stick. The power of the process comes from avoiding the treatment of mere symptoms, and in isolating the fundamental cause of any problem.

An outbreak of MRSA provides a straightforward example of this sort of analysis. This analysis goes through five 'whys' to find the answer (typically five has been found to be sufficient).

So, why did the outbreak occur?

It transpired that the nurse failed to undertake MRSA screening on admission.

Why?

She was not aware this was a requirement for emergency admissions.

Why?

This was not covered in her orientation to the Medical Admission Unit.

Why?

Infection Prevention and Control was not included in the induction training for new starters.

Why?

The trust has no hospital-wide approach toward induction programmes.

And so we arrive at the root cause of the outbreak. It might have been *symptomatically* attributed to the nurse and her personal failing, but at its heart the training of new staff was at fault, and was a systemic problem. The obvious answer of disciplining the nurse would have had little impact on future outbreaks, and instead would have damaged a career, been financially and emotionally costly, and stressed other nurses now worried over their jobs. The root answer here was for the trust to ensure all new nurses received essential training, in this case to screen emergency admissions for MRSA. Root cause analysis provided the space for thought, located the deeper connections, and produced a workable solution.

This sort of analysis does not of course solve all the problems of the world, but it is useful in the right circumstances. Yet, most organisations spend far more time looking for culprits than causes. Because of this misdirected effort, they seldom gain the benefit they could from understanding the foundation of the unwanted situation. Root cause analysis is conceptually simple and is often best done with a group of people involved and knowledgeable in the area of concern, along with someone to prod for the fresh thinking and to bring organisational expertise. The clever part is in understanding how that particular organisation ticks and the linkages between cause and effect.

To continue our exploration we are going to look back to the last government to lose an election (in 2010) and find out, at root, why. Please put the politics to one side – again. You might love or loathe that government. Our purpose here is not to cast political judgements, but to find organisational insights.

We should pause to set the context for our analysis here. The entire period of the 1997–2010 government is described in *An Organisational Life Story of One Government* to be found on the website www.treatyforgovernment.org. To summarise, we observe how the new government started amidst much hope and expectation with its formidable team, its rigorously prepared policies, and its control of Downing Street. Major victories are declared – in funding for the health service and in one of the world's longest-running conflicts, in Northern Ireland. The government started too with a bang with democracy: devolution to Scotland, Wales, and London, proportional representation for these elections, some executive mayors, abolition of hereditary peers in the House of Lords; and then it stopped. An inward-turning organisation does not see much outside. Personal power for those at the top is not a condition for redistributing power to others.

Quite quickly the government bumped into the obstacles of the Civil Service and its supermarket trolley, and its own celebrity status, insularity, events, and non-existent competition. Successes continued but the major error count commenced, the government evolved, delivery was a struggle, capacity constraints were ignored, junior ministers emulated quarks, and party ill discipline resurfaced in the least expected place – at the top. The consequences of unconstrained psychological flaws came to the fore: the constitution provides no superego.

Decisions were taken by fewer and fewer people. Leaders grew mould but stayed, the Parliamentary Party of MPs did nothing. The cult of the leader lived on, the ministerial reshuffle rate was upped, power continued to reside in the wrong places, and self-delusion reigned. The loyalty card was played. The government was tired, stuck, and long in the tooth. The party faithful flocked to their armchairs. They think it's all over. It is. It's 2010 and the election was lost.

In case you are tempted to jump back to politics to explain this loss, bear in mind that the present coalition is being allowed by our system to make unnecessary mistakes. It has made good but limited reforms to the system of government. But a word of warning to any party wishing to use this analysis to bolster its own case for election. The Conservative Party does have one major advantage over Labour in its governance. But apart from that, it is following much the same organisational course as its predecessor administration, with inevitably the major error count rising, very limited real reform of public services, and a limited useful lifespan.

The Tories' advantage here lies in the rules both for feeding backbench concerns to the leader and Cabinet, and for changing the leader or prime minister. As we will see, good governance often lies behind organisational success and bad governance behind failure. Many make the mistake of associating success with the particular chief executive, chairman, prime minister, or leader in office at the time. Very occasionally exceptional leaders are the exception, for good or ill (Churchill or Hitler), but, usually, the capability of the people who happen to occupy high office is secondary to the quality of the system in which they work. Constitutions matter more than most of us ever see, as this chapter will, I hope, make plain.

Let's get on with the analysis. Nineteen causes of loss have been identified from research, interviews, and observation. These are categorised into policy, delivery, people, and political causes.

Policy Causes

Cause 1: The government lost because it bought dirty banking.

Why did it buy dirty banking? As one Labour lord said: 'It was the fashion.' Politicians are as much prey to fashions as anyone, and swashbuckling banking was in vogue. We all bought it. People had been given money for the privatisation of their building societies. They paid handsomely for it in the long run through higher mortgage rates, lower savings rates, and a bigger financial crash in 2008.

But whilst we are all at fault, governments should think. As part of the Thatcher belief in privatising all things regardless, the 1986 Building Societies Act allowed the conversion of ownership by its members to plc. shareholdings. Top managements were of course seriously rewarded, or more correctly de facto bribed, for conversion. Five of the ten former societies were part of the banking crash, including two of the very largest, and all five converted after the 1997 election. It would have been a bold and decisive act to scrap the 1986 Act on day one of government in the face of the mood of that time. This would not have stopped those conversions in progress as their members had majority voted in favour. But, Bradford and Bingley and Birmingham Midshires would not have become part of the banking crash to the stress of those with savings there. We pay people in government for judgement. It would have been right to abolish the act. With the support and credibility it had at the time, the government could have done it. It did not. In 2010 in the Mutual Manifesto, the Labour Party notes the value of building societies and the strength and diversity that a healthy mutual sector brings to financial services. Shame it had not concluded thus in 1997 and acted upon it.

Besides the building societies' cull, why was the rest of banking allowed free rein? Because of erectile dysfunction regulation.

Cause 2: The government lost because of its 'debt and spend' economic policy.

Why did it adopt this policy? Because it enabled Gordon Brown's highest priority – an expanding state – which he believed to be right. Because the policy was popular in expanding services without much extra tax (once freed from the 1997 election commitment to stick with the previous government's expenditure plans).

Why did the Cabinet accept the policy? It did not. Brown did not ask, and no one in the party held him to account for his policy. Presumably he justified the policy to himself and others through 'post-neoclassical endogenous growth theory' and more prosaically 'no more boom or bust'. The latter ignored the essential (although unpleasant) role of recessions in shaking up companies and public sector bodies made complacent by too much growth. We have all experienced them. Recessions do not have to be a 'bust'. Bust is what the Conservatives produced in the late 1980s.

Why are governments allowed to adopt unproven economic theories as they wish? Because nothing exists to stop them, with too few or ineffective checks and balances, added to the over-concentration of power at the centre. (Some economic decisions have been taken out of politics, notably the setting of interest rates. This has produced greater stability. The Office of Budget Responsibility is now intended to provide the 'debt and spend' discipline.)

Eventually the debt policy ran out of road with the banking crash and the economic downturn. Its unsustainability was found out.

But why is unsustainable debt allowed? Because nothing in our rules for government says no. Gordon Brown introduced a voluntary 'golden' rule – right. And then avoided it – wrong.

Cause 3: The government lost because of the policy and practice of immigration.[11]

Why was so unpopular a policy pursued? Because it was perceived as central to the economic miracle of sustained growth with no boom nor bust. Thus, to meet demand and to grow, companies wanted the educated and motivated employees to be found in East Europe and elsewhere, as well as the basic low-wage workers,

---

11   A subject now open for discussion, and not just by consenting adults in private. There was a time when to talk of it was to be 'racist': the invariable destination of political correctness is to control

often from Africa, for menial jobs. The policy was perceived as essential to support future state funded pensions, mainly for public sector employees. An expanding working population meant the hot-potato issues of retirement age and the value and funding of public sector pensions could be avoided. It was both a convenient policy and one with immediate GDP benefits. But in its calculation it was an equation which ignored and omitted key variables on the basis they were inconvenient: employment exclusion, population growth, congestion, infrastructure and public service costs for immigrants, social housing allocation, house prices, quality of schools, displacement of existing people, social immobility, the rate of absorption and adaptation, and what it means to be British. But whilst government ignored the inconvenient variables, in their lives the public noticed them. The applied intellect of the woman and man in the street far exceeded that of ministers, senior civil servants, and policy wonks.

The flawed policy came as much from the Institute of Public Policy Research as from government.[12] Accountancy firms are sued for millions when audits go wrong. Think tanks should be grateful the same disciplines on advice do not apply to them.

A further cause for the de facto pursuit of the policy and thus mass immigration was the inability of the Home Office to control

---

12   The IPPR reports and advice of the time were driven largely by the 'dependency ratio'. This is the ratio of the working to the non-working population. With the standard retirement age deemed fixed at 65 for men and 60 for women, with life expectancy increasing, and with birth rates flat, the dependency ratio was increasing. The result was proportionately fewer people of working age and thus fewer paying for public services and for pensions. (Around the same time the IPPR also reported on the need for more babies – reminiscent of Singaporean attempts to raise birth rates by raising marriage rates by running dating games on a ship.) Their answer was more economic migration to increase the working population and reduce the dependency ratio, and thus to maintain the public purse, with the added benefit of employers welcoming a policy which gave them a better labour supply. Those displaced by the educated, skilled, and motivated immigrants were thought mainly to be the socially excluded no-hopers and a permanent underclass whose welfare cost would be covered by the economic activity of the new economic migrants. A virtuous circle that only required us all to be remarkably tolerant of a perpetually growing total population, congestion, and a large number of often very different cultures, for it to work.

the inflow of immigrants, legal and illegal. The Home Office could not keep a cow out of a house, nor distinguish between a cow and a butterfly. The cause of this was the unreformed Civil Service, its monopoly on power, and its lack of management and delivery capability.

The policy also fitted well with Labour's desire for a social conscience and to feel holier than thou – all immigrants being seen to be in the needy category.

Finally, the government pursued this policy by accident. The policy was never set out, although Blair defended it in the 2005 election. Mainly taken by advisers and civil servants, a series of apparently minor decisions to let in workers from the A8 Eastern European countries from 2004 (whilst Germany opted for the latest date of 2011[13]) was based on another Civil Service car crash and poor Home Office and Foreign Office research that concluded only a minor flow was in store. In practice, this accumulated to a migration jackpot.

Why could such a major error be made? Because most policy is made in private.

Unfortunately, the circle was as virtuous as its analysis, with holes everywhere. Far from being set in stone, the dependency ratio is variable. The standard retirement age of 65 and 60 was fixed when life expectancy was about five years longer, compared with an average of about 20 years, now. The Beveridge welfare state was modelled on a post-retirement-age life expectancy of 5 years. Today, sixty is the new forty, with people both able and often wanting to work well beyond, as well as containing the skilled, educated and motivated labour employers want. Encouraging more women back into work both part-time and full-time has and would further improve the dependency ratio.

Bringing the 'socially excluded' back into work is not easy, but it becomes almost impossible when the demand side of their equation falls to zero as employers can fill their needs with off-the-shelf migrants. The Smith Institute, in its report on the Young Offenders Programme led by National Grid Transco for gas operatives, and the North Wales lifesavers, show how some of the excluded can be brought back into work – an end in itself and an alternative source to migrant workers.

13   Evidently German civil servants can add up. And model.

Cause 4: The government lost because it made too many major errors.

The electorate's tolerance of large mistakes becomes exhausted when the cumulative error count or rate exceeds n. From the £1 million political donation by Bernie Ecclestone, to the Dome, to the abolition of the 10p tax rate, to the absence of weapons of mass destruction, to floating the prospect of an election without a credible plan B, mistakes of this scale stick. Why did it make such large mistakes? Because it was insular, relying on the small court of advisers and central party figures for its understanding of the many issues which hit government, and failing to use the wider and specialist expertise available to it.

Why was it insular? Because Downing Street is so dominant in the system of government. Working there conveys a sense of power and importance with no countervailing requirement to check decisions. Reaching out takes humility and an appreciation of one's own limitations.

Delivery Causes

Cause 5: The government lost because for most electors it was not achieving much any more.

The government was, in many respects, a tale of two halves. In the first, much was achieved, such as Northern Ireland, Sure Start, the devolutionary measures, NHS and education funding and so on, even if these actions were not to your political taste. In the second, little was achieved; indeed it is hard to recall anything of lasting value – the smoking ban in public places in 2007 stands out, albeit with its dictatorial excesses.

Why was it achieving so little any more? The government had run out of steam, it was tired, the internal battles were taking up energy, mistakes were not being learnt from, often it was simply unaware that little was changing on the ground.

Why had it run out of steam? The combination of a full diary followed by the nightly red boxes is a punishing schedule. But why take decisions via red boxes? First, history – that's the way it has always been done and it has the aroma of the empire when Britain was great – still an organisational aphrodisiac for some. Second, control – ministers are kept in check by the administrative process. It is an absurd way to make good decisions. No other quality government or major organisation does it.

And why were mistakes not being learnt from? Partly because governing in Britain is so skewed to the first part of change, i.e. policy and legislation. The paucity of feedback means government is usually unaware, and often would rather not know, of the outcomes of its legislation or new programme. In government, once the policy leaves Westminster it is of limited interest.

Partly too, mistakes were not being learnt from because the old guard was still in power and too busy defending its record. A new guard would have been free to learn from things that had not worked.

But why was the old guard still in power when it was no longer of much use to the country? Because when in office, Labour has no mechanism to change the guard.

Cause 6: The government lost because of poor delivery.

Why? Because our political parties concentrate on policy and believe this to be the reason for their election, not delivery. The coalition's education minister Michael Gove has said: 'I think that the election campaign should be conducted on the basis of policy versus policy.' No Michael, we're paying you actually to change something for the better. Why else would we vote?

Why this obsession with policy? For a century or more, politics has been mainly about distribution of wealth and income, about advantage and disadvantage, about the balance in rights and powers between the haves and the have-nots. Policy prevailed. Today's world is no longer about major redistribution, but about maintaining our wealth relative to the rest of the world, fair chances, running public services well, and about the myriad of issues and events which arise. Today's politicians have to know as much and more about how to get things done as they do about their policies. But, they do not.

Why do politicians not know about delivery? Because the recruitment routes for MPs are so narrow. Four of the five leadership candidates in 2010 had little or no experience outside of politics generally and central government specifically. Some

MPs have experience of local government, usually as a councillor, some even as staff or managers, but deep and varied experience of organisations providing products or services to demanding citizens and consumers, or experience of real life in the private sector, or as a sole trader living off one's wits and talent and adapting to shifting markets, is rare. To become an MP the younger you start in the Westminster village the better your chances are as you grow your network, secure patronage, and receive early notice of jobs and seats. Ministers and MPs always need bright, energetic and loyal advisers and researchers with experience in the intensely political Westminster world and media. Unfortunately, almost none of this experience is at all useful in successful delivery. Most politicians also make the mistake of only seeing the world through a political lens. Politics, its trade-offs, its judgements, its presentation, and its connections are a highly skilled occupation that should carry danger money. After all, politicians are the repositories of our hypocrisies. But today's politicians have to know the boundary between politics and organisation, where the expert in one is the liability in the other. New Labour was famed for its political skill. In its early days it had and valued deliverers too. But, as the internal battles took hold and in the absence of the governance necessary to prevent it, politics became the dominant game once more. It is not that organisation is more or less important or clever than politics, but that good government and therefore winning elections requires much more of it.

Why else do politicians know little about delivery? Because they hope that the Civil Service does. For at least half a century, the Civil Service has been living off the politicians' desire for a simple life with just policy to decide upon and never to experience the harsh reality of trying to put it into effect. The kindly Civil Service takes that off the politician's hands with the reassurance not only that they will do the delivery but also that they own the role constitutionally. It is out of bounds to the grubbily elected. Unbelievably, the concept of politicians taking and being responsible for implementing the policies on which they have won an election is still labelled 'politicisation' by a biddable media. It uses any excuse to sneer at and correct the political classes. Politicisation is ranked alongside corruption in the perceived ethics of government.

Why is the Civil Service still in charge of delivery? In the face of all the evidence, this quite astonishing role reversal has been achieved by the First Division Association (representing the top 7,000 civil servants) whose purpose is to maintain the status quo in the employment, job security, and power of the existing civil servants. Its general secretary is no less a high quality spin-doctor in this cause than any working for a prime minister. He would be – the stakes are high.

Why was the Civil Service not gripped, given that over the last fifty years, ministerial memoirs have concluded that the Civil Service had been a major obstacle to delivering the manifesto, and needed major reform? Because only once they had arrived in Downing Street did this become clear. It took Blair six months to conclude so, by which time it was too late, because the disruption to be caused by the wholesale reform needed would delay the government's programme by months and years.

Why else did they fail in delivery? Because not having any education or training in organisation they ignore such fundamentals as capacity constraints, prioritisation, and focus. Quantity not quality.

Cause 7: The government lost because it was over-reliant on legislation as an agent of change.

Why was it over-reliant on legislation? Partly because of habit – that's what governments do. Partly because of ego – passing laws feels important. Partly because of media and public pressure of the type 'it must never happen again' (it always does), so a law against it is passed. Partly because governments want to feel they are doing something and legislation gives the impression of action. Partly because the alternative means to achieve change are harder. Partly because legislation is not policed. The effectiveness of legislation in cost and benefit terms is not collected, fed back to Parliament, nor published.

Cause 8: The government lost because media management became more important than delivery.

Why did the news media take priority over actuality? Because the 24-hour news machine came to the fore during its time in office and

New Labour became its partner. Because political success became perceived to be more and more about good media coverage. Because New Labour was so good at media management, and organisations tend to concentrate on things they are good at, even if counter-productive in the end. Because the government would rarely go against Murdoch and his ciphers in the newspapers.

But why could one media owner wield so much power over politics? Because no constitutional safeguards exist to prevent their inappropriate influence.

People Causes

Cause 9: The government lost because they had a leader who was not going to win.

Quite quickly after his appointment, it was apparent that the British people did not want the type of prime minister that was Gordon Brown. Many who supported him thought his non-celebrity status and dour competence were the right contrast. The non-fashionable Angela Merkel in Germany had shown the way, taking over in November 2005. That judgement turned out to be wrong. Why did it have the wrong leader? Your reply might be it was unable to change the leader. But, why was it unable to change the leader? Because its governance is not able to make changes when needed.

Why inadequate governance? Because, in response to mass ill discipline by members in the 1980s, party organisation had been built around maximising control at the centre and limiting any forums for formal dissent. And because Labour MPs have limited appreciation of the essential role of good governance in these circumstances, and have never taken this role unto themselves. And because there is less ruthlessness and courage in them than is needed. And because they enjoy the plotting, speculating, being courted, offers of power, and gossiping that goes with unstructured challenges to the leader.

The Parliamentary Labour Party is all of its MPs. This is the only group that could exercise discipline and accountability for the leadership, and make changes when needed. General elections exist for the country to judge the government. Parliament exists to judge governments between elections. The political party has to judge its choice of leader. The PLP did nothing, and is the real villain of the whole story. But, it knows no better, not even that its role should be to hold its leadership to account and to change it when needed. If it did and it had, the party could still be in power.

Where was the governance that should have kept the leadership in check? The Conservative Party has its 1922 Committee, comprised only of backbenchers, to call a halt to its overdue leaders. In this forum, its MPs are able to speak truth unto power on those limited occasions needed for the party and for the country. The Labour Party has no such forum. It relies on conspiring, deals, calculating who will come out on top, courage of the few, those without a ministerial future exceeding those with or with hope, message placement in the media, spin and anti-spin, hoping someone else will put their hand up, playing off both sides, the whips recalling past misdemeanours, patronage, etc. This can be very exciting at the time for those involved, but for all the transparency and integrity of this process, the potential candidates might as well offer straight financial rather than power bribes. For a party with a belief in its moral superiority over the opposition, how is it that power politicking on this scale, involving such low cunning and guile, can be considered in any way superior to the straight and grown-up governance of the Conservative Party?

Beside the comparative ethics of the processes, the outcomes show that the Conservative Party removes its leaders fairly promptly in relation to their value to the party and the country (even ejecting Thatcher in 1990), and the Labour Party does not. Is it a coincidence that since the establishment of the 1922 Committee, the prime minister has been Conservative for 62% of the time and Labour for 38% (excluding Ramsay MacDonald's four years as non-dom prime minister alongside the majority Conservatives)? Many other factors pertain, but Blair should have gone before the 2005 election, Brown should have gone within a year of taking office, and Neil Kinnock should never had the opportunity to lose two rather than one elections, especially when John Smith would have been so much more credible with the electorate. The Conservative Party would have made those changes.

Cause 10: The government lost because the old guard hung on too long.

Why did the old guard hang on too long? Partly because of inadequate governance. Partly because of the psychological needs of those at the top – they need personal power, they have large egos to satiate, and could neither give up the power voluntarily nor suppress the ego. Prime ministers are not time-limited in the UK. Partly because too many at the centre of the party had invested too much in the New Labour project to see that its day was done. Change would only have come with fresh people at the centre.

Both Blair and Brown stayed – to the detriment of the party, MPs and staff, the government and the country. In both cases MPs knew change was needed. Tony Blair should have gone when his political instincts and desire told him to – before the 2005 election. But the people around him who depended on his patronage for their jobs, both ministers and advisers, persuaded him to stay. Once Brown started hammering at the door, Blair's own competitive and stubborn side made him not want to concede. By this time too, his ego dominated his decision-making frame, alongside the lure of being prime minister for a decade and the achievement in his own mind of 'finishing the job'.

The construction of the Cabinet was no longer based on competence and political pull with the public (in other words when the selection criteria had most to do with governing well), it was now based upon the survival of the prime minister (a wholly different objective which mainly pointed in the direction of not governing well). If any reader should doubt the overwhelming importance of good governance to good government, then this example of a lame prime minister using a weak constitution to remain in office with a lottery of ministerial competence may convince those doubters.

There is a certain irony in comparing the availability of special measures for failing schools with the non-availability of any measures to deal with the failing organisation of the then government. Blair presided over a failing organisation whilst proposing yet more public service reform for others.

Why did so few in the centre of the party see the need for big change? Because the feedback mechanisms in government did not make clear how little was working and thus that fresh thinking was required which would have forced the change in personnel, too. Because, too, the people in charge came to see the organisation as themselves – New Labour became a Boys' Own Club, and not something that had an existence beyond them.

Cause 11: The government lost because of the ill discipline and division at the top.

The party experienced the most sustained bout of ill discipline since the early 1980s. This was not caused by the militant tendency, nor union activists, nor Old Labour purists, but by the leadership. Far too much energy was consumed by the battle between Blair and Brown, both over policy and over leadership. They displayed an extraordinary lack of discipline in pursuit of domination. Power and survival took precedence over good government. Ministers were reshuffled to maintain power and not to govern well. Why? Because both the country's constitution and the party's governance allowed them free rein to indulge in this orgy of self-delusion.

The behaviour at the top was first disbelieved as stories of briefing battles surfaced – planting black propaganda about personal opponents in the news media. Surely, we thought, these leaders could not be so foolish as to leak electoral goodwill with mutual slander? Surely their ethics were better than this? Yes, politics is for the thick-skinned, but who benefits from the self-mutilation of the organisation? What possible short-term goal could justify the long-term damage? But here we had a leadership out of control, thoroughly turning off their most loyal and active party members. Clearly something was wrong here with the organisational context of British prime ministers (and much more so with the likes of Berlusconi in Italy, Putin in Russia, and many others around the democratic world).

They believed in what they were fighting for, both their roles and their policies, but the PLP and the wider party had no mechanisms to hold them to account for their behaviour, nor for their policies, and nor for their effect. Top-down discipline and control was all, with no space for upwards or peer discipline. With a monopoly on power whilst the Conservative Party was out of action, the long stop of electoral control had gone. They ran riot, so much so that by the third term much of their energy was devoted to their personal battles.

Competition between individuals in an organisation is powerful when directed at its purpose or output. It can provide much of the dynamic for improvement, always alongside the collaborative energy essential for success. Gladstone and Disraeli may never have achieved individually what they did without their intense personal rivalry. But the Blair–Brown feud went way beyond healthy competition. Their lack of self-control was every bit as culpable as any seen throughout the party's history.

Why was it ill-disciplined? Because outside of national elections, no one was holding the leadership to account. Because our constitution is weak in holding any government to account. Because the centrality of a constitution to organisational performance was not understood. Because once in place the leaders will rarely make their lives harder by proposing tighter accountabilities for themselves. This is always the job of its immediate constituency, in this case Parliament. It was also ill-disciplined because the opposition was weak and it could get away with it.

Cause 12: The government lost because it was overtaken in its ability to read the public's mind.

Why was it overtaken? Because, after having had a clear lead in public mind reading in the first half, it rested on its laurels, and then failed completely to spot that the Conservatives had started reading minds better once David Cameron and his emotionally literate mind-reader Steve Hilton arrived.

Along with much that New Labour *did* get right organisationally was the appointment of Philip Gould as its public mind reader. He was fresh from Bill Clinton's winning campaign in 1992. Amongst the many Clinton innovations were rebuttal, rapid access to 200,000 news outlets across the US via email, and the mantra 'speed [of rebuttal] kills Bush'. These were crucial campaign firsts. Clinton also had a new kind of pollster who went behind the immediate responses to questions to gain a more sophisticated understanding of voter's motivations. Philip Gould worked on this campaign and imported and developed these techniques, built around deep polling, focus groups and intense listening.

Clinton also had a very tight campaign organisation centred on the 'war room' – a single operational space that, before ubiquitous mobile phones, texts, and twitter, made for fast communication and fine motivation. The central team met in that room every morning at 7 a.m. With this and more imported into the operation, a formidable Labour machine was built that, at its height, scared the willies out of the opposition.

So, why did the party become complacent and rest on its mind-reading laurels? Because the competition was weak due to 'first past the post' and, again, because the governance does not exist to refresh the people at the top of the party.

Cause 13: The government lost because its party headquarters was underperforming.

Why was it underperforming? As with everything else, standards had slipped in the second half. What was a clear lead in party organisation in 1997, from direct mail to analytic canvassing tools and Excalibur (the rebuttal system), had not developed. Why? The drive and ambition of the headquarters slipped with the complacency of power. It lived off of its past. The governance of the party apparatus by the National Executive Committee was ineffective. Politics and politicking was all. The party HQ became there for itself, protecting the jobs and pensions of the staff incumbents.

Direct mail was impersonal and unprofessional, and no one central noticed nor was looking. The letters became increasingly frantic calls to arms in the form of canvassing and donations with yet another old hector from 'Harriet Harman'. All Tories were labelled evil, the only distinction being that some were more evil than others – as if that was useful, held sway with voters, or even accurate. Communicating with members by rant is not where I am. Meantime, the Lib Dems had worked out that members might just like to feel involved with what the party was discussing, proposing, and now, in government, is actually doing, and might like to use their brains. Their communications are engaging. Labour remains afraid of its members.

The HQ thought it was providing 'air cover' with targeted mail shots to marginal constituencies. It may have had some effect, but its connection with some MPs at least was as poor as with members. Almost none of the modern voter and member highly personal electronic communications, used to good effect by Obama, were in place. Direct mail ruled, seemingly driven by a contract, and nothing new was countenanced. This all felt like the Walworth Road headquarters in 1993, before the revolution there two years later.

A further cause of stasis in the HQ was the terms and conditions. Far from encouraging fresh ideas and dynamism, by being institutional and setting job security and permanence as over-riding objectives, so survival becomes all. The party needs terms and conditions suited to fairly rapid turnover and the fresh thinking and energy this brings. The HQ is too small to carry politicking staff past their shelf lives.

The world of political party competition never stands still. If campaigning practice does not change, often radically, between elections, then something is wrong. The flaw will become fatal. Development should be the norm amongst the HQ management. It should be a sacking offence to oppose change. In the 1992–3 organisation review for John Smith, I and others reported on a very large number of factors that were preventing or limiting change. Many were dealt with by Smith and then Blair, and the 1997 election was won. But today, although their nature has changed, plenty of fresh obstacles have emerged.

Political Causes

Cause 14: The government lost because it lost touch with the electorate.

Why did it lose touch? Ministers usually start out well but their separation from the people is often rapid. Physically it occurs through bulletproof cars, first-class travel, and high-security offices. Perceptually it happens as civil servants filter information about the outside world through their lenses of convenience and risk-avoidance. The minister's few advisers provide a broader perspective but one inevitably limited by their own experiences, which these days is usually a working lifetime in the political world.

A minister's diary is typically crammed, sometimes with highly managed photo shoots, a process designed to get the best press but one which inadvertently reinforces in their minds their own success: good media coverage equals good job. Immediately, this is good politics, but the effect only continues if a good press reflects the reality on the ground. In the long run, photo shoots are terminally self-deluding. The diary provides little time for thinking or reflection. When arriving home later at night, out comes a peculiarly British invention, the red box, to keep one away from the public and in the hands of the Civil Service.

Why are the red box and these other barriers accepted? Because politicians do not know any better and feel obliged to accept arcane practice. And because much of it is good for the ego.

Cause 15: The government lost because its base became increasingly narrow.

By the 2010 election, one canvasser reported that the only people consistently supporting the party were public sector employees. By then, the New Labour coalition consisted of these employees and: trade unions, local government councillors, the North London political sect, an immigration coalition of charities, immigrant-benefiting employers, the empathetically inclusive, the disabled, and ethnic minorities.

Why had its base become so narrow? Because it could not face dealing with the problems that had once been Labour solutions. As the rest of the electorate continued to fund the public sector without it responding with productivity and service improvements, they felt they were paying without any of the benefit. The public sector pensions arithmetic was unsustainable, but the immigration 'solution' was sprouting many obvious costs that the electorate was rejecting. The party was unable to let go of its faith in minorities. The government ducked the welfare failings too and ducked reforming the public sector trade unions (except the fire brigade's), the party's major remaining funder. By protecting 'its own' it lost the rest.

Cause 16: The government lost because it neglected or offended too many 'micro' constituencies.

Why did it neglect or offend these constituencies? Because it became trapped in a set of beliefs and assumptions that led it to privilege big business, banking, the media, immigrants, benefit recipients, public sector employees, and the disabled. It forgot the white working class, took the professional classes for granted, and offended private pension holders, recreational drug users, lovers of liberty, and rural living. Usually another constituency was viewed as taking a higher priority, as in the case of public sector pensions versus private; or because of the government's narrow experiential base, it had no understanding of life on the other side, as was the case with the rural population. Labour had only five rural constituencies in the last parliament, and these MPs were not in any inner sanctum. The Countryside Alliance may have been composed of people not like us, but they had legitimate concerns about the flip side of animal welfare and the non-paying performance of the Rural Payments Agency (another Civil Service car crash, but one which should have had ministerial priority to fix). The issue of rural mobile phone coverage was lost on them – due to the absence of mast sharing one electrician needs four different mobile phones and carriers to get coverage at his various customers' properties. The closest many in the leadership and advisers got to rural life was a weekend cottage, or Hampstead Heath (or Chequers). This was in stark contrast to when New Labour started MP targeting rural issues in the mid-1990s with MPs like Gavin Strang.

Being largely driven by polling, with its emphasis on majority views (and thus its lack of emphasis on minority views, except those with conscience status in the party), and with satisfying the news media and the majority agendas of their readerships, several minorities became expendable. Thus it was with recreational drugs. In the first half of the administration, a pragmatic and non-hysterical approach had resulted in the marginalisation of cannabis possession in the criminal justice system, downgraded from Class B to C in 2004. In the second half, running scared, the government jumped to media hysteria once more, and cannabis was sent back to Class B. (It is a curiosity that governments stop seeing people who it characterises as lawbreakers. They do not count, possibly because the House of Commons has OCD about legislation coupled with the mandatory homily that the law must be upheld. The consequence is that those so characterized are politically ignored, even though they continue to be electors, taxpayers, and citizens. The many smokers desperate for a fag on an open station platform and the millions of drug users simply disappear from political calculations.)

A further cause of offending these various minorities is the absence of systematic vetting, by Parliament and others, of proposed government decisions that would at least delay and sometimes prevent knee-jerk decisions. Such vetting would provide the politicians with significant protection against the news media and gut-reaction campaigns in favour of the wrong, the ineffective, the wasteful, the nonsense, and the damaging.

Cause 17: The government lost because it did not know what it was for any more.

Why did it not know? The old certainties of redistribution, disadvantage, and oppression were gone, but New Labour remained a prisoner of its history in the form of labour and the trade union link. It had achieved what it was going to in the first six years or so in terms of the social justice/economic efficiency formula. As their recipes for public service reform and expansion seized up, as the thinking dried up, as the reshuffles became dominant, New Labour became an empty shell.

Cause 18: The government lost because of the absence of proportional representation.

Why? The absence of PR after 1997 meant that the government could continue to wield power with little competitive pressure. Limited competition leads to low standards. Low standards lead, eventually, to election losses. Electoral systems that produce higher standards lead to longer-lasting parties in government.

Why does the absence of PR inhibit competition? First-past-the-post delivers a majority on a minority of support, and limits the choice of governing party to two (albeit a third party can occasionally play a part, but never the lead). It is a barrier to entry in market terms. Political parties in decline can continue when it would be preferable if they withered and new parties took over. This is far from a free market.

Why was PR not introduced in the first term, as its manifesto indicated? Because of the psychological needs for personal power of those at the top. Once in power, sharing power with others was anathema. The same can be seen in those opposing AV in the referendum in May 2011. The Labour supporters for FPTP top the 'psychologically flawed' table. They need the personal power most. Watch them.

Cause 19: The government lost because its funds were much less than those of the Conservatives.

Why? Because fickle corporate donors ceased donating as power receded, because the 'loans for honours' debacle and police investigations in 2006–7 scared off rich individuals, and because the large deficit in the defined benefit pension scheme for party staff took campaigning funds. For the 2010 election, the Electoral Commission reported that the Conservatives spent £16.7 million (£17.9 million in 2005), Labour £8 million (also £17.9 million in 2005), and the Lib Dems £4.8 million (£4.3 million). Labour's current income is around £4.7 million from the unions and £5.7 million of Short money[14] (increasing the latter was a long-sighted act by the Blair government).

The opportunity came to equalise funding but was spurned. In March 2006, former civil servant Sir Hayden Phillips was charged with setting up an inquiry to come up with proposals for reform. The inquiry reported a year later, and recommended capping individual donations at £50,000 and capping spending for political campaigns. It also suggested increasing state funding by £25 million and expanding its reach.

Why did the government not accept and implement these proposals? The causes are several. First, it had become accustomed

---

14   In 1974, at a time when the parties received no state funding to perform the role of an Opposition (usually Labour), minister Edward Short introduced funding for the parliamentary party and the leader's office, to enable it to employ the staff and do the research to be more effective – a gain for democracy. The funding was not for party pension deficits or election campaigns.

to being the highest-funded party, and made the mistake of thinking this was the new status quo. Second, it would have meant ditching block funding from trade unions with all of the implications for further distancing. Third, its self-delusion and tiredness made it unable to take a good decision. As Professor Justin Fisher says in the Hansard Society's review of the 2010 election, 'normal service resumed', i.e. the Conservatives had double the finance of Labour, an imbalance that will not change until Labour is back in power. It is difficult to overstate just how short-sighted was this decision not to endorse these proposals.

Who is to Blame?

Let's try and pull all this together – the context, what's wrong, the nineteen causes. The roots of failure may seem many and diverse; but the themes are common.

We all criticise government. Many say we should not be so harsh. Certainly, if you or I worked in that system we would struggle to do any better. But all the criticism of the system is justified. To use a chant from the football terraces – it's crap and it doesn't know it is.

In the course of writing this book I have come to realise that the current system demands cash for honours, and requires secret deals with news media empires. That is the price of election, not the occasional product of a sleazy prime minister or two. The current system leaves ministers and civil servants wide open to preferential lobbies that are, therefore, rife – any industry lobby usually gets what it wants at our expense. And leaves these industries soft and flabby and globally uncompetitive – a pretty poor industrial policy. And, in its effect, the constitution insists on bulk spinning – everyone becomes a spinner. It does not have to be this way, but that is the system we have.

I have come to realise the contribution to government failure made by the systems according to which party leaders are elected, and of the way parties are funded; of the maldistribution of political authority, of over-politicisation and apoliticisation, and misplaced power all also generating failure.

The consequent concentrations of power creep up on us – in party politics, in government, in banking, in large companies, in the news media, and in large public sector organisations and their cousins running government services in the private sector. At first we accept it as an inevitable and acceptable price to pay – for efficient business, for example. But it never stops and eventually it goes way too far. It is currently rated 'taking the piss'. Parts of these functionaries of our country behave well, but far too many do not, and their behaviour dominates in many adverse ways – seen and unseen.

The problem is not that politicians are only in it for the personal power (although some are), or that senior civil servants are clinging on to their status and cashmere terms and conditions (although they do), or that if only a different party were in power all would be well (it never is), or that public sector staff are too used to warm and fluffy work lives (although many are). We find politics in the wrong places, like scorekeeping, and kept out of the right places, like making things happen. All of this behaviour is the product of what the system of government demands and allows – the rules that stipulate how government should work. Slack rules allow slack behaviour, what you can get away with, duck, or bodge. There is nothing to say it should be otherwise. No controls, no imperatives, no disciplines … on governments (not on us). All organisations need these. Who is to blame?

The fundamental conclusion is that the reason governments fail is because they have not been designed. They have not been designed to succeed. They fail because they have far too much authority, far too little discipline on what they do, and too few rock solid obligations written into tamper-free constitutions. They fail not primarily because of the leaders and policies of the parties, but because the system in which they operate is so out of date that failure is inevitable. They and we are locked into a government system of vast dysfunction, with a default setting for muddle and error. What surprises me is when things work.

Why, then, do we continue to use the old banger for governments to ride in? Because the rules for governments – as distinct from the rules for us – insist on it. This is the point to talk about the C-word. Constitutions lay down how governments should work, what they can and can't do, the obligations on them. Our constitution is the rulebook for those in power. It should never be left solely to the political classes and academics to debate and amend, as happens now.

Constitutions are like the rules for a game – and we know if the rules are good the game is too, and if they aren't we give up on it. Constitutions have to be obeyed by governments – the courts and the judiciary stand at their end to enforce them. Our constitution needs to work much harder. If we raise the bar then we raise what is demanded of government.

Organisation starts (and often stops) with its constitution. Indeed, the hidden hand of a constitution is found at the heart of much organisational success and failure. A constitution is a set of fundamental principles according to which a state is governed: what is required of a government; what is allowed and not allowed; how power is deployed; the independence of the judiciary; rights and responsibilities. Why are our constitutions so inadequate in such important areas? Because the constitutions of governments were written or originated a long time ago, and the remit of government has expanded very considerably in the last century or so. Their scale today would astonish nineteenth-century rulers.

Most constitutions were designed or had their origins 200 years or more ago, from the American (1787) to the French (1958, and with eighteen subsequent amendments). Magna Carta – the best constitution Britain has ever had – was written in 1297 in the form still partly on the statute book. These constitutions were designed to ensure democracy, the rule of law, and human rights. Good. But just ponder that since those objectives became enshrined, little has changed other than very limited attempts at extra 'check and balance' on government decision, introduced usually in response to some crisis or other.

Then think about how much has changed in the world of government in the last hundred years, and even the last sixty. Decision-complexity has risen exponentially with population, with the number of countries, with globalisation and the scale of country to country competition, with global finance, with technology and with science; the power of bodies influencing government for better or worse is out of all former proportion, at times seemingly unstoppable – financial institutions, large businesses, and the news media; the pressure on resources is biting; and, if that were not enough, climate chaos is set to grow. What's more, less is up for political judgement and more for professional delivery as experiments in capitalism versus socialism, inherited versus social justice, have reached their conclusion.

Consequently, governments have not been designed for their modern primary purposes. Today they run very large public services and regulate major industries. Governments have become major doers and deliverers and they are expected to solve most problems. The bureaucracies of delivery have an inevitable tendency to become ends to themselves rather than servants of society – they become inward turning in the absence of forces that make them look outside. When the constitutions were written, governments delivered hardly any services, and faced none of these issues of direct delivery.

Constitutions were never invented to control corporate power. The rights of man came about to protect the individual from arbitrary acts of absolute monarchs. Every democratic constitution in the world has these provisions, and the concomitant independence of the judiciary. In the days when constitutions were being thought about very hard and instituted, marauding corporates did not exist. If they had, the founding fathers here and everywhere else would have had a substantial part of the constitution devoted to protection of the individual against unrestrained or insufficiently restrained corporates, be they legal or illegal. Businesses of current scale are a modern occurrence and their power has grown with their size. Some are near totalitarian in outlook. They lobby in private to prevent increased competition, to maintain an armlock on a common need like pensions or food, and to see off the interests of the public.

Neither were constitutions designed to handle the disproportionate power wielded by today's news media. The news media has become pervasive with the means of distribution multiplying – a huge leap in scale and therefore influence from the original printed sheets for the few who could read. Deals for political support in exchange for business benefit are standard practice on a small and large scale. For as long as government decisions are skewed towards corporate, media and other sectional interests, citizens and consumers will come a long way last.

Governments were not designed with today's debt in mind. Historically, debt was incurred to wage war. If it was left to grow and comparative excess prevailed, countries went bust or revolutions broke out, as in France in 1789. Thus controls were grim but effective. Today they are not, debt is easier to obtain, and it is used to finance much more than war. The advent of the welfare state and increasing longevity expanding those supported by it has made the politics of debt hard to resist. Politicians hope that the financial boil will not burst whilst they are in office, but will remain for future generations to lance. No constitutional safeguards envisaged this dilemma.

Neither were constitutions originated when life spans were such that putting off hard choices would benefit one generation at the potentially enormous expense of later ones – choices about who funds pensions and when, and whether at least on a precautionary basis climate chaos is to be taken seriously.

The task of government has expanded seismically. Governments' capacity for beneficial change is far exceeded by the demands on them. None of these constitutions were designed for this multi-mission of government. No current government in the world has been explicitly designed to succeed. None has been designed according to modern organisational theory and practice. We should marvel that organisations so out of date manage to function at all. This is neurosurgery with a torque wrench. If something has not been designed for purpose then it comes as no surprise when it doesn't work; so why on earth should we expect undesigned government to work?

At this point, we need to introduce the concept of political authority. As we shall find later, this is where much of the system has gone wrong, and lies at the node of putting it right. Political authority is broadly what we give to a government on election 'to run the country'. Someone or somebody has to take the myriad of decisions and do the myriad of actions required of any modern government. This is essential – 30 million voters acting collectively could not do it. But that authority is distributed – it doesn't all go to the government (except in dictatorships). Under the present system authority is distributed from the executive to provide some check on government actions – this is such power that parliamentary committees can muster to vet proposed legislation and to review past action, to the second chamber, to independent assessors like the National Audit Office and Office for National Statistics, to the Civil Service, and to the judiciary (although in the UK this 'separation of powers' between the executive and the legislature is scrambled). Political authority is usually split between national, regional and local governments. The powers resting at each vary considerably between countries.

But our constitutions have large holes in them. The political authority of governments includes much score-keeping simply because our constitutions are silent on it. Watch how politicians debate the numbers. Governments wriggle and squirm to spin every number from crime statistics to debt levels to employment to immigration. But maths really should not be a matter of politics. Absurdly, it largely is. About once a decade small steps in the right direction are made via the independence of the Office for National Statistics and the creation of the Office for Budget Responsibility, both charged with producing valid and not politicised figures.

Next the holed constitution places no obligation to evaluate dispassionately and objectively the result or outcome of every policy, programme, law, institution, expenditure, or agent of government. The results of government are either uncollected or are a matter of argument. Results should never be matters of political judgement accept where they are not clear. But in the absence of any systematic assessment, tabloid opinion, urban myth, prejudice, misinformation, spun defence, and most often simple ignorance substitute. Equally large holes exist as governments do not have any obligations to deliver beneficial change effectively. Too much becomes left to politics and lobbying, crowding out what should be matters of the quality of decision-making and of good organisation. Civil servants and ministers are usually ignorant of the subjects on which they are being lobbied and bend to the best or loudest argument. The government has masses of political authority to take the wrong decision on a lobby's behalf, all in private.

Amongst the elites with the political authority, is a pervasive self-serving culture that the complexities of government are way beyond the common person: only they have the abilities to govern. They are wrong, but the tendency has been for authority to be smuggled quietly to the centre. But much has been learnt about how to make decisions well in organisations. None of this new knowledge is reflected in the way that governments are constituted. Governments can still make decisions in any way that they please.

So what fills the constitutional void? Politics and politicisation. The original house was built soundly, but wings have been added successively without applying a building code – the foundations of representative democracy, justice, and rights remains standing, but the rest is flawed. It leaks and disenchants. The consequences of this laissez–faire political authority lie all around us in the form of the nonsenses that are deemed irreformable in practice or that we have to accept in the name of some apparently greater good.

This book makes the connections between performance and a constitution, between the rules for government and lived experiences, and therefore the central place of its constitution in a society. The analysis is organisational, the solution is constitutional, and the change will be political.

Rather as Gandhi said when asked what he thought of British civilisation – 'I look forward to it' – so I look forward to a British constitution. What passes for one now is the so-called unwritten or more correctly uncodified constitution – a mixture of custom and practice, what the Civil Service can get you to believe, academic interpretations of precedent, and the periodic judgements and misjudgements of the courts – alongside the laws that have given some shape: the Bill of Rights 1689, accompanied by Magna Carta, the Petition of Right, Habeas Corpus Act 1679, Parliament Acts 1911 and 1949, and more recently the Human Rights Act and the Freedom of Information Act. This is piecemeal, not a coherent system designed to deliver. Read the Swiss constitution and, without necessarily agreeing with it all and noting its omissions by comparison with the Treaty, decide if it is not a far better set of rules to govern a country than the obscure and fungible rules of the UK – in fact the latter is a set of rules for a muddle with pockets of high privilege, which is precisely what we have. We return to the point that the constitution and ethos of any entity are what determine its performance and behaviour.

My ambition is to create the concept of, and the desire for, world-class government. This would stem from a twenty-first century constitution, and an ethos amongst leaders to strive for the best. The constitution would embrace the main pillars of effective government, not just what government was 200 years ago.

So, what would a design for successful government look like? What are the essential building blocks? The rest of the book sets these out.

PART 3

THE DESIGN FOR SUCCESSFUL GOVERNMENT

7

The Treaty For Government

It is not the strongest of the species that survives, nor the most intelligent, but the one most responsive to change.

Charles Darwin

In the mid-1990s, I had a meeting in Lausanne with the then number two at the International Olympic Committee, the lawyer and Director General, Francois Carrard. As consultants we would often take ideas to clients in the hope that they would then engage us for the project. In preparing a report on London's Olympic Challenge and how to win a bid to stage them, I'd noticed how often the same problems occurred – every Games used to be marred by late construction, mismanaged ticketing and poorly run road transport. (The latter was so bad at Atlanta that a few competitors even missed their races.)

I drew this to the attention of the IOC in a note entitled 'Not Re-inventing the Wheel'. Each winning city to stage the Olympics had never run one before – so the wheel of how to set up and manage them was endlessly reinvented, often barely turning. All sorts of posing, politicking, power plays, ego expressing, holy alliances, unholy alliances, and last-minuteism came together in a mixture of random quality and amateurism.

The IOC had seen all of this before and had the knowledge – if only it wished to deploy it – as to how each wheel should be made. My proposal was that they should specify how an Olympics should be mounted in order to avoid these repetitive failures. Being based in Switzerland, where they understand how useful constitutions can be, the IOC went further and designed the organisational system to deliver a Games successfully. And the design is written into law – in effect the constitution for delivering Olympic facilities and operations. Knowledge transfer is part of it too – Beijing spent four days with the London team debriefing on its experiences. All successful institutions have effective learning engines. The reason the London Olympics worked was because the system designed for them worked. Yes, we were fortunate in having Tessa Jowell as lead minster, and mayor of London Ken Livingstone, two very capable deliverers, and Lord Coe played a blinder in the politics of winning the bid and is a wunnerful human being – but it was the system wot did it.

One critical part of this system is this: 'The IOC make Opposition support a precondition of bidding – something that would not be replicated for other projects – but the Olympic experience underlines the value of political continuity and preventing major project delivery from becoming a political football.'[15] The IOC has seen the very public and dire consequences of zigzag government on staging an Olympics.

At much the same time as visiting Lausanne, I was designing the central organisation of the Labour Party for John Smith. I needed to know what its objectives were – organisations are designed (or should be) for a purpose. 'What are they?' I asked. Silence. The notion that a political party should have objectives other than the political seemed foreign. 'What about winning elections and governing well?' I suggested. These were accepted. The new design, along with a lot of work and changes by many others, turned Labour into a formidable campaigning machine, and it did govern well for a while.

I hope the case has been made that the failures of government are caused first and foremost by how it is organised. Which political party is in office is secondary. Most of our problems can be traced back not to the political parties, which are only products of the system, but to the system itself. It is tottering and it is up to us to sort it out.

Objectives

So, we need urgently a design for successful government – one designed for its objectives, and aligned internally. We've seen

---

15   *Making the Games: What Government Can Learn from London 2012*, Institute for Government (2013).

what's wrong with what happens now, and thus what to avoid. These failures are the symptoms. We need to cure the root causes of the malaise, and the cure is the Treaty.

What, then, are its objectives? Essentially, a system is needed that generates the best decisions and policies; that implements these well, and preferably really well; that runs the many day-to-day bodies it has at high levels of service judged by the consumers/ citizens and at high and growing productivity; that is satisfying to work in; that does not fund itself on unsustainable debt; that is fair in its decisions and operations between the rich and others, big organisations and individuals, in the application of its laws, in the distribution of welfare, in the raising of taxes, and between current and future generations. The system should provide routes for us as individuals to influence and understand its decisions – when we want to – that doesn't have to be fought to contribute to solving a public problem, and that takes the noise out of the relationship between government and individuals; in other words, to rebalance power between the citizen and the government.

Let's remember too that such a system should exclude ideology and prejudice for their own sake; should proscribe preferential lobbying; should reduce the power and influence of corporates, banks, and the news media, counterbalanced with citizen power; should pins noses to results, not spin doctors; should stop as much as it starts, achieve more and attempt less; should demand more of public sector bodies and their close relatives in the private sector contracted to government; and should minimise waste. It should attract different kinds of politicians with contrasting formative experiences and the experience and temperament to get things done, and should prevent the psychological flaws of the politicians and civil servants dominating. Government should not be a freak show in private. This is the point where ego confronts democracy, where the psychology of leaders eyeballs the needs of the people, and where the constitution should mediate between the two.

This new system would also limit the obligation on politicians to talk bollocks; would immunise them against business power, gut reactions, and media frenzy; and eliminate cash for honours.

These are fine objectives, but how do get them delivered?

Why Constitutions Matter

In developing a constitution designed to produce successful government and replace repetitive representative voting, we are trying something new. Constitutions have never had this purpose. It is an ambitious agenda, but new constitutions have always been written at times of high ambition.

Constitutions make or break organisations. In their current form, they also prevent dictators and all their horrors. They specify how our representatives are to be elected, for how long, and who has the vote. They bestow further human rights upon us. They ensure separation of powers between the executive, the legislature, and the judiciary to provide checks and balances. They scrutinise performance and behaviour, and minimise corruption. They secure free speech. They prescribe which decisions are for the representative bodies and which for referendum. They specify where and what power is held at levels other than central government.

Long-standing democratic countries take these rules as read. Debates arise around the effectiveness of the checks and balances, devolution, and voting methods. The rulebook is relatively settled. Think of a game: if the rules are wrong, the game does not work. If one player cheats, the others lose interest. If the rules are biased, one player always wins (as in a casino). We can see all these faults at play in our constitutions with debt where the rules are wrong, soft corruption where the protected species are cheating and the non-voters opt out, and lobbying where the rules and the benefits are biased to corporates.

That is the reason a constitution is so fundamental to organisational performance – if the rules are changed, you get different behaviour and different players. The new treaty would produce new politicians and new politics and new behaviour. The tricky bit is designing the various elements to fulfil the objectives.

A recent experience with a new rule for government – the Golden Rule – is instructive. Introduced in 1998 in the UK, it was intended to stop the government racking up debt by stating that government should only borrow to invest and not to fund current spending. It was and is a very good rule. The problem was that its inventor, Gordon Brown, was in effect left to apply it himself. As he sought more political wiggle room, the rulebook changed, and the game eventually fell apart. The rule was written in such broad terms as to be voluntary. Rulers can never referee themselves.

Its successor government ditched the Golden Rule. After all, it was a product of its political opponents and therefore wrong – a classic case of zigzag – and had also been discredited through misuse. Meanwhile, post the credit crisis and responding to failure, four other countries are adding the Golden Rule to their constitutions – France, Germany, Spain and Italy.

Evidently these countries see writing the Golden Rule into the constitution as the means to good accounting. The golden rule removes from the political playing field decisions on the quantity of debt. The constitution sets the ceiling. It will then depend on the tightness of definitions and the effectiveness of enforcement. So here the decision on the debt cap has been depoliticised. What decisions would the British Chancellor have taken in the good times of the mid-2000s with this level of control over him? What shape would the UK economy be in now? To put it bluntly, the government would not been have allowed to piss away money we did not have, and are now slowly paying back. Good government depends at least as much on disciplining the decisions of those at the top as it does on their inherent quality. With the right controls they perform better in the job.

What else would be better if it were removed from politics? And what would be better for being *within* the political remit? How should our rules for government be developed to get the best out of the system and the people in it? How should the power be separated?

What is Political and What is Not?

Let's remind ourselves that at present once our vote is cast, the political authority invested in the representatives who form the government presumes very wide competence (and goodwill) on their part, if it is to be exercised properly. History shows that too much reliance is placed on this laissez-faire political authority.

There are so many aspects of government that should be: matters of fact, or conclusions arrived at independently, or policies made using all of the knowledge now known about good decision-taking, or modern organisational theory and practice applied in running public services. Politics occupies too much space – space that should be taken by the system and by organisation.

Where decisions are still matters of political judgement or trade-offs or about genuine differences regarding the human condition, a vision for society, or what matters, then the political process would continue. Gay marriage, much of foreign affairs, and a Good Friday Agreement are political judgements. Where else? Wherever constitutional imperatives, feedback, and policy vetting leave the solution unclear. How often will that be? Not as often as you might imagine. Elsewhere, covering broad swathes of what is now political only by default of silent or absent constitutions, the authority would be vested in the system of government, not the party.

Starting with a blank sheet of paper, where would our political authority now be placed to best realise the objectives set out above? Do we want it to go to the government and to a political process? Do we want it to go to non-political bodies with separate duties? Or do we want it to go to a fixed rule? It's not black and white, so what should go where?

We have seen that to prevent unsustainable debt – one of the objectives for the Treaty – decisions on this have to be depoliticised. In other words, when we vote we would not be allocating this part of our political authority to our political representatives but to a fixed and tamper-proof rule. Let us then take one of our examples of past government failure from Part 2 of this book and now a new objective – a decent pension system for all. We are certainly not leaving that all to politics to do. The overall objective would be enshrined in a fixed rule. Thus governments would *have* to provide this. The policy to realise this objective would be developed by the government of the day. But not by any random means they chose – because the *process* for developing policy would be specified and vetted. Whilst policies and decisions would continue to be a matter for the government, the process for achieving the right policies would *not* be political. In other words, while governments will propose decisions, the way they have come to that decision and the factors included in coming to it, would be vetted by the system. And if the policy fails the vetting process, then it would be sent back for correction.

Once decisions have been made, future politics will be mostly about government performance. Competent delivery would be a big part of why we elect a government. Delivery is a matter of politics and should be repoliticised, and thus taken out of the de facto control of the Civil Service. Making all the changes work set out in the new pension policy would be the responsibility of the government and ministers. No ducking this one.

Then would come the sharpest control of them all – feedback. Has your party produced better results? Convince us that your party has produced precision-guided welfare that does not pollute on impact. Can you run the trains? Cut public expenditure and produce greater outcomes simultaneously? Have you hard-regulated the banks back on to planet Earth? To return to our example, in practice, is your design and delivery producing the objective of fair pensions for all? And feedback – results and facts – is most definitely not political. Here, our political authority would be allocated to independent scorekeepers.

For PSOs, whilst results and facts are not political, doing something about them is. Thus underperformance would trigger government action; otherwise the PSOs would be left to get on with it, confident that effective feedback would keep an eye on them.

In summary: objectives as rules, the policymaking process, and feedback and scorekeeping would be depoliticised. Delivery, the delivery system, and priority reform would be politicised. Most public sector bodies would be running in business-as-usual mode, without political input, unless triggered.

I should emphasise that the depoliticisation of aspects of government is not to place them in the hands of some technocratic elite to decide as they think fit as the only alternative to failed politics and governments. Our Treaty provides a system for right decision-making under our jurisdiction where we set the objectives and process.

One further decision for our deployment – we will want to reclaim some political authority between elections on big issues, through the right to referendum, both nationally and locally. How often this is done would be up to us – possibly once in ten years with issues on the scale of membership of the EU. But we might, in time, get a taste for making decisions, as the Swiss do, and hold referenda more often.

In terms of where the power would go then less for the prime minister and Cabinet, less for the senior Civil Service, less for powerful lobbies, less for party funders, less for PSOs. More for the Commons and the Lords, more for independent scrutineers and scorekeepers, more for elected executives, more for other political parties, more for the public, and more for real local government. In practice, governments would achieve more, and therefore ministers would achieve more and therefore be more powerful in a literal and not psychological sense (and crucially, it would be controlled and directed power).

Summary of the Treaty

This Treaty would be put to the people to deliberate, and thence to vote on as a package. Then it would be put into practice through a new set of rules for government and some new roles. It would cover the redistribution of power, the depoliticisation and institutionalisation of comprehensive feedback on results and performance of every sphere of government, and the politicisation of delivery with executive ministers and a new Civil Service (with a modern name) employing the right people for the right roles.

To make the whole system work organisationally, these are the building blocks or the design:

1. Feedback
2. Abandonment programme
3. Policy vetting
4. Operations
5. People
6. Competitive democracy
7. Separation of powers, behaviours, tamper-proof rules, custodian role
8. Intergenerational fairness, and responsibility deal

First we need feedback and government by results. This means feedback of results or outcomes on anything and everything done by or for the state, including legislation, regulation, statutory duties, policies and programmes, public sector services and bodies including the government private sector. Results equals judgement day awaiting every government proposal – its results will be examined and measured, regularly and publicly. This is an overdue discipline on everyone in government. And on corporate lobbies. And on us.

Second, alongside results would come the abandonment programme. Wherever something is not working or is not going to work, it would halt quickly alongside its costs. Policy termination would be the norm, not the exception.

Third, the stuff going into the pipeline must have a far higher chance of coming out the other end. The way policy is made and decisions are taken would change. Thus policies and decisions would be vetted and, if not up to standard, rejected. Ten tests would be applied. These would obliterate ideology, prejudice, initiativitis, something (anything) must be done, preferential lobbying, and the second, third and fourth rate. Learning from others would become the everyday means of working. Transparency would be common, not rare. Perpetuating the status quo and vested interests would become 'proscribed' activities.

Fourth, for turning policy into practice, getting it done – the operations of government, a set of duties including one of straight speak would apply to all public sector bodies and to their private sector relatives and to everyone working there. The approach to getting performance and value out of the public sector would go well beyond the current method of New Public Management and its offshoots. Rigorous feedback and results would of themselves make a huge difference, along with renewable terms of office for heads and chief executives, changing boards of management, effective supervision of regulators and PSOs, the search for and application of best organisational practice (for example, 'benchmarking' how other countries enforce planning permissions on rogue developers), and harmonised and fair terms and conditions across the public sector. Real local government – which looks nothing like the sham we have now – is all part of creating responsive, functioning and cost-effective government and would be run according to the same conditions of the Treaty. Delivery would be dispersed to where it can, on balance, achieve the most. In time public services would be run with world-class ambition and achievement.

Fifth, all of this means some big changes in the type and experiences of people in government. We need governments to get things done, which means people in them who know how to get things done. The Treaty proposes executive ministers, specialisation and training of politicians, maximum terms of eight years for prime ministers, four-year terms for governments, and new rules for changing party leaders. A new breed of politicians would emerge from executive roles in the public sector and elsewhere, and obtain their 'coaching' qualifications for government. With political authority in the right place, at last the Civil Service would be effectively reformed and split in two.

Sixth, we need high standards of competition amongst political parties through full proportional representation, fair funding of political parties including limited state funding and banning large donations, the right to referendum, free assembly and expression, and public deliberation and engagement.

Seventh, these roles must be in the right place to work. Just as the scores are not left to the managers to assert, spin, and argue over in sport, so governments cannot rate themselves. Thus a fourth and fifth separation of powers are needed, beyond the power held by the executive, the legislature, and the judiciary. In acceding our political authority to the state, we would be allocating these new powers not to the executive but to the revitalised House of Lords for results – the Resulture – and to the House of Commons for policy vetting. The independent score keepers – the NAO and the ONS – would be offspring of the House of Lords, not of the government and not of the Commons. This is a major change. The Lords would have to acquire the vision, ambition, and energy to reform government and to organise themselves to establish the Resulture. The Resulture would be staffed independently of the government's administrative Civil Service, as would the other independent bodies. The comparator here is the judiciary.

The House of Lords would also have the role of setting and disciplining the behaviour and standards applicable to ministers and others in the system. This would include relationships with news media owners and editors.

Our Treaty has to be looked after and its rules applied without tampering. Our custodian would be an essentially apolitical 'stakeholder'-based House of Lords. In effect, and by chance and some design, this is nearly what we now have. We are lucky indeed. Hurdles for changing the Treaty would be set too.

Eighth and finally is the intergenerational, fairness, and responsibility deal whereby no transfers in costs to future generations would be allowed for current account debt, pensions, or climate chaos; fair pension provision for all; fair taxation; new rules for corporate behaviour; and a Congress for the Future with clout would be run annually.

We are starting to see an aligned organisation with each part facing in the same direction. We have put politics in the right places and taken them out of the wrong. Power is balanced and can no longer be appropriated by the wealthy. We have a competitive market for government – and one that lives or dies by the results for us. We have reclaimed much political authority through the visibility and thus accountability of the whole system, by the right to referendum and engagement, through stakeholder policymaking, and most notably in time through the restoration of real local government. Policies and decisions would be taken to deal effectively with issues, not to indulge an ideology or lazily bat a problem into the long grass. The operations in the middle to deliver these decisions and policies have delivery itself as their objective, rather than their own existence. The people coming into the system would increasingly be those that can deliver and do the job. The priorities of political parties would change from: policy, power, and delivery (coming a long way last); to power, delivery, and policy.

This is the architecture of good and world-class government. Is it complex? Of course – although far less so than at present. Will it take commitment and ambition to build, and time for its full benefits to show? Of course. Will there still be failures? Of course – but many fewer.

8

Knowing Where You Are

The Secret Life of Chaos, a television programme presented by Professor Jim Al-Khalili, describes the extraordinary self-organising capacity of cells to develop to a complete human being and all of nature. The mathematical equations that govern this self-organisation are quite simple and yet result in order and chaos, patterns and the unpredictable, from the spots on a cow to the ridges on desert sand dunes, from the fractals of a lung to storms and tornadoes. To create order and beauty and function, feedback is essential. At each stage of development, the output from one equation forms the input for the next cycle. The organisms self-correct and self-develop.

The same principle is true of organisations: the greater the feedback, the more it and each person in it will respond and self-correct. Feedback matters. It is a discipline on the other end of the pipe: if you put garbage in you will no longer be able to spin your way out of that decision. If your delivery is poor, you will no longer by able to duck and dive your way through years of underperformance before some accountability appears – usually fleeting. It will cut many needless arguments in areas such as welfare, where the objective is not either/or but how much and how. Feedback cuts the pointless, the fruitless, the unintended, the perverse, and forces their abandonment. It means you don't have to wait years for public pressure or a media campaign or a change of government to do what needed doing all along. It focuses minds on priorities and on efficiency, and cuts out managerialism and proceduralism for their own sake, thereby saving money and taxes. It highlights issues – like unfit people – and compels change.

It serves another vital purpose: feedback that is public educates the electorate, dents my prejudices and yours, and infuses democracy with intelligence.

Ignorance of the Result is No Defence

Feedback is not a private matter between the PSO or its private equivalent and the ministry. Transparency is essential to good government. Secrecy is only needed for war.

What types of feedback would be needed to make government work? Think about what types of feedback are used by organisations working in the competitive world. They are many and various precisely because to survive and to prosper, organisations need to know what is going on in many ways: sales, income, profits, costs, customer satisfaction, time to market, staff morale, supplier relations, brand image, advertising effectiveness, IT performance, etc., subdivided by product, geography, division, or however the company is structured, with external analysts comparing performance within and across industries. Government will need a similar volume. Bear in mind it is spending 40% of GDP, and therefore could reasonably be expected to be producing 40% of the feedback. The cost of this government 'results industry' will be significant – but a fraction of the cost in waste and inefficiency that comes from not having it. The very best investment a parliament can make is in feedback.

Imagine no more flying blind, no secrecy, removing the invisibility cloak, sharing knowledge. Imagine using strong and transparent feedback loops to stimulate improvement, open information systems promoting accountability to the funder – to you and me. Imagine the leap from 'Have you delivered the right procedures?' to 'Have you delivered the right results?' Imagine the savings in overheads and administration and annoyance as results takes the place of layers of management and buckets of procedure. This should be the future.

Feedback is necessary for anything and everything done by or for the state: legislation, regulations, statutory duties; policies and programmes; and all public sector services and organisations, including the government private sector. What would that look like?

Legislation, Regulation, Statutory Duties

'Does this legislation work?' is a good place to start, and how well or how badly.[16] League tables of legislation would take each Act, ascribe a purpose to it, assess to what extent the purpose has been realised, and estimate its costs – both for government and for non-government in the shape of individuals and organisations – to run. Such estimates would be broad brush, not matters of precision accounting, but good enough to work out whether a law is worth keeping.

The league table would place those laws with the highest result-to-cost ratio at the top. The bottom half would then be the place to consider abandonment. In some cases the answer will be screamingly obvious – i.e. the law is a total waste of time and money – in other cases it will take some thought or further investigation. Each law abandoned would save money and complexity both for government and the public. Alternatives to ineffective legislation would be found: in Australia, littering was successfully tackled through subtle communication, peer pressure, and campaigning, rather than a failed law.

In some cases, a law is ineffective because the means of enforcement are flawed. The appropriate course then would be to change the enforcement method rather than to abandon the law, if different means of enforcement would work. Planning breaches by developers and builders are a case in point. The US uses a 'parking ticket' approach: when a developer breaches a planning condition and an enforcement issued, non-compliance results in a fine. If it is unpaid, it increases.

Rigorous examination of each law would also throw into sharp relief where a field of law overall has gone astray. London is said to be the libel and divorce capital of the world. Does this tell us anything about the legislative health of these two fields? Chancery law is too complicated to be understandable (and is ultra expensive to apply) – what is its purpose, and is it fulfilling it? Family law is still adversarial and not inquisitorial, held in secret, and presumes that a legal process can resolve the complexities of family life. The

---

16   The House of Lords is moving in this direction, albeit with the glacial pace of reform Westminster considers normal: 'We recommend the appointment of an ad hoc post-legislative scrutiny committee to examine the Children and Adoption Act 2006 and the Adoption and Children Act 2002, to report in a timely manner, so as to allow for evaluation of the committee's work before the end of the 2012–13 Session.'

same questions should be posed. Employment law has become an expensive minefield courtesy mainly of a judiciary without relevant knowledge. Again, what is its purpose, and is it achieving it? Is there a better/cheaper way? We sign contracts as long as the Bible to buy a piece of software. Why?

The case for a wall-to-wall assessment of these areas of law is absolute. All of these problems have existed for a long time. Essentially nothing changes, I think, for four reasons. First, the judiciary periodically has to fight off the government of the day attempting to reduce their independence. The judges become habituated to resist change. They are obviously right to maintain their independence, but not to resist change. Second, the legal profession believes that all of life is reducible to a legal process. It is unable to see beyond its own profession and the many other ways of resolving a dispute. Third, the legal profession has a huge vested interest in the status quo. It is a high-pay, high-status, and high-power career with limited accountability. Fourth, few people outside it understand it sufficiently to mount a credible challenge. Internal reform will not happen, particularly with so many representatives in government. What would a ruthless examination of results find here?

As with legislation, so with regulation – every example should be similarly vetted regularly for its value and cost, and justified (or not) by its benefit versus cost. In some cases of poor value the regulation would still be needed but the cost of application would be reduced. Much regulation should be applied through well-designed and easy to use websites.

Statutory duties of public bodies would be reviewed periodically to check whether they remain appropriate in today's circumstances. Climate chaos should, but often does not, change the priorities of all those public bodies with some remit for the environment, from national parks to ecology monitors.

Policies and Programmes

Take a policy, any policy, and ask if it is achieving its objectives. Unbundling the local loop, child poverty, vetting, safeguarding, disability benefit, fishing, cycling safety, money laundering, watchdogs for trading standards – any policy or programme large or small. There are thousands, some long forgotten and still going. Start with the easier to assess and the more likely to be having little effect, or those operating indiscriminately.

Let's have a think about what this might mean for a country's policy on welfare, for instance. What would a ruthless examination of its results against its objectives generate? Well, what are its objectives?

The first is to disentangle the insured from the needy from the fraudulent from the demotivated from the perversely incentivised from those who will always struggle from those who would benefit by being trained from the dependent victims of the welfare state. People classified as being in need will have various motivations, not necessarily good. They may take undeserved assistance from the state, or not support themselves at the earliest opportunity, or be motivated to not support themselves by the benefits, or take something that is not theirs. The notional sanctification of all poorer people neither accords with reality nor does them any favours. Improving people's lives has rarely resulted from permanent benefits. Universal benefits will always be regressive in their outcome.

What then might be the results we are intending? Sufficient income during job transition arising from the bad luck of enforced redundancy? How long for? Is fairness the test? Or job availability? And where? Sufficient income for those who will always struggle – substantially physically or mentally disabled? Education and training and thus a job and a sound economy through tying benefits to courses? These segments are relatively straightforward.

But what about teenage pregnancies? Too low a level of support may mean the child has less life chances, or worse. Too high and benefits are motivating childbirth and population increase.

And what about those whose underlying benefit dependency has more to do with their own psychopathology? Is this a case of a victim mentality? And how will money help or even cure that or improve this person's life? A crash course in cognitive behavioural therapy might achieve better results. Giving people a purpose – building their own home, training in a skill, working on the land, specific support and mentoring – may well be the way out of benefits.

Naturally this is pretty complicated. My purpose here is not to design a new welfare system but to start down the road of clarity of purpose and the *ruthless examination of results* – all without coming at the issue from polarised history.

Government Bodies

For government bodies of all sorts a broad assessment of performance by every stakeholder would provide prima facie evidence of a well-run or poorly body. The best example of this method is the PROGRESS Process developed by the charity Antidote to improve schools. This involves pupils, staff, and parent surveys using an online reporting tool to describe their experience of the organisation, and then using the data that emerges to have conversations with each other to develop an explanation about what it means and a strategy for improving things. Every school should engage in this sort of process every year. League tables of GCSE results are too blunt an instrument, and unlike the PROGRESS Process do not point to solutions as well as to the problems. Confidential reporting prevents the syndrome of the untouchable but largely useless head, too. All government agencies should find out how their stakeholders experience the organisation in this sort of way and be held to account for responding to the findings. Board members would then have the judgement of the people and organisations they are there for, and not some partial airbrushed data from management in the annual review.

We can learn from the Internet here, which continues to develop its capacity for non-governmental moderation and regulation, built into business models. The more obvious examples are the feedback from consumers, for example on eBay, which acts as probably a more effective control on sellers than any government regulator. Such feedback is open to misinformation through such novelty metaphors as 'astro turfing' and 'sock puppeting', but countered by 'stack overflow' and technology message boards.

Would regulation built into the business model have done a better job than the Financial Services Authority, the Bank of England and the Treasury at exposing and controlling the scams if banking products had been sold over the Internet? EBay is built on maximum transparency. The banking system is built on maximum opacity. This world hides behind commercial confidentiality and competitive advantage. This is largely nonsense. The intriguing question is how can the mechanisms of effective business–model–based regulation from the Internet be applied to the banking industry – at much lower cost, of course, than current institution–based regulation.

Regulators would be part of this stakeholder assessment also, along with all bodies substantially funded by government – charities and the government private sector, those companies contracted to undertake public sector operations. Where individuals are the objects of the policy, then feedback is needed on them, and the agency concerned would record it. The criminal justice system is the most notable absconder here. The presenting circumstances, the offender history, the sentence given, and the reoffending or rehabilitation record are needed both to determine whether the treatment has achieved the result, and to better select future sentences for other offenders. This would be a learning system, aimed at improving the effectiveness of the CJS in reducing reoffending.

Instant feedback provides the information for staff to act upon quickly, for the authorities above managements to pick up on when necessary, and for the public to see their experience of government expressed accurately, not suppressed nor spun. At present, poor performance only becomes an issue about which something may be done well after the event. Effective feedback is continuous, not isolated. I am reminded of the toilets on a ferry from Holyhead to Dublin. As you leave, a press-button panel invites you to score the loos as good, OK or poor. Simple. It does not require a questionnaire of varying design quality to be completed and posted somewhere. It is real time and avoids the time lag of days or more before urgent cleaning is undertaken. One feels under no social pressure either to give feedback or to avoid it. Many bureaucracies would improve through instant visible feedback. A simple press the button on exit – good, bad, average- would be relayed straight back on such services as airport passport control, for train travel, for the Fort William roadworks. I wonder what a 'ticker tape' display of results would look like in the House of Lords open areas, or above the entrances to town halls across the country.

A variant on instant feedback would centre on feedback forums. These would open in order to take a specific failure, for example a late train or repetitively late trains on the same line, and identify the root causes and thus the solutions. Such forums would be built on a blame-free environment and the duty of straight speak.

Of all this feedback, little would be based on performance indicators as the public sector has come to experience them in the last thirty years, and much more on answering the question 'What happened?' – what happened when a food regulation was changed; what happened when the corporation tax rate was reduced? However, performance measures do have an important place – but they should not be a matter of politics, nor of ignorance and insufficient training.

To watch UK governments zigzag with performance measures and targets over the last decades is to observe a dysfunctional classroom. We have had the following and all points in between: no measures (this is simply foolish – we need to know, for example, parent and pupil satisfaction with a teacher, passenger satisfaction with a train line); lots of measures (inevitable with so many services); targets (by and large self-defeating, as the New York mayor Rudy Giuliani concluded in the 1990s – they distort); dumb measures (as per Labour's introduction of quantity-only measures for operations with no reference to quality – meeting a target of 100 hip replacements, even if they became infected or had to be repeated, represented success); indiscriminate measures (offences brought to justice by the police score a teenager with cannabis equally with a gangland head with a crack-cocaine empire); and 'what gets measured gets done' (partially true – but as the sign hanging in Einstein's office at Princeton said, 'Not everything that counts can be counted, and not everything that can be counted counts.')

The political classes argue and stumble over performance measures from a position of ignorance, prejudice, and psychological need. After thirty years of their experiential learning, still too few of them have a coherent or balanced understanding of the role of measures in organisational performance. Is it too much to ask of our politicians that this, amongst other core knowledge, be an entry criterion to government? SATs for politicians?

Good feedback lets everyone know what happened: what did we do, how well did we do it, has anyone benefited. Some results will be 100% clear-cut, some fuzzy, but even the latter reduce the uncertainty and aid decision-making. The next crucial issue is who should command the body of feedback.

The Resulture

The separation of powers is taken for granted in modern discussions of government and implemented in many constitutions throughout the world. To prevent one branch from becoming supreme, protect the 'opulent minority' from the majority, and to induce the branches to cooperate, government systems that employ a separation of powers need a way to balance each of the branches. Typically this was accomplished through a system of 'checks and balances', the origin of which, like separation of powers itself, is credited to Montesquieu. Checks and balances allow for a system-based regulation that allows one branch to limit another, such as the power of Congress in the US to alter the composition and jurisdiction of the federal courts.

Just as powers are divided between the judiciary, the executive, and the legislature, so the vital missing separation essential for any government to succeed is the 'Resulture'. The Resulture would be the part of the system of government responsible for feedback. Feedback of results and outcomes is not a matter of politics but a matter of fact. This cannot be a job for the executive − it would be rating itself, and the process would thus have no credibility. The task needs to be independent of the executive, and would be the responsibility of the second chamber − commonly termed the Senate or in the UK the House of Lords. Thus the second chamber would be the custodian of the public's experience of government and of all public sector bodies, here to represent the citizen. The second chamber would thus gain a clear, unambiguous, and vital role. And it would need to get organised in order to exercise the necessary powers to ensure accurate, independent feedback exists.

The various 'independent scorekeepers' of statistics and outcomes from crime, to GDP, to debt, to unemployment, to tax yields, health, and immigration would form part of the Resulture, responsible to the second chamber, including:

1   NICE, the National Institute for Health and Care Excellence, which produces vital feedback on medical treatments and procedures, and is something of a feedback role model.

2   ONS, the Office for National Statistics, whose independence and remit has developed successfully over the last ten years.

3   NAO, the National Audit Office, that would have to develop some of its ineffective legacy methods to bring it up to standard, or be restricted to financial auditing only. I had a number of interactions with them and the previous Comptroller and Auditor General to think about and develop more effective methods of improving government performance from their zero harm gladiatorial exhibitions at the Public Accounts Committee (including some of the proposals here, like legislation league tables). Nothing happened.

4   Existing feedback agents, i.e. universities, think tanks, and independent institutes that get commissions from public funders and usually produce good to excellent information but with somewhat random targets, would be cohered through the Resulture.

None of these bodies would ever be staffed by the Civil Service, and would have no connection with them. Each would hire and develop its own fit-for-purpose staff. Independence of feedback is not possible with common staffing.

It is noteworthy that the Freedom of Information Act has become an excellent feedback mechanism, but we should not have to prise results from an unwilling government. It should produce them, and want to. In a design for success, FoI should be unnecessary, but clearly must remain and be strengthened if needed, for now.

Accounting standards, a key determinant of accurate information would be here too, including therefore Golden Rules on debt. The second chamber would become a hive of activity and information, fulfilling this role for the people and for society, the 'ticker tapes' of results pouring through. Once you are monitoring and using feedback you really are performing a vital role in 'running the country'. Indeed, the role is as important as the executive and the legislature.

The Resulture would also have the role of recommending abandonment of a body, programme, regulation, law, etc. The executive's role would be to decide. The House of Lords would become energised with a sense of achievement rather than a sense of importance.

As part of our new system, we need to decide from where the members of the House of Lords or second chamber would come, and this is covered in Chapter 11, 'Fit People'.

Of course, similar although far smaller scale arrangements would operate for real local government with comprehensive coverage and independence.

Once feedback mechanisms are embedded and functioning, much will change in the public sector simply because results, and particularly trends in results, will be visible. No longer would a government or initiating minister be able to ignore non-performance and failure, or hide behind partial statistics or spun anecdotes, or defend the indefensible. The ambience in Parliament should shift away from adversarial 'proving' right and wrong by whatever means, and towards some collective inquiry and endeavour. With results doing the talking, in the early days much needless activity and procedure would be dropped, and zero-outcome legislation, regulation, statutory duty, central instruction, programme, initiative, and policy abandoned. Savings would be substantial. Government would become less complicated. Public sector bodies would start to look outward to the results as judged by others, and become less internal and less ends to themselves.

Politicians will hate this discipline of feedback based not on political jousting but on real outcomes – until they see its value. The news media will too. Corporates will lose power and become more competitive. We will get better government. The irony is that feedback is a strong discipline on governments and parliaments, but it also buys some immunity for politicians from vested interests, powerful lobbies, and the news media. And it buys real power in that more is actually changed for good rather than central hyperactivity. For the public as citizens and consumers it buys results for us and for society as a whole and a lot less cost.

'Government by Results'. Sounds rather overdue.

9

Policy by Design

Next up for the Treaty are policymaking and the means to get many more good decisions produced by the system of government. Stringent feedback is of itself a powerful control on the quality and quantity of policymaking and decision taking. Knowing that poor results will come back to bite you would discipline governments, ministers, civil servants, lobbies, newspapers, advisers, academics, and think tanks. This is vital – but after the event. Policy discipline would be there to get more right in the first place. The more we get right going into the pipe, the less needs to be corrected at the other end. 'Policy by design' is intended to get as much right as possible going in.So how do we get good decisions?

The Monetary Policy Committee's model for decision-making is instructive: It was set up to depoliticise the task of setting interest rates. Five members are from the top posts of the Bank of England, and four are appointed by the Chancellor of the Exchequer. It meets monthly. Its members discuss and vote. The minutes and votes of each member are published – disagreements, opposing views, changes of mind. It is transparent. Expert commentators join this dialogue through the press, and in explanations to parliamentary committees. Each member's personal constituency joins too back at the university, bank, partnership, or other place of work. Transparency brings a lot of knowledge, experience, and brain power to bear. Challenge and difference are encouraged. (How grown up.) At the end of the meeting members vote, and the majority set the rate for that month. Round we go again, in wide deliberation and learning, to the next month's decision. Here we have a pre-determined decision-making process, not politics.

In the commercial world there is the discipline of due diligence. When one company wants to buy another, it conducts checks on the subject's health and future. There are the obvious inside examinations of the accounts and other management information to check their veracity and to see what careful analysis might throw up; and the less obvious but no less important assessment of its market and customers and competitors. Are its products in demand, ahead of the competition, exceeding consumers' expectations, going to be sidelined by new technology, and so on. Good due diligence is systematic with set checks that have been found to get a decision as right as possible, and a professional institute requirement.

Norman Strauss, one of the most original organisational thinkers, proposes this about policymaking:

> Ethos – defined as the characteristic spirit and genius of a society, culture, policy, system or idea – or an amalgam of them – embraces the summation of what we stand for today; it is also tomorrow's vision of what we want to stand for then. Stafford Beer called these two distinct positions 'the inside and now' and the 'outside and then'. Thinking about them requires successive utilization of divergent and convergent multi-disciplinary thinking, together with abstraction, transduction, and learning skills, if change is to be managed successfully.

> So one can redefine governance as continuing ethos management from now to then; as eras are created and fashions and zeitgeists pass. Or, at its simplest, if what was promised in an election is to be delivered in office … The need is both to take in more inputs and to understand how to manage the contradictions, paradigms, systems of thought and analysis, complexities, alternative values, potential policy shifts and conflicts of opinion which their variety provides. Ultimately, I expect we will need to define another governmental separation of state power – beyond the executive, legislative and judiciary to become skilled in the ongoing variety all of this. I know of no country or institution which does this well, so there is a pressing need to create one *ab initio*. We could call this fourth separation of power the 'Plurality' – *E pluribus unum*; out of many (ideas) to one.

Without such continuous, because institutionalized, organic thinking across all aspects of society, government (and/or regulation) will not be matched to the complexities of preventing the emergence of critical national and global problems that require urgent solving – if not first prevented in a 'just in time' or 'well before they become urgent' way.

The number of upset countries, distraught citizens, failing companies and failed leaders thrown up by the global financial crisis proves just how much such basic reappraisal of our bandwidth in governing, regulatory, organisational, structural, constitutional, institutional and leadership systems is still required.

Opposing opinions must be reconciled more effectively by institutions learning to practice higher order unifying concepts, such as ethos, so that all of the best available knowledge is properly evaluated and absorbed by the governing system ... According to Stafford Beer, it is ethos alone that can unite disparate policy functions, purposes, meanings, and motivations clearly, to summate what an organization, nation, or political party stands for. In my view, good government is Ethos Management, and I suspect he would agree.

Perhaps the modern democratic state needs to be redesigned around these precepts if vision, policies, values and multiple motivations are to be captured in a distinctive ethos, enacted by a Viable System and coupled with the effective governance that leads to optimized citizen engagement and satisfaction for the majority, without alienating too many minorities. Then we could hope that we have at last created an organisation and operating culture, that is best suited to carry out the ruling values, derived from the distinctive ethos, which summates the critical policies that citizens voted for.

Strauss, the Monetary Policy Committee, due diligence, and the Treaty are all pointing in the same direction: a pre-determined process, tests, and governance to make policies work.

Ten Tests to Make Policies Work

There are ten tests to check if a policy has been developed properly: what is the point of this policy, is it consumer/citizen based, is it based on insider information and experience, has the public been engaged in its development, have all the stakeholders' interests been considered, are other countries' experiences the answer, have all factors and influences been taken account of through systems thinking, have the mechanisms for effective delivery been designed, and what will it cost. By exception the final experimental test would come into play.

1. Point test

What is the point of this decision, policy, law, regulation, programme? What is it intended to achieve, what results are desired (against which, of course, the feedback will be set)? Is the point of one aspect of welfare policy to support the broken poor or to enable the aspirant poor, to quote the *Big Issue*? What is the point of aid? Relief of starvation, building water supplies, giving cash to governments to do something useful with? If the latter, what would a ruthless examination find? That aid feeds corruption? Many decisions and policies would fail and fall by the wayside of wasted government at the point of the point test.

2. Consumer/citizen test

Has the policy been developed from the consumers/citizens it is supposed to be aimed at? It must start from the cohort that is the object of the policy, understand their motivations, incentives, the conditions around them. Why do they behave as they do? What changes would improve their lot or change their behaviour in ways that would realise the policy objectives? Segmentation starts here.

Welfare policies should start in the families of those they are aimed at, with the policymakers working in those families, often using the techniques of consumer strategy.[17] Fishing policy starts on

---

17   The switch for MPs from travelling in the remote first-class carriages to standard class on trains diminishes paperwork time but connects with many more real lives.

a fishing boat. Policymakers would spend much of their time out in the field and far from a desk. Successful public services start with a real knowledge of the people and their needs that they are serving.

Some consumer analysis of domestic violence illustrates what can be found. We despair at the stories of a wife and mother enduring abuse for years, but never leaving her partner, and, in effect, going back for more. Why stay? The routes out provided by the state to the woman are first to criminalise the father of their children, second to put the father of their children in prison, and finally to take the children into care. What an offer! The alternative of a regular punching is, sadly, the rational choice. A consumer-based policy would look very different to the state's current offer.

Adoption policies should follow successful and failed adoptions through the several bodies and procedures to determine what happens and how in practice, not on paper. Adoption is one of a considerable range of social problems – underachievement, tax-negative families, poverty, low aspirations, homelessness, teenage pregnancy, long-term unemployment, social exclusion, career criminals, disability, family breakdown – that can only be understood by being as close as possible to the lives of those with these problems. Living their lives, even for a short period, is the best means to grasp their motivations, cultures, and barriers, and to experience the public services they receive and their positive and negative or neutral impact. Front-line staff often are the closest you will get to these lives. Sitting at a desk, surrounded by broad statistics, or seeking the best argument to support your political label or moral preference rarely solves social problems. If you really want to know the results for recipients of housing and other benefits, go and sit with people receiving them.

3. Insider test

This is the equivalent to the consumer/citizen test but for organisations. We will never get to grips with something as complex as rogue banking unless we have a deep grasp of life inside these organisations, why people behave as they do. Some have argued that in European financial services, the only people who really know what is going on, and thus what needs monitoring or preventing, are the financial institutions themselves. Knowing how these industries work on the inside is essential to being able to regulate them successfully. This means deep expertise from inside from current employees willing to talk straight, ex-staff, specialist deep journalists from the likes of the *Investors Chronicle*, and/or analysts experienced at getting inside the minds of people inside their organisations.

4. Engagement test

This is a useful point to introduce DAD and EDD. Decide–Announce–Defend is the traditional government decision-making process in many countries. It is the top-down, expert model with which we are accustomed. From big decisions like the use of nuclear power and the route of a new train line, to local decisions like high-street remodelling, a planning decision, hospital closure and a flood-defence scheme, the arm of government with the powers looks at options in private, may do some public one-way consultation, reaches a decision, announces it publicly and holds its breath. Often, the stakeholders of various shapes react, and the management of the government body goes into defence mode. Sometimes, the decision is forced through, sometimes dropped and sometimes the battle wages for years. Defending the decision is a high-cost and time-consuming process. But it is how decisions have been taken in an authoritarian world and it appeals of course to those taking them with high control needs in the case of ministers, or oversized intellectual egos in the case of civil servants.

Engage–Deliberate–Decide is how the Canadian government went about its health-service changes.[18] The first step is to engage with the public on the problem without bias. Is there a problem? If so, what is its nature? Next start the education so people are as well informed as reasonable before making up their minds. Surprise surprise, people often change their minds once they are properly informed. The most vociferous critics can become local champions. Then, ask the people interested to produce options. And finally, ask them to decide on one. By this means, the level of agreement reached is usually higher and consensus is achieved. Implementation is much easier and quicker with a committed

---

18   See www.treatyforgovernment.org for details.

public, the decisions are often better because no distant centralised government body can possibly hold all the information relevant to a decision, and whilst engagement costs money the end-to-end cost and time is less. It takes time, and it is a learning journey, but the more contentious the decision to be taken, the more engagement is worthwhile.

EDD takes a fundamental shift in attitude by public sector management. The public is not stupid. The public comes in many forms. Different interests and needs underpin the stated position. But, once properly engaged and informed, the public will identify responsible, workable solutions, which reflect the whole system they experience in a way the remote policymaker or manager has neither the time nor the knowledge to replicate.

Constituency surgeries are a very odd lens on the world, representing little. Opinion polls are very limited engagement and provide little understanding of real lives. Statistical averages analysed in think tanks are not engagement, and never produce workable solutions.[19] Talking, listening, enquiring, experiencing the lives of others by being with them; service sampling through working on the front line of services; consumer analysis and strategy; and the tools of facilitation – all these will shed light and insight and produce workable solutions.

Public engagement would be appropriate in some and perhaps many cases. Proper engagement would necessarily meet the stakeholder, insider, and consumer tests, and is thus fully aligned in purpose. For big complex changes, like reform of the health service, substantial engagement along the Canadian health reform model would be needed. (The coalition government would not be having the trouble it is if it had engaged on its NHS reforms.)

Lastly, engagement has a value in itself in a modern society: it extends democracy to specific decisions (and some research concludes that there is a causal correlation between the extent of democracy and happiness); and is an antidote to preferential lobbying. Closed-door deals of convenience to the business and

---

19   As an important aside, think tanks need to expand their repertoire to cover much more than the limited set of issues in which they have expertise, including for example technical ones like tunnelling for power lines, the speed of road building, and construction pollution.

to the politicians or civil servants cannot be done. EDD has a lot going for it. Perhaps most importantly, contrary to the dismissive opinions of experts in government, the public is very capable of both grasping the issues and of bringing much-needed knowledge and expertise to the table themselves. Properly engaged, I would trust an EDD decision much more than a DAD decision. Let's remember our starting point for the Treaty: government fails.

5. Stakeholder test

This would be applied to determine how those impacted by the policy fare, and whether their interests have been represented in the process. It would consequently exclude any policies that created de facto franchises to print money be they oligopolies of pension fund providers, or a closed Civil Service. Preferential lobbying would also be outed.

To explore how this test might apply in practice, let's look at a really contentious issue – immigration – from a stakeholder standpoint. My purpose in selecting such a difficult problem is to see where a cool and unprejudiced assessment might lead us.

Many countries in Europe have experienced the rise of right-wing parties with strong anti-immigration agendas. Liberal minds tend to worry furiously about them, urge better explanations of the value and need for labour migration, indulge in statistical warfare, or otherwise blast them for being racist and of course plain wrong.

Now where do the displaced 'indigenous people' go for representation? Who is looking out for their interests? The established political classes have written them off. This is how the left-wing blog Liberal Conspiracy put it in making sense of the statistics and rebutting the hysteria of the *Daily Mail* and others: 'In 1991, just after the end of the Thatcher decade, two out of every seven jobs in the UK labour market were in the non-service sector. By the time New Labour took office in 1997, this had fallen to one in four and by 2008 it was only one in five. That's what's really hurt the white working class in Britain, their failure/inability to adapt to the changing labour market, and the rise in the number of foreign-born workers during this period is, for the most part, a by-product of that failure, not its cause.' So that's OK then – it's their own fault.

But does 'their failure/inability' mean that this group of stakeholders does not count? Or cannot see that access to 'their jobs' is cut off? Or that housing allocation criteria based on 'need' in practice privileges immigrants over them? And do they still have the vote? Or are they to be put in a siding somewhere and forgotten? And is Liberal Conspiracy a wing of the Tea Party?

Perhaps this Liberal Conspiracy paragraph does more to explain the rise of the BNP than anything. Since the minimum wage, has there been a single policy specifically for the white working class? In ignoring the stakeholders called 'displaced existing citizens', governments have driven people into the arms of the right-wing parties. Where else could they go? Their traditional representatives in left-wing, working-class, social democratic, and liberal parties had all deserted them. In ignoring inconvenient variables, the government gave rebirth to the BNP. The BNP became the equivalent to the Migrants' Rights Network – a fine charity with government funding that exists to further the rights of migrants. Where is the equivalent body furthering the rights of existing citizens who become internal refugees or who are otherwise affected by migration? In practice, this exclusive role is taken by the BNP. In the accepted order of things, it is perfectly all right for the MRN to work solely and preferentially for one group, but not for the BNP to do the same for the other. Immigration is often a zero-sum game: one person's gain is another's loss.

The EU has free movement of people as a cornerstone of its free-market vision. At the macroeconomic level, this should maximise growth and produce the integrated, borderless, thriving, diverse, Europe of our dreams. At once we would be Italian, German and French. Brilliant. But post-neoclassical endogenous growth theory takes no account of feelings – feelings of ownership, of nationality, of identity, of responsibility – nor of the time to adjust to something new. In pursuing free movement of labour throughout the EU – an economic policy – the economists, of course, missed out people.

Humans take time to change and adapt to new things. We react to change, usually adversely at first, even when it is beneficial. From family upheaval to mass redundancy, people follow the well-established path of shock, denial, depression, anger, resignation, acceptance, and understanding. Mass immigration is a major change and takes time to adapt to. There is a rate of absorption that is exceeded by the *c*.500,000 immigrants (plus illegals) to the UK in 2007, which cannot be gainsaid by the left blogs explaining that net migration is well down. The policy has been treated as a switch thrower, when it is a slow migration, in more than one sense.

Possibly the most xenophobic European country is France, and here the tensions produced by the mass arrival of foreign cultures and values appear at their strongest. All countries regard themselves as the best in the world, but France has always had perhaps the strongest identity with what being French means. Impose on that Rumanian, Albanian, Iranian, Ugandan, and Indonesian values and see what you get. Suddenly, the whole foundations of being French, following an extraordinary period of post-war prosperity, social harmony, and peace, are shaken. Does the existing population want them shaken? Would you? Has anyone asked them? Free movement of labour is positive at the margin, but immigration brings not just people but cultures too. Sometimes the mass arrival of foreign cultures can feel threatening. And the Islamic colonialists mean it to.

Collections of lifelong neo-Nazis may be waiting out there for their moment, but mostly people's attitudes are the product of their experienced environment. The EU economists have destabilised national cultural identities, and people feel uneasy. Should the new French identity jettison that which has been held fine for so long? How is the new identity to be decided upon? By referendum? Or will it emerge serendipitously from the melting pot, undesigned and unchosen? Will the new one be better, preferable, or worse? And will communities hold together in the way they have for years? The French cannot have felt this disturbed since the Second World War (an objective and not inflammatory comment). People do not take kindly to invasions: and mass immigration can feel like a legalised invasion.

Identity is another subject of complexity. I only observe here that humans seem to need to identify with something including place, that place includes a country, and that identity then lends stability to that place. If it is exploited or ignited then xenophobia can result, and indeed war. But pan-national organisations exist to limit the excesses of national identity, from NATO to the Latin American Integration Association. Mass or rushed immigration is destabilising.

The fault in generating extreme nationalist parties lies with the economists and their exclusion of many stakeholders, and with the liberal minds who believe immigration should flourish without reference to its effect on those who have lived in a place for generations. In their world, it is the current population's job to put up with as much disruption as occurs without complaint, and the penalty for objection is to be branded racist, bigot, politically incorrect in the use of language, or whatever. The white refugees from Tower Hamlets have no rights. The EU would do well to put its 'free movement of labour' objective on hold until this has been worked out and factored in. I worry.

One final point. Whether you or I agree or disagree with these arguments does not really matter. The fact is that right-wing parties with significant support exist, and substantial opposition to immigration exists. Telling these supporters they are wrong, or bad people, will not change that. It may well be that you and I are more sophisticated in our adaptation to change, or just 'better' people. Or we would like to think so. Or the antis have been more affected than you or I, and have lost more. Or are more concerned about the loss of national culture. None of this matters in the sense that sufficient people exist who, rightly or wrongly, oppose the existing scale of immigration for this to be a problem for us all. They vote, they are stakeholders, and they matter just as much in a democracy as you or I. This rate of change will always produce a major reaction, which cannot be wished away.

A balanced, progressive and sustainable policy for immigration would take into account *all* the stakeholders and *all* the costs and outcomes. Tomorrow's immigration is not about whether, but about how much, when, at what rate, and the adaptation deal between immigrant and resident. Immigration is one of those policies that cannot be imposed successfully on various unwilling sections of the public for the very obvious reason that this big a change cannot proceed without collective commitment. Like it or not, it's called real democracy. Variables will not be kept out of the equation for ever simply because they are inconvenient.

6. 'Other countries' test

Globalisation has its problems and its benefits. World-class manufacturing has brought us all untold riches of consumer durables. Modern government has been running long enough for similar-country-based practice to be assessed, learnt form, and used at least to inform home policies. The world has been using a variety of models in each sector and sub-sector – from health to financial regulation to adoption – for long enough for usually one to be worth using. Increasingly, successful policies from other countries would simply be lifted and used (subject of course to the other tests here, in case unseen factors not present in the UK are key to its success, or factors present in the UK would make it unfit for purpose). If someone else has tried it and it works, that represents a prima facie policy from which any diversion can only be justified by excellent analysis. Why would you not adopt from the US the enforcement method for planning breaches when the UK method is so ineffective? Other countries' experience is the quickest and cheapest way to sort many of the easy improvements.

International comparisons have driven huge improvements in the products and services we get from companies. They should be the norm for policymaking for governments with the humility to know they do not have all the answers, with the vision to understand that experimentation and diversity lie at the heart of success, and with the curiosity to find out what others do. Being an island nation has benefits, but it limits the citizen-learning that occurs more easily in continental Europe as different practices in every field are sampled whenever crossing a border. We in the UK have to try harder for this valuable source of experience.

I wonder what other countries' experience would tell us about schools? This thought was triggered by the surprise of an Italian as to the extent of private schooling here. In his country private schools are only for the 'mad and the bad'. Interesting. How come they seem to have consistently good schools? What if theirs were looked at not simply from a structural perspective – selective versus comprehensive, local authority versus free schools, etc. – but from all angles. How well aligned are they? Is the local population hard-wired to the school? Do they have real local government and therefore real accountability? Teacher training? Pay? Turnover? Curriculum? Results?

7. Systems thinking test

No policy/decision works in isolation from its context. Exogenous factors always impact the point. This is the test to determine if the policy takes account of the inconvenient variables, if it is joined up, if it is holistic, if it has considered the knock-on effects and the unintended consequences. This is what is called systems thinking, and it is a powerful discipline.

Let's have a look at a contentious policy area (or perhaps I mean take a look at it contentiously) – the reduction, by government, of activity that is harmful to the health of those who engage in it freely.

Governments can be quite sophisticated in their thinking. They can also suffer from tunnel vision, or if not a tunnel then a deep gorge. The tendency is to take a single issue – smoking, say – analyse how to reduce it, and focus hard on the solution. In many circumstances focus is what is needed to deliver change, but only when the analysis has looked at the wider landscape. What is over the other side of the ridge? If we do implement this policy, what are the knock-on effects?

Smoking is undoubtedly bad for us. Many have thankfully and successfully given it up for good. The public health campaign has been a remarkable success. But, taking a system-wide view, what would we find? Are some of us doomed to smoke, or be fat?

Whilst many have given up smoking, in the last forty years the 'pandemic' of obesity has gone the other way. Obesity has similar morbidity, health costs, and productivity costs to smoking. Of course, effective government action for obesity itself (as happens in Denmark, where legislation restricts the use of trans-fatty acids in food production) looks overdue. The addictive qualities of fats and sugars could be taxed to the same extent as are those of tobacco. Is it an outrage to wonder if an apple should become cheaper than its calorific equivalent provided by addictive foodstuffs? Pricing has some affect. There is no point in allowing crap to be sold so cheaply.

Welfare benefits are used to buy addictive foods for babies and children, starting them early on the escalator to obesity. This is one of the strangest uses of public expenditure. Government is effectively funding obesity. What would be the advantages and disadvantages of conditional benefits in the form of vouchers, which could only be redeemable for healthy food? It feels uncomfortable, but presumably less than the discomfort the child will suffer if obese in the future.

Governments are often impotent in matters of human behaviour. Education, education, and education are the best they can do. As with recreational drugs and young people, the most effective strategy is to ensure the effects of each drug are well known. Prohibition does not work. Nor does the war on drugs. A consistent policy for harmful substances would be to add addictive foods to the list of Class A drugs, making their possession a criminal offence. But it also raises the question as to whether and how policy should seek to control behaviour. (It will not succeed, of course, but often this is not the objective.)

In the way public policy debate is framed in some countries, human vices are not allowed. The widespread pretence, even in our own heads, is that we should live by some higher calling or superior morality, which excludes vice. Thus, anything that alters our consciousness, such as alcohol or cannabis or magic mushrooms, or potentially damages our health, is wrong. But, in an otherwise hard and unfulfilling life, in a low-paid job and poor housing, with a lost or stressed family life, the only pleasures for some are alcohol, cigarettes and recreational drugs. The consumer is quite aware that these are 'bad' for him or her, but consumes them nevertheless. Is that the 'wrong' choice? Who am I to make that judgement? Is it a judgement for government?

An alternative basis for policy decisions is to accept that humans do have vices, and to enjoy. For all of history humans have sought out so-called 'mind-altering' substances precisely to alter their minds. Is this a 'vice' or a fact of the human condition? Educate, persuade, offer, prevent the wild excesses of capitalism, and do not dole out money for negative consequences. Do what you can. Otherwise accept a 'flawed' society.

A more general word on policies aimed at stopping people dying, as embodied in the state's life-prolongment programmes: they should recognise one of the more obvious facts – everyone dies. Some die before they want to. Whilst understandable, the war on dying may be as useful as the wars on drugs or terror (and as destructive and costly – it's killing the NHS). The purpose of living is not 'not to die', as some policymakers seem to believe. We are all trying to navigate life by finding a balance between what is good for us and what we enjoy, between prevention and cure, between duty and freedom, between ecstasy and boredom, always aware that good and bad luck may be around the corner, and conscious that we will never know whether our choices have given us a better or worse life than our neighbours. The narrow pursuit of 'not dying' represents a narrow understanding of life.

In terms of systems thinking, five factors are in play. 'Groupthink', on a national scale, is the first – smoking is bad for you and we all got caught up in believing it was right to reduce it and by whatever means. The second is the fatal attraction of simple policies (I wonder what is the psychology of this?). The third is the psychology of the moral high ground. Some people are strongly motivated by moral superiority over others. Saving lives, especially saving people from themselves, as with stopping them smoking, represents high moral worth. The fourth is the pressure felt by government to do something, even though it may be ineffectual. Fifth, governments are free to take decisions in any way they want. Political pressure is the only restraint. Decisions can be made on no information, flawed analysis, prejudice, or an anecdote on the 10.47 from Pitlochry.

So if the lone smoking policy had been checked for its systems thinking, the voters would have found a number of ignored variables: substitute pleasures like eating and their cost to government and society, the underlying causes of smoking and obesity and thus enduring prevention, consistent taxation, use of benefits, quality of living, vice as perhaps an ineradicable component of the human condition, and the value of waging a war on dying. Quite a lot. And now we are experiencing an obesity epidemic.

For successful government, disciplines must exist to ensure the decision process is based on evidence, that the evidence represents real lives, the analysis is comprehensive, and the objective clear. Is the objective to save lives through stopping smoking? Or to save lives in total? If person X lives longer by stopping smoking but dies prematurely through obesity, is that a result or a waste of persuasion money? The scope here to spend and fail is considerable.

8. Delivery test

Will the policy deliver the proposed results? If so, how, and what evidence is there to show this? Much legislation would find its way straight into the bin at this point. Are public places cleaner when dropping litter is made illegal? Or are there other ways? This test is about the 'how' of turning the policy into practice. Is the delivery method a) proven to have worked elsewhere, or b) worked out thoroughly (in terms of how to get from 'now' to 'then', to use Strauss's phrase), and c) aligned?

9. Cost test

What would the policy cost to execute? A reasonable estimate needs to be made of direct costs to all arms of public sector, and to individuals and companies – for example whole costs of money laundering for children, hospital closure, a specific tax change. The benefits would be estimated here. In some cases the need for the policy will be so obvious as to remove any need to justify by measuring its benefit, but in other cases a proper cost–benefit analysis would be required to pass this test. Fundability would be tested here too – is there sufficient government funding for it, or would some other public expenditure have to be reduced to make way for this higher priority? Vetting here would extend to the 'one in, one out' policy for legislation and regulation, leading to old laws or programmes being abandoned.

10. Experimental test

Some policies and decisions will not have the comfort of past practice, feedback, other countries' experience, and engagement. Some policies are by necessity experimental. This is entirely appropriate, and governments should be free to say so. Some issues – the so-called wicked problems – remain tough to solve: social mobility, secondary schooling, social disadvantage, and so on. As in other disciplines, an experimental policy would be monitored to see if it is working or not. Governments are expected to solve some very difficult problems. Science faces difficult problems too. Science conducts experiments where the answer is not known.

Much of the task of government fits into the 'not known' box. Why on earth does government not routinely experiment?

It is entirely legitimate for government to analyse and produce a theory for a solution, just as science does. However, science does not accept the theory as the answer until it is experimentally confirmed. Governments routinely omit this rather crucial step. Randomised trials[20], the norm in scientific experiments, and other approaches used by NICE would be applied.

By default, experimentation does occur because different countries often use and implement different policies. This diversity in thinking and solution is potentially a very rich source of proof. One of the benefits of devolution (as to Scotland and Wales, and to the states and Länder in the US and Germany) is that different solutions can be and are tried. The Whitehall 'answer' is no longer the only option.

Experimentation is key. Conducting makeshift evaluations to prove a policy works is not. Nor is defending what you've done is not either. The Human Rights Act is essential, but in practice it has proved to be wrong in a few places, not least because of the way our courts interpret these things. So change the wrong bits. What are the actual chances of getting a law like this, plus the court interpretation, 100% right? Zero. So why does government behave as if it has? Learning is essential.

Who Owns Policy?

Those then are our ten tests. How do we make sure they are applied properly?

Under the Treaty no one would have a monopoly of policy – not politicians, civil servants, or PSOs. Policymaking would not be 'owned' by the government or the Civil Service. The custodian is actually the ten tests. Policy and decision-making would be an open process – both to prevent cake capture and to produce better decisions that are better understood. Yes to private discussions of all sorts of options, but the formulation of the finished policy requires openness. This requires adult behaviour with everything on the

---

20   Randomised trials of government policies are being promoted by some in the current UK Cabinet Office

table and thus some easy headlines of mock outrage. But the media will grow up, as they and we have done over the marital affairs of politicians. The Treaty is intended to generate the mindset of 'we all own the decision' – the objective is to get the right decision. In this system, more democracy improves the quality of decisions.

Fifth Separation of Powers

How do we make this happen? Applying the disciplines to get it right would be the fifth separation of powers after the executive, judiciary, legislature, and Resulture. Policy vetting would follow the existing course of legislation through the Commons and the Lords but would be provided by separate and powerful committees with the ability and remit to refer back to the executive those policies failing the ten tests. Select committees would support the vetting committees through their specialist knowledge. Providing it acts with the emerging independence of mind seen in its recently freed select committees, the Commons can perform this vital role effectively.[21] If it cannot, then this power would have to rest solely with the second chamber. The 'ten tests' policy and decision process would be supported and reinforced by the administrative 'Northcote–Trevelyan' Civil Service. This separate arm is described in Chapter 11. The tests are of course a stimulant to learning. This will gradually get everyone used to this very new way of thinking, so that think tanks start presenting their proposals already tested. Expertise on policymaking will be built in Parliament, becoming a specialised career for some MPs and lords. In time we may see certified policymakers.

Operating all this vetting represents a lot of work, given the policies and decisions streaming out of government. Care would have to be taken at the start not to suffer the experience of Japan when it introduced some vetting in a similar vein. Selection and

---

21   Until 2010 the prime minister and coterie controlled select committees through their hold over appointments of their chairmen and members. They were part of the system of executive patronage. After the 2010 election, all MPs voted via secret ballot for the chairs and members. These committees have become rather more useful, although have much ground to make up to fulfill their proper role in the system of government, and have nowhere near the bite of their US counterparts.

the right to retrospective vetting might be needed for a time. But, first, the overloaded stream would reduce perhaps not to a trickle but at least to an ordered flow by the discipline of policy vetting, reducing the quantity of wasted or misplaced policies and its cost. Initiativitis would be obliterated. Huge savings are available with this upfront work. Second, policies are only worth their effect on the ground, they have no value in themselves. Putting time and effort into getting policies right is essential. What is the alternative? Continue to fire ill-conceived policies with all the enormous costs and failings described earlier at the citizens, consumers, businesses, etc.? What joy. Or invest time and thought to get it right first time? A no-brainer.

These ten tests would immunise government against media-frenzy policies, and against the psychopathologies of politicians in the form of the need to be right, the need for personal power, and the need to control. The tests also stop prejudice dead in its tracks, along with preferential lobbying, overload, the 'something (anything) must be done' approach, 'reform' for the sake of it, and legislative OCD. Clarity in policy design relegates moral questions too.

To crudely adapt a workplace homily: 'Professional policymaking prevents piss-poor performance.'

10

Delivery with Zero Defects

Now we come to things actually happening – the delivery of government services.

Thus far under the Treaty, we have built feedback so the system knows what is actually occurring, and policy vetting so that the intention of the changes is clear and the chances of them working well are very much higher. These two building blocks of our design will, of themselves, improve delivery. In an aligned system, the parts in between – the operations – need mechanisms to get the best out of them.

We want public sector operations to work, and at a reasonable cost. So, for example, we want good regulation that prevents death and injury at work, or food poisoning, or being ripped off by the banks. But we don't want to be unnecessarily constrained in our lives by petty rules, our time thoughtlessly consumed by useless procedures, we don't want blanket bans applying to everyone when the problem is caused by the few, and we don't want to be on the end of bureaucrats on power trips. PSOs must not be ends to themselves. We want all schools to provide a reasonable education in its broadest sense, a responsive health service that deals with people as adults, trains that consistently run on time, roads built quickly. Etc. So how can our System of government provide them without defects? (One caveat first: the Treaty makes no mention of whether something should be privately provided or publicly. Both can and do work, and the policymaking section takes care of this choice. But even when a service is contracted to the private sector there always remains a major task for government to manage the contract or regulate the industry.)

Do we want zero defects in air travel, for example? Fairly obviously the answer is yes. A plane crash is a terrible experience for all. Let's have a look first at the safest airline in the world.

Why does it deliver to such a high standard? The lessons from this industry have much to teach governments. The Australian airline Qantas is an example of how to produce effective outcomes. As an outcome, not crashing is as important as they come, and Qantas has not had a fatal crash since 1951. Could this be down to a policy prescribing lots of forms and procedures, or is something else afoot?

The civil aviation industry grew out of military air forces where strict hierarchy of command was paramount: the captain was considered God. By contrast, the Australian culture is no respecter of rank or position. Flat relationships pertain. Thus on the Qantas flight deck if the captain was coming in too quickly, or slowly, or at the wrong altitude, the co-pilot or engineer would be quick to say so. On the stiff-upper-lip deck, no such instant feedback would be provided. Thus Qantas crew benefit from the collective wisdom of the crew and immediate course corrections. Two heads are better than one. Feedback cultivates an atmosphere where learning is the norm and no shame or loss of status attaches to it (in contrast to so many other organisational and educational environments). The learning continues in the canteen after the flight. As well as being an expert on military psychology, Norman Dixon also researched the psychological causes of aviation accidents, and concluded that this feedback culture lay at the root of Qantas' safety record. The cultural norm of speaking out, or disobedience, causes an enviable safety record, over and above that achieved by statistical quality control in manufacture and engine monitoring, zero-defects maintenance with lots of results-driven procedures, and a strong sense of personal accountability.

The various health and safety regulators show no sign of understanding the existence or the relevance of this experience. Locked within procedure as the tool of choice, the notion that institutional disobedience is crucial to saving lives is beyond them. Furthermore in the aviation industry, the system of investigating crashes shows a culture of determination to get to the root cause. One never hears of an attempt to cover it up or to deflect blame. Transparency in the answer makes the learning unencumbered, and therefore the prevention of further mistakes is the norm. There are no axes to grind with air crashes. Everyone's interests are aligned – the staff, the management, the passengers, the shareholders, government, the manufacturers, and society all want zero defects. Further failure is in no one's interest.

Like flying, working in the construction industry will always carry risks, although much can be done to limit them – adequate scaffolding, hard hats, knowing where old gas and electricity mains run, checking for asbestos in buildings to be demolished, maintaining temporary lifts and hoists properly, and so on. 'Knowing' what to do is essential. 'Doing' it is where lives are lost or saved, and is where the proceduralists look to forms and where the culturalists look to openness, honest feedback, and the absence of hierarchical constraints. Thus far, no legislation requires cultural and psychological assessments. It should. It would save an awful lot of worthless paper. The origin of the policy (in this case producing a set of regulations) to deliver safety lies in a flawed set of assumptions about how the right things get done in organisations. By contrast the approach proposed here would be both more demanding in terms of results and better to work in.

The term 'zero defects' was born in the Japanese manufacturing industry. Previously components would be machined and usually some returned for costly and delaying rework in order to correct inaccurate machining. In the engineering factories I worked in the late 1970s this inaccuracy was considered the norm. Anyone suggesting zero defects would have been laughed at as totally unrealistic. Pioneers in modern manufacturing took a different view. If you start with an expectation of 20% rework culturally that is what you will get, and 'only 80% correct' becomes the standard (rather like our trains where ten minutes late does not count as late). But if you start with an ambition of zero rework and use statistical quality control and other techniques to establish the cause of faults and to eliminate them, then zero defects is achievable. All the time. Ambition and techniques, all within a demanding framework of imperatives that rewards high standards through success in a market, are crucial.

Feedback and policy testing would have a significant and sometimes dramatic effect on the quality of delivery. The question then is what else would contribute to improving operational performance – a form of proxy for market imperatives – to create a zero-defects culture in PSOs.

Imperatives

'Imperatives' are all of those aspects of organisation that make or force the body to perform. All organisations rise and fall, float and drift, come and go. They are incapable of permanent good performance without external stimulus. Perhaps the most obvious recent example is with mobile devices where the top brand has changed four times in fifteen years: Motorola, Nokia, BlackBerry, Apple. This has been driven by the exploitation of emerging technologies. Just as one company established pre-eminence, rested on its laurels, and took its eye off of the customer, so another took the chance to innovate and change the game being played for consumers.

The difficulty for most public sector bodies is that such technological advance and the competitive pressures to exploit it do not exist. Further, these bodies become institutions – in government's mind they exist in perpetuity. Health care *is* the National Health Service. Criminal justice *is* the police and the courts. Health and safety *is* the Health and Safety Executive. Local government *is* city councils. Any organisation that comes to regard itself as a fixture will atrophy. All organisations need imperatives; they are difficult to produce in the absence of competition and bankruptcy, but essential to stop bureaucracies becoming ends to themselves.

The Treaty has six imperatives: local feedback, the funding mechanism, supervision, power to change the board and/or management, regular appraisal of purpose, and abandonment.

Local Feedback

The first is feedback of results as described earlier, but with every PSO having local feedback on everything it does. The focus on results would mean dismantling the entire costly central directing and mandating of procedure and anything else that is not about purpose and therefore results. The intent is to drive intelligence and accountability down, not decision-making up.

Funding Mechanism

The second imperative would stem from the funding mechanism to apply increased accountability of the PSO to the people who are paying, i.e. companies and individuals, through consistent funding, an end to derivative funding for real local government, central government becoming a social investment banker, and complete transparency in the money–go–round.

Consistent funding would follow from less adversarial politics as a result of a) the Treaty generally, and b) proportional representation specifically. Coalitions would be the norm, thus preventing zigzag government, and end our bipolar political party disorder. Funding would not go up and down as the maniacs and the depressives alternated power with the huge costs of their U–turns, and over– and under–funding.

In the 1960s, 75% of a local authorities' spending came from the rates, i.e. from its local citizens and businesses. Other than redistributed and other central government funds, the money had travelled the minimum distance between the taxpayer and the user, who would often be the same person. The taxpayers had the satisfaction of seeing their money spent on services all around them. The taxpayers were also the electors who could change their votes depending on how well they thought their money was being used. This is about as close we get in public expenditure to money changing hands for a good or service.

Real local government would be funded locally (with some redistribution), and accountable locally. 'No taxation without representation' is a slogan originating around the 1750s that summarised a primary grievance of the British colonists, which was one of the major causes of the American Revolution. They were paying taxes but went unrepresented in government. Equally there can be no representation without taxation – or if you are not paying you won't be interested. (If you are not paying for your local services directly, then you will have no great interest in who is in power and representing you in the council; conversely, if your council tax was four times its current size – which is on average what each council spends – then you would be very interested, active and demanding.)

In general today funding of PSOs is based on incremental budgeting and pleading your case. The Treaty would change this method from marginal changes annually based on the quality of pleading by each department or agency, to funding being an investment in achieving an outcome. Funding would have to be earned on the back of feedback of results. National funding from the Ministry of Finance or Treasury would be based on results. If these are being delivered then funding would continue, if not then funding would drop, with permutations between these extremes. Funding of public sector bodies should be about investment, not routine continuance. Where is the best social return on each public pound invested? We need a cadre of public investment specialists, and not the mentality of the existing HM Treasury operating like a ship's purser.

Lastly, there is some good news from the coalition government and its introduction of substantive transparency of public money and what it is being spent on. This really is a step forward. The Treaty would simply take this further so that all costs in every body are publically visible.

Supervision

The third imperative would come in the form of effective supervision of every PSO on our behalf. Each common grouping of bodies would have the equivalent of the Supervisory Executive overseeing them.[22] Each supervisory executive would supervise a portfolio of agencies, and specialise in knowing why each is performing as it is, with specialists in agency turnaround, and specialists in regulator turnaround. Thus industry regulators as a group would have specialists supervising them – not to second guess their decisions but to keep an expert eye on them, to warn of any softening, and to reform when necessary. The old demarcations of departments controlling or sponsoring the bodies within their sector remit would go. This is a matter of operations and of operational excellence brought about by knowing 'how to', and applying, in this example, industry regulation expertise which crosses sector boundaries. Effective supervision takes the right people, the right

22   The Supervisory Executive, established in 2003, manages a cross-Whitehall portfolio of businesses and has responsibility for project-managing the government's asset-management programme.

information and transparency, with an element of being ruthless in decision and humane in execution.

Power to Change the Board and/or Management

This is the fourth imperative, and would be a decision proposed by the Supervisory Executive and approved by the minister. All head or chief executive jobs in publicly funded bodies would be subject to a 'four-year rule'. Essentially, every four years, the board would be required to take a positive decision to keep the head or chief executive in that job. This would be a balanced assessment of performance driven by feedback – external and internal. It would be the opportunity for an adult conversation, and be the time to make a change when needed. Most often this would be a comparatively quick and simple confirmation. But its purpose would be to avoid the head who is failing but clinging on because no one wants to do the deed, or has insufficient knowledge to mount a case, or does not have the time for the hassle, or does not want a fight. Thus the board would be enabled to act in a 'business as usual' way in declining to confirm a head in that role. The maximum of six months redundancy terms would then apply (see below). All top public appointments would be initially for two years, and the board would be required to decide positively to retain the incumbent. Subsequently the same positive decision would be required every four years.

These jobs are not there for the post holder. They are too important. They are there for the stakeholders. Top people get more recognition and more money and should take more risk in their tenure. And that is the point. It would be as easy to make the right change as it is to keep the right person. This is not about hiring and firing at will. It is about balancing the interests of the head with the interests of the pupils, parents, citizens and other stakeholders on the wrong end of the wrong top person.

Regular Appraisal of Purpose

The fifth imperative would be a regular appraisal of the purpose of the body, its *raison d'être*, its remit, statutory duties, and regulatory requirements both on it and by it. Why are we here?

Is this remit possible? Does it help? Does it work? Is it sufficient? The Supervisory Executives would examine these ruthlessly, and recommend to the government those to be abandoned, including whole agencies. Public sector organisations must get used to justifying their existence.

Abandonment

Abandonment or closure would be the sixth imperative. No public sector body should regard itself as a fixture in society. Feedback would be institutionalised, but never a body. Abolition has its part to play. A good example of improving performance through closing an existing body was the abolition of the Greater London Council in 1986 (as I mentioned at the start of the book, Thatcher's anti-democratic reasons were all wrong, but the decision was right). As an irreformable institution it needed to go, but it should have been immediately replaced with today's executive mayor and the Greater London Assembly, rather than after twenty years. (The limbo was another product of our adversarial politics and 'first past the post' system.) My point is that abolition was essential.

Now as irreformable as was the GLC, of note today is the Metropolitan Police – today a curious mixture of a media business, customer-service operation and home to some dodgy ethics along with some good policing – whose non-performing, non-accountable culture can only be resolved by abolition. The obvious answer would be to split it in four and merge these with the outlying forces. Several of the departments of state are candidates. The Home Office, in the words of one of its recent ministers, is 'not fit for purpose'. Can it ever be? Perhaps it could at last be put out of its misery, and thereby put us out of its misery.

Such is its profound incompetence, MoD procurement is another case where change to bring UK weapons procurement up to the standards of the Israeli equivalent, for example, will only occur through abolition and a new and aligned body. When will this happen?

The coalition's abolition of some 'quangos' has seen some stuck organisations go, and this can only be good, yet it arose from crisis. Under the Treaty, 'government as usual' would see regular consideration of all public sector bodies and their value to the taxpayer/citizen. Again, Peter Drucker reached this conclusion long ago in 1969 in 'The Sickness of Government', in which he said:

> We may build into government an automatic abandonment process. Instead of starting with the assumption that any program, any agency, and any activity is likely to be eternal, we might start out with the opposite assumption: that each is short- lived and temporary. We might, from the beginning, assume that it will come to an end within five or ten years unless specifically renewed. And we may discipline ourselves not to renew any program unless it has the results that it promised when first started. We may, let us hope, eventually build into government the capacity to appraise results and systematically to abandon yesterday's tasks.

Forty years of experience has taught us that we must do this.

Public Sector Duties

The next part of the new approach would be in a set of duties to provide personal motivation to everyone in the public sector that has all of the power of something written into the constitution. What are or should be the principles applicable to working in the public sector? Is it ethical simply to ask for more and simply to defend the status quo in funding and outcome? Or should these organisations and people have duties to work out how to do the same for less, for example? Then be awarded more? Where (and what) are the principles in play here?

We must be clear what is expected of all PSOs and the people working in them, including the government private sector, through a set of statutory duties:

- Deliver results.
- Use the best process to achieve those results.
- Otherwise, use controlled experiments.
- Minimise costs of the service.

- Deliver within the whole of public sector and not in silos or fiefdoms.
- Balance power in relation to consumers and citizens.
- Be proportionate in public services with regard to health and safety, speed cameras, etc.
- Be transparent.
- Speak straight. This would see an end to corporate speak, spin, obfuscation, evasion, gagging clauses, and straight lying. All staff and management would have a duty to say publically what is really going on, and thus to contribute to improving services. This duty would go well beyond a whistle-blowers' charter and the proposed duty of candour for NHS inquiries. Bent speaking would replace straight speaking as a potential cause of disciplinary action or dismissal. (The duty of straight speak would further reinforce the discipline of dealing in reality and results. This would of course be encouraged by failure investigations wanting to learn, and replace guilt-seeking inquests. The latter inevitably promote bent speak. Straight speak would announce 'The train is crammed due to our lack of planning, and due to our slack contract specified and managed by the Department for Transport.' Attributing a delay to signal failure when the true cause is the cause of the signal failure would go the same way. Thus would commence the change in cultures needed in much of the public sector, closing down the self-excusing wiggle room, and opening up the collective intention to reduce errors and to improve. The accountability on the individual would be for straight speak, and not to obey management edict to deny.)
- Maintain an attitude to work of enquiry and learning, to produce something useful to society.
- Adopt fair harmonised mid-point terms and conditions throughout the public sector – a policy of both fairness and equal opportunities, as well as facilitating movement across the sector and the transfer of knowledge and experience with this movement. Pay would vary as it

does now, between jobs, bodies, and geographies. But the terms and conditions would represent a uniform mid-point in the current distribution. Redundancy terms should not be prohibitive and should be fair to the employee: a maximum of six months' pay would meet these criteria – and all those hideous pay-outs for the managerialists would end. Pensions should be funded, invested with the Universities Superannuation Scheme or similar, and based on contributions not defined benefits, and be entirely transferable across all government bodies. Harmonised pensions at least across the public and Civil Service would promote beneficial movement between public bodies. Harmonised pensions across all sectors would not only be a rather important equality, it would also increase the flow of people between sectors and organisations, transferring knowledge, practice, skill, and understanding in all directions. Equality in recruitment should be established too with organisations like the BBC opening most of its vacancies to outsiders.

- Sample the PSO's services in order to experience these services as the public do.
- Abandon the ineffective.

These duties would serve several purposes, prime amongst them the creation of something like the sense of personal accountability sought by a former head of the British Olympic Team amongst everyone working for it. The athletes had an obvious motivation, but the staff did not. Thus he sought to instil in each member of staff the desire to do a good job always. PSO staff today are largely demotivated by the organisations in which they work – top down, directive, forms, checklists, managerialism, protective terms and conditions. These and their demotivating effect would go and the new duties would provide some of the positive motivation by pointing staff in the right direction, mandating thought, and directing their attention to the PSO's purpose and to customers and citizens, not internally to the bureaucracy.

Best Organisational Practice

The Swiss constitution has this to say on the responsibility for organisation: 'The Federal Government directs the Federal Administration. It provides for an effective organisation and goal-oriented fulfilment of the tasks.' Would you like some of that? I would. In other words, there is a clear public constitutional duty on the government to organise its PSOs effectively. The final part of the Operations system is in applying best organisational practice for each public sector body: alignment, benchmarking processes from around the world, utilising proven concepts, and default decentralisation. Each PSO would have the duty to organise in this way.

Alignment of Each PSO

First up is aligning the body so that all its components point in the same direction. This may sound complicated to do, but any misalignment is remarkably easy to spot. And change.

Benchmarking

Second would be benchmarking processes from around the world. What is the best way of enforcing planning conditions? What is the best way of collecting company taxes? What is the best way of controlling air pollution? There are thousands of small processes, and much variety from which to learn and to choose. The default attitude amongst many in the public sector is to ignore or to reject the experience of other countries. I have always found this inexplicable, but presumed it is partly the nation's ego at work, partly a desire for a quiet life, and partly a sense of having little to learn from anywhere. This is all nonsense, of course. To learn is to change, and learning comes from many sources. Being highly centralised, little variation is found between local governments in Britain. Regional government does not exist – although devolution to Scotland and Wales means other methods are appearing slowly. Inter-government learning commences here. Meantime the rest of the world has many of the same objectives and needs as the

UK. International learning from one country to another is not only legitimate but also essential for anyone taking the duties above seriously. It is usually fascinating too. It implies change and ambition. And humility.

Utilising Proven Concepts

The third would be utilising proven concepts with applicability in the public sector. Results-based accountability is one such. Zero defects is another. Zero defects says that in each step of a process the aim is no errors. This always seemed impossible to me until it was put this way: how many eggs is it acceptable to drop in a packing station? And how many babies is it acceptable to drop in a maternity ward? The point is that errors are a matter of attitude to the task in hand, and it is proven that if you expect errors they will come, whereas if you aim for none, performance improves.

Default Decentralisation and Real Local Government

Fourth under organisation is default decentralisation. Almost every public service in the UK is now centralised either under a single body like the Court Service or through British 'local government' (i.e. largely administration by officials directed from Whitehall). This is not local government. Nor democracy. Nor local responsibility. The country is largely out of practice of real local government, which is very different in operation and experience than the pretence in the UK.

Under the Treaty, local government would be re-established not as we know it today but with all the purpose, competence, and energy created by the model proposed here. Re-establishing local government after such a long absence will take time and learning. For local people it will be about much more than simply voting periodically.

Good quality, real local government is a science to be learnt in each locale. As in life, as much learning will come from making mistakes as in getting things right. Executive mayors are the *sine qua non* of local government, elected by PR, along with local tax raising and national redistribution, feedback, policy vetting, operational excellence, transparency, and decision-specific democracy. Just how active the local citizens will become, time will tell, but it will be far more than the neutered electorate's practice at present.

Looking around the world, an approximate maximum size for effective government is a population of 7 million – a Finland or a Scotland as a nation government, or the states of the US or the regions of Germany. The federal governments in these larger countries cover many more than 7 million of course, but their role is limited and much government delivery occurs at the state and local level. Wales and Scotland now have the chance for good government. The Westminster/Whitehall set-up is simply too large and too complex. English regional government seems out of the question. Real local government is essential.

Real local government also means electing more of other types of local public chief executives, and electing primarily for their capacity to deliver. Many services, from national parks to courts, need the fresh dynamic a new method for acquiring executive power would bring.

Of course with decentralisation comes diversity. The way a service is delivered in Bury may well be different to that in Bromley. Through diversity comes experimentation, particularly in all of those public services where finding solutions is so complex. Here Engage–Deliberate–Decide, or engaged experimentation, is essential.[23] Life changes too along with what is possible technologically and from the market. Local innovation blossoms. Once the best solution has emerged or emerged for now, the vital next step is every other local body adopting this practice. The Treaty provides for this. Thus standards rise. With the other factors of motivation and responsiveness active too, standards will rise faster than through central direction and control. Intelligence is driven down, rather than decisions up.

Some say that citizens should receive the identical service in Bury or Bromley, the same standard of operation in the same time with the same care – otherwise the 'postcode lottery' occurs and that is unfair. Such lotteries proliferate now, even with the government's highly centralised system attempting and failing to produce universality. Life is, of course, in part a postcode lottery

---

23 Some local authorities are experimenting with participative budgeting, prioritising road maintenance schemes, for example.

and fortunately always will be – living in an urban area with twenty inches of rain a year is a very different experience from living in a rural area with 200 inches. People are both born into and choose different existences. Some variation is the price to be paid for real local government. But the variation arising from local decision-making will produce competing solutions – rather than the Whitehall answer forever more – from which the best will gradually be widely adopted. Diversity and learning produces higher standards of service overall than attempts at Westminster/ Whitehall centrally driven uniformity.   We need to take delight in experimentation and diversity, and in the potential universal uptake of the successes.

The Swiss constitution puts it thus: 'The Federation only undertakes tasks that the Cantons are unable to perform or which require uniform regulation by the Federation.'

Some of the current national bodies would remain centralised – there seems little benefit in devolving the processing of driving licences – but others would not. The organisational conundrum goes like this. The larger the organisation the more difficult it is to run well, the further away it becomes from the consumer and citizen, and the chains of accountability to the people become so stretched as to be meaningless. Front-line workers delivering services top down are demotivated by directive, and procedural management. The more distant the direction from the users or consumers, the less responsive and adaptable the service will be. Sometimes it will be plain wrong. Workers with latitude to respond and design and deliver services will, within the framework of this Treaty, be both motivated and responsive. The Treaty would prevent former lax standards of the staff serving the staff.

Let's remind ourselves of which of all of these operations is political and which not. Delivery is political and so is making the operational system work. But once working, most bodies would be in a business-as-usual mode and left to get on with it. Ministers would intervene where reform, change, or abandonment was needed, and provide the political leadership to do that. But government capacity is limited. Any successful government would concentrate its resources on priority reform only. Most public sector bodies would be left alone to run, with all the comfort of rigorous feedback and effective supervision for the executive to see all is well. Governments would start less and finish more.

- Will operations be perfect? No, nothing is.
- Will they be vastly better than now, both to receive and to work in? Yes.
- Will they cost a lot less? Yes.
- Will we do it ... ?

11

Fit People

Is it possible to design government to get more of the right type of people into the top jobs? And once they are in the seat, can the framework be constructed so as to get the best out of them?

It has been said many times, and in many contexts, that 'it is against the system, and not against individuals that we raise our objection', to quote Sir Stafford Northcote and Sir Charles Trevelyan to the Lords of HM Treasury in 1855, when introducing their reform of the Civil Service: it is not a people problem but a system problem. A different system will both attract people with different skills than today and will demand different skills (as has been the case whenever the Civil Service is reformed). The people who succeed under the Treaty will succeed for different reasons. Principally these will be their capacity to deliver results successfully, and to make more right decisions rather than fewer. Some of these with the right mind and experience are MPs and others in the System already. But most are not.

Thus far we have designed a system with feedback, policymaking, and delivery. These, of themselves, will promote the acquisition and development of the right people with the right education, experience, training, and attitude to do the many tasks in government. But there are also aspects of our design specific to the people. These people will be working in a system where our political authority has been carefully arranged, where power has been redistributed, and where the external disciplines are strong. We will no longer have to fear an over-mighty executive indulging its prejudices, egos, and friends, and could thus be optimistic about placing more power here.

It is self-evident that for any organisation to succeed, the mandatory ingredients are people with the necessary experience doing the right jobs working in a well-motivated culture, an aligned organisation, and without obstacles to collective endeavour. These conditions exist in a few corners of government at present. This chapter is about power in the right places for the various groups of people in the system to do the right things. These groups are the politicians, the civil servants, and the members of the House of Lords. Our role is crucial too, as electors.

So, first, what can be done about the politicians?

Politicians That Do

One cannot do anything without power. And one cannot do anything without effective delivery. In the new world of politics made by the Treaty, successful parties would need the five literacies: delivery, policy, political, media, and emotional. Today, many put policy first, power second, and delivery a long way third. Under the Treaty, it would no longer be 'whether' or 'what' first, but how. The consequence of this principle is potentially profound.

Executive Ministers

Avoiding responsibility for delivery is a luxury the electorate can no longer afford in its politicians (if we ever could). We are not paying governments for anything other than getting something worthwhile done. A declining proportion of a politician's remit is policymaking and an increasing proportion is delivery. Delivery would be politicised and the direct responsibility of the politicians. The presumption that the Civil Service will do it has been shown to be false. We need a political class who first and foremost can get things done. Political leadership means a minister being given full responsibility for a specific change; being in post long enough to have impact; the minister having the skills to lead and deliver; having the freedom to appoint a small specialist team for the task and not being landed with an unchosen lump of the traditional Civil Service; being able to engage with stakeholders and users by more efficient and effective means than large formal meetings; and being time limited so this does not end up being a permanent consumer of resource until a change of government or a major efficiency wave. To give them a name, it means executive ministers.

Executive ministers would know how and be able to lead and run those public services and changes for which they are responsible. This does not mean they are managing the service, but it does mean they are responsible for it and will therefore need to know how to get the service to deliver and to perform. In bringing about change large and small, from pensions to planning enforcement, executive ministers would provide the consistent political leadership to make it happen. This cannot be subcontracted to civil servants. The point that delivery is political cannot be overstated.

Good government needs executive ministers with ambition – the ambition to fix something, and to have developed the knowledge to fix it, or to know the need and get the right people with the right experience and knowledge to fix it. Who wants to sort out joke road junctions, electricity regulation, or adversarial divorce? The job of an executive minister, like an executive mayor, would be not just to chair the odd meeting that their diary allows and turn up for a photo shoot, but to lead and drive the effective implementation of a report, to worry about it at night, and to feel personally responsible for an issue like child Internet safety. The fluff of a typical junior minister's job would go.

From where would this new breed of executive ministers be sourced? They would arrive with formative experiences in organisations that deliver, be they in the third sector, real local government, agencies, or companies and often from roles as executive mayors in local government. Many future politicians would develop in real local government as executive mayors. Thus local (delivery) politics would be a vital gene pool for national politicians. The established breeding grounds of think tank, political party, and adviser roles would shrink in relevance and value. Elected representatives would be there to do what is agreed and known. Little is left of 'our policies are better than yours' regarding ends, for example in criminal justice. The difference is in means and the quality of delivery.

With delivery becoming a clear responsibility of politicians and of politics, governments will need the power to appoint people with the right experience to get these tasks done. Robert McNamara's condition for accepting the job of US Secretary for Defense in 1961 was that he could select his own team. Comprehensive feedback will generate the requirement to appoint experts, not political mates. As a minister your performance would be judged on your results. If you appoint someone unsuited to that job, it will show. A crucial part of being an executive politician is in having the skills to recruit and select people to manage a stream of reform or delivery. One chief operations officer of a major professional services organisation concluded that his main contribution, far from daily controlling, was recruitment: get the right people in the right roles and success follows.

Training

These jobs are serious, and taking them seriously means training for them. This would be akin to the coaching certificate required for sports coaches before taking up the post. Core competences are necessary in all the fields described here – organisation, operations, statistics, policymaking – plus regular specialist learning every year: continuing education for politicians. The current system rewards political skills, not results, knowledge, or learning. This should change. NICE has an excellent approach to bringing subject specialists up to speed in its methods of analysis for its specialist evaluations – an approach of wide applicability to politicians. MPs could do worse than start with *Democracy 3*, a computer game currently giving twelve-year-olds a good grounding in the complexities of policy development.

Specialist Politicians

Outside the executive ministerial ranks, politicians would have no lesser roles. They would develop specialisms for example in policy vetting, regulation, supervision, particular industry or sectors. Through specialising on select committees, MPs would develop their policy expertise in an applied and results-based way. This would then prepare them to take on ministerial roles requiring this formation, like pensions minister. The quantum of relevant experience that politicians have can increase or decrease their power – the wrong experience means they become dependent on the civil servants, the right experience means they can achieve more. Some political careers would be spent in Parliament without the need for a ministerial post, such would be the power and influence located here.

The days of junior ministerial jobs being distributed as rewards and punishments for political support or disobedience, with people in the role for an average of one year and initiatives being the best output, would be gone. These jobs would matter – to the public.

Directly Elected Heads of PSOs

In general, the more directly elected executive heads there are of government bodies, the greater the accountability to the public and the better the performance. Other conditions have to be right too, but local government executive mayors would be the norm (and the public asked to judge their comparative value once they have experienced them for several years far more than to judge their expectation). We need executive politicians, executive ministers, executive mayors, and executives directly elected to head agencies where this makes sense of the accountabilities.

Limited Terms of Office

As shown around the world, limited terms of office are essential – two terms of four years in all elected leader roles, especially prime ministers. Many countries impose this shelf life through a mandatory maximum term of office. Term limits have a long history. Ancient Greece and Rome, two civilisations with elected offices, both imposed limits on some positions. In Latin America today term limits are common, and of course they operate in the US presidency.

In today's world, political leaders are also celebrities. Our fascination and their capacity to hold our interest wanes. The greater the exposure, the sooner boredom sets in (and political leaders seek and experience ultra-high exposure).

Power is seductive – and hard to let go of. Depending on the organisational context, leaders can become tired, stuck, and long in the tooth. Top jobs are very demanding. At any one time, a senior politician will be working long and unsocial hours, thinking and reflecting time is limited, 'events dear boy' can become exhausting, the price of continued office is eternal vigilance for attack from the opposition and news media, and driving implementation takes much energy. At this point, fresh legs are essential. But governments often soldier on. A further consequence of outstaying your effectiveness is that you move from attacking the problem to owning it. Time and energy is spent in defending policies rather than accepting that some worked and some did not. Tired, defensive, and ego-driven people only have the energy to continue with the same policies, when fresh legs would bring fresh thinking without owning the past.

After having been chair of Relate for six years, I contemplated whether to continue for two more or stand aside. Much had been achieved in transforming Relate from a largely voluntary monopoly provider of relationship counselling into a multi-service competitive professional agency. But much remained to be done. Whilst my position was not terminal, my tool bag was only so big, and people get tired of your voice and style. I stood down, a new chair was elected, and the transformation continued.

The change in style between my successor and me was particularly effective. I was the right person to light fires, demonstrate the urgency of change, develop the strategy, and push it into existence. My successor brought far better skills of running a stable charity and finding workable compromises. He was easier to live with.

Whilst on a very much grander scale, the same applies to prime ministers – effective lifespan is limited, you can only do so much, and others can do a different but equally effective job. Both Margaret Thatcher and Tony Blair would have been better remembered, and probably in better health, had they gone after eight years.

This is my iron rule of power: the scale of a leader's autocracy is directly proportional to time in office and difficulty of removal. Empirically, eight years gives plenty of scope to achieve whatever that person is going to, and by that time will have reached the autocracy cap.

New Civil Service

Under the Treaty, the existence of the Civil Service as a separate self-governing institution with, in its own mind, a constitutional role that gives it power independent of government, would cease. The ends of delivery and of democracy require that it be largely sublimated to the elected government, with one key exception. Earlier in Part 1 we found how the Civil Service has survived in the Northcote–Trevelyan model because of the excessive concentration of power in the executive branch – the government – and reform would mean yet more power here. With the Treaty, executive power would be redistributed and reduced.

Traditional Civil Servants

However, still remaining within the Northcote–Trevelyan model would be the administration of the parliamentary, political, and legislative roles. This means ensuring the government operates according to the rules for developing legislation, answering parliamentary questions, responding to select committees, and so on. This role would be reinforced to include standards of policy and decision-making. The Northcote–Trevelyan Civil Service job would not be to make the policy but to ensure it is done to the ten tests before it goes to Parliament. It would recruit and appoint independently and serve impartially. The rules for recruitment would be set by the House of Lords in its role as custodian of the Treaty (see below).

New Civil Servants with Meaningful Names

But it is clear madness to presume that government delivery and policy can ever be run successfully according to the Northcote–Trevelyan model. It can't. Thus the existing remit of the Civil Service would be split in two. Accountability of elected politicians and governments demands they have the power to deliver and that includes very much their management and the motivation of staff. This is a fundamental issue of alignment. How differently employees behave towards the minister when they know who feeds them, determines their recruitment, pay, development, assignment, promotion, and termination. Balanced and fair terms and conditions would be in place such that staff would be properly accountable for their performance. Aligned employment is right for democracy and accountability. This does not mean regular sackings, nor wholesale changes, nor minsters appointing the cleaners. In practice ministers will appoint a key few people at the top. But their authority would be clear. And the statutory duties of public sector employees would apply here too, of course.

The people recruited for these jobs of delivery would vary greatly, from straight managers of services to experienced industry regulators, from professional contract managers to a new cadre of service fixers, from PSO supervisors to expert tax collectors. None would be report writers recruited straight from university by examination and assessment centres, but professional doers working to and with the political leaders/executive ministers. The existing Civil Service norms of regular job churn and 'grow your own' would cease.

Thus would be born the new civil servants (who would not have that inappropriate and archaic name). The Civil Service as we know it would disappear, although those current civil servants engaged in tasks at which they do excel and have real competence would remain in parliamentary administration. The rest would go from the centre.

There would be no lifetime-tenured civil servants with a quasi-constitutional role. Government staff would be recruited and moved as normal organisations do: for the task not for the service. The Treaty would get the politics in the right place, guard against politicisation in the wrong place, and provide the defence against corruption with high standards of transparency. None of this is a role for a modern Civil Service.

Once the new Civil Service is in place, turnover would be limited to normal organisational standards. This would be the case too after general elections, when only those brought in for specific reforms – for example to transform the pensions system, or to take charge of a priority agency – would be explicit 'political' appointments. Politicians would, however, have the right to appoint anyone.

Those responsible for supervising the various public bodies would have the power to remove the whole board and/or the whole of the top management following the same rationale, subject to ministerial approval.

House of Lords

Deep within the panelled corridors and ermine robes of the Palace of Westminster lies an organisation going in the right direction. Collectively it does not suffer from an ideological hangover, nor an excess of politics and spin, and is more representative than the elected Commons. It contains quite a broad spread of specialist knowledge. Most of its members have had jobs outside Westminster for long periods of their lives. They are older than average, but as in some very successful societies, they form a sort of group of elders bringing all the wisdom age can give. Their personal agendas are limited – none is bent on ruling the world. And they have been successful in improving the performance of governments, mainly in stopping or amending poor legislation. Ladies and gentlemen, I give you the Contemporary House of Lords.

The peers now come from many corners. Even the political party appointees have the life experience to know that all governments tend to get a lot wrong. And they are there for life so owe their continuance to no one. And therefore show limited party loyalty in the face of ideological nonsense, ministerial ego, or plain incompetence. As Dr Meg Russell shows in her book[24] the House of Lords is a revelation compared with its pre-1999 role as Conservative 'throwback nodder' when its party was in government, and 'blocker' when it was Labour. In analysing the system of government I had pondered whether the House of Lords was part of the problem or part of the solution. Its image said the former, but my intuition said the latter. Dr Russell's book confirmed my intuition.

Recently the Lib Dems proposed an elected Lords. This is conventional and seemingly modern against our arcane method of appointment. But who would want another chunk of our system given over to the bipolar political party disorder? Who would want this branch politicised? As a major check and balance, and under the Treaty the body with the absolutely critical roles of being both the Resulture and custodian of the Treaty, how could any of this be done with politics all over it? It could not. Results are to be depoliticised, the Treaty is constitutional not political. It should be the home of experience, wisdom, and independence of mind, and not another vehicle for political parties. So where should our lords come from?

---

24   *The Contemporary House of Lords: Westminster Bicameralism Revived* (Oxford University Press, 2013).

Well, the present starting point is good. In effect a mixture of political appointments, but of people either not politicians or past driving personal ambition, and those from the 'senior ranks of their professional fields, among which the largest today include business, banking and finance, the law, higher education'. This has quietly become a 'stakeholder' second chamber, to use the jargon. This is an aspect of the new system where we need to look around the world and find the most effective second chamber and why, but at this point my proposal is that the stakeholder concept works within the Treaty.

My view at present is that we should continue with the current membership, find means to reduce its size, and maintain the connection to party politics but cap political appointments at 25% of the total, and reflect approximately voting under proportional representation. The stakeholders would be widened. Few technical professions are found there. Nor many of the front-line occupations where stuff actually happens, from electricians to nurses to teachers to office dwellers.

The question then comes as to who would appoint the stakeholder group. Once again the lords are already there. They have an Appointment Commission with strict criteria and invite applications (did you know you can apply to be a Lord?). It would, however, be separated from any government influence or control and be established constitutionally as part of the Treaty. It could usefully widen its catchment to include recommendations from professional bodies, third sector bodies, local governments, religious bodies, PSOs, the media, business, and indeed the Brownies. The types of people to be put forward would usually be older and thus have made more mistakes and have shown the capacity to learn from them, would have a wider grasp of how things get done than just their occupation, would bring open-mindedness and humility, and would eschew any commitment to their nominating body. Their job is to bring knowledge, not a sectional mandate. Their oath would be to the system and the constitution, and not to their origins.

Subject to anyone coming up with a better composition, this would build on the values found now in the House of Lords, and widen its understanding and grasp. It would give it the legitimacy to fulfil the tough roles the Treaty requires of it. The second chamber has to feel legitimate to us in exercising these powers. We have to have the confidence that, although we may not like a decision, nevertheless the lords have been appointed to produce an expert and independent chamber – that works better than one directly elected by us. The stakeholder concept would therefore be subject to particularly extensive deliberation with the public before the Treaty vote. One essential design criterion for any future-proof system of governance is in preventing what might be termed 'perverting the course of an institution' – which is, broadly, what has happened to the EU bureaucracy and is the underlying cause of much of the current public disaffection – we must design in means to ensure the Lords are not perverted.

The House of Lords would need its own resources to build the Resulture, and it would need some sort of lead group to organise all of this. The Federal Council of Switzerland is a good model. It would then need to employ some top-quality managers to set up and run and cohere its scorekeepers and results finders.

Electors

Finally there is us. Electors have a big role to play in the system and in generating successful government. We will learn through active democracy, feedback, and open policymaking. This will challenge our own prejudices, and develop our capacity to elect the right people – not people who tickle our fancy but those who get good things done. We will get much slicker at electing the right people for the job.

As has been said many times, people get the governments they deserve. How good do we want ours to be?

12

Competitive Democracy

Rarely are the benefits of competition talked of in relation to democracy. Yes for companies but not governments. Competition matters here just as much. Not just for political parties, but for policies, decisions, solutions, and for people in government jobs – including leaders. This is not just about competition raising standards and learning, it's also about what it stops – zigzag government, preferential lobbying, 'secret policymaking' disasters.

Politics and government in democracies is a competitive market. This can be a major stimulant to improvement. Part of the point of the analysis is to determine how the principles of competition can be used more effectively in government. In Britain and the US proper competition is stymied by first past the post electoral systems producing duopolies in the political parties of government, and the dismal choice. Monopoly Civil Services prevent or limit competition in policymaking and in delivery and, as we have seen, government is typically cut off from the beneficial effect of these forces by smoke and mirrors. One of the challenges for a modern system of government is to harness the power of competition at the political party level. Our current system limits competition as much as it can without becoming an elective dictatorship. Our design needs to go in the opposite direction.

A developing society in a complex world depends as much for its future on solution diversity and experimentation as does the natural world on biodiversity. A similar truth applies also to lifestyles. I used to wonder why I felt so strongly about the *Daily Mail*, then realised that it has always had such a narrow idea of acceptable lifestyles that it has been the nearest the UK has had to a fascist party since Oswald Mosley's (fascism seeks uniformity – and hence why it always fails). We need diversity of lifestyles and power precisely because we cannot know which will turn out to work best in the future, or indeed even survive. Diverse societies are resilient societies.

Diversity is key throughout systems of government. The greater the diversity the more likely to find an answer to some really complex problems. Thus far we have incorporated into our system diversity and competition through real local government, and diversity and competition in policies through engagement, using other countries experiences, and experimentation. Now we come to the political parties and their leaders.

Here, the Treaty has five clauses, all essential to functioning competitive democracy: full political party competition through full proportional voting; effective means to change the party leader/prime minister, and backbench governance; equality in party funding; maximum four-year terms for governments; and the right to referendum. All of these apply to the UK (some countries already have proper PR and fair funding of political parties).

Proportional Voting

Every country needs proportional representation at every level of government. This would not be the rather fey interpretation called the additional vote, but straight PR based on the transferable vote, requiring a minimum percentage (typically 5%) to be represented in Parliament. PR buys you higher standards of political parties and of politicians and ministers; an end to zigzag government and its costs; pruned ideologies; fresh thinking; wider and better representation of interests and objectives (for example the response to climate chaos); and insulation from powerful lobbies. It also provides some significant inoculation against news-media hobbling and its hold over governments through the plurality of parties and the norm of coalitions. The more parties you have to buy, the harder it is. Two-party states are far easier to fix than multi-party. Murdoch has always opposed PR.

Usually at this point, a politician (trying hard to mask his patronising tone) will stress how important is strong and decisive government and thus first past the post. At this point too we should think about just who are these people attracted to these top positions of great power, and their motivations. Are these the people of our dreams of balanced mind and sound judgement, possessed of clear vision, committed to our good as citizens, able to operationalise their objectives swiftly and without the unexpected? Or something else? Once a politician explains a decision by the need for strong government, you can be certain this is someone at the top end of power needs. As expected, we heard this in relation to the Alternative Vote referendum by those opposed to power sharing – 'we need the strong government that only first past the post can give' and, by inference, not the namby-pamby wimp-type government from coalitions and other inadequates. Sounds good, does it not? Flutters the spine? Makes one stand up straight? From time to time, we have experienced strong government, most potently with Thatcher. She drove some changes through which we would all agree with, in hindsight, like building the M25. She drove some necessary change but punitively and with destructive speed, like the mine closures. She also drove hard some major errors, like the poll tax.

I never saw the point of strong government, when strong can and does lead to such high costs. I want right government, not strong government. Right government may from time to time be bold and courageous, and it may also be considered, cautious, careful, and experimental. Strong is just an excuse for the more psychologically flawed. Its end game is Stalin, Mao Tse-tung, and Hitler. And a Thatcher would never have been necessary to resolve the worst excesses of the UK's ideological hangover in the factories if we had had the plurality of proportional voting. First past the post produced both the problem *and* the strong and costly solution. It maintains a country in a permanent state of civilian civil war. No first past the post – no problem – no need for Thatcher. What joy.

Changing a Prime Minister and Backbench Governance

How a political party changes its leader might be thought of as solely for the party to decide. But political parties are part of the system of government and sometimes those leaders are prime ministers. Thus changing the leader is part of the Treaty. Let us contrast two systems for this – that of the Labour Party and that of the Conservatives. These are the rules for a challenge to the leader of the Conservatives. A leadership election is triggered either by the resignation of the party leader, or following a vote of 'no confidence' by Conservative MPs. To secure a confidence vote, 15% of Conservative MPs must submit a request for such a vote, in writing, to the chairman of the 1922 Committee. This can be done either collectively or separately. The names of the signatories would not be disclosed. The chairman, in consultation with the leader, then determines the date of such a vote 'as soon as possible in the circumstances prevailing'. If the incumbent leader wins the support of a simple majority in any such vote, they would remain leader and no further vote could be called for a period of twelve months from the date of the ballot. If the leader were to lose such a vote (again, on a simple majority basis) they must resign, and they may not stand in the leadership election that is then triggered.

Labour changes its leaders like FIFA selects World Cup venues. The rules for a challenge to the leader of the Labour Party when also prime minister are these: 'When the PLP is in government and the leader and/or deputy leader are prime minister and/or in Cabinet, an election shall proceed only if requested by a majority of party conference on a card vote of the individual members, MPs, and trade union members.' Thus a party conference has to be called first, then a vote held in public. The political consequences of such a divisive and 'dirty washing in public' event are such that in practice the chances of a party conference voting to call a leadership election with a sitting Labour prime minister are zero. In other words, when in government, the Labour prime minister cannot be challenged. He or she is there until resignation or election loss. Ousting a Labour prime minister becomes a tortuously long process that debilitates government and saps public confidence, as seen both with Blair and Brown. Personal power politicking takes over.

The Partnership in Power report applied from 1997 necessarily took the power at conference to set policy and elect NEC members away from individual party members and from the trade unions. A sense of order and calm was established – essential to electability. However, this power went to the leadership, and not to the party's MPs. Thus the leader – and in government the prime minister – became *less* accountable.

Before 1965, leaders of the Conservative Party were not elected, but 'emerged' after discussion among Conservative MPs, a system that is described by one academic as 'an opaque process of negotiation and soundings involving senior party figures'.[25] The leadership race that took place at the 1963 Conservative Party Conference following Macmillan's resignation through ill health proved most controversial, and prompted Ian Macleod's reference in an article for the *Spectator* in 1964 to the 'magic circle' within the party.

When asked about the 2010 Labour leader election, one former Cabinet minister said, 'We have decided David [Miliband] will be the next leader.' Labour now had its own magic circle and opaque process worthy of the Tories before 1965. But this Cabinet minister had forgotten that the election of a new leader did involve an open process, albeit with flaws. Ironically, Ed Miliband benefited from a desire amongst some to end the dominance of the New Labour establishment, voting him in rather than David. From an organisational perspective, recruitment, as appointing a leader is called, is never an exact process. No matter how careful the job and candidate specification, the incisiveness of the interviews, the precision of the psychometric tests, the revelations of the assessment centres, or whatever means is used to select, only when the job is being done will you know whether that recruit will succeed or not. The sin in recruitment is not in making a mistake in selection but in not acknowledging and acting on a mistake once made. This should be an organisational hanging offence. Of course, too many appointers see their political stock falling if a mistake has to be acknowledged. But the alternative is labouring on under a failing leader with a failing organisation. Good governance needs to be there to force the organisation to confront and resolve difficult issues.

The Conservative Party is able to change its leader when it needs to because the 1922 Committee is a forum where the performance and electability of the prime minister/leader can be discussed without looking over one's shoulder too much. The committee comprises all Conservative private Members. When in government, that means the entire backbench membership (i.e. all bar ministers) of the party. In Opposition, it comprises all Conservative Members bar the leader. It is chaired by a senior backbencher, who enjoys access to the party leader and keeps the

---

25   Paul Webb, *The Modern British Party System*, pp. 197–8 (SAGE Publications, 2000).

leadership informed of backbench opinion. Other office-holders are elected annually to form, with the chairman, an Executive Committee. The committee acts as a 'sounding board' of opinion among Conservative Members. The press often refers to the committee as 'the influential 1922 Committee', and indeed it is influential, although not so much in terms of policy. Philip (now Lord) Norton alluded to the popular presumption that a visit from a delegation of the 1922 – dubbed the 'men in grey suits' – constitutes the traditional means of removing a leader, but he went on to state: 'In practice, no leader had ever gone as a result of any such visit; nonetheless, this mythology has helped underpin the influence of the 1922 Committee.'

As a footnote, when David Cameron became prime minister in 2010, he sought to widen the membership of the 1922 Committee to ministers. In other words, those being governed would now be part of the governing. None of us particularly welcome others checking up on what we are doing. Cameron's proposal was understandable as a human being. The prime minister did not want this particular check and balance hanging over him – it would diminish his personal power – and he could neuter it by being at the meetings, implicitly threatening any criticism by his presence and his power of patronage as prime minister. Anyone who has ever sat on a board, be it of the largest company or of a small charity, will know that the conversation is very different with the management present and with them not. Even without the corporate politics to contend with, people are much more open, direct, and honest in their criticisms without their subjects present. To the credit of the party, this proposal was rejected. The institutional memory was sufficient to know why the 1922 Committee comprised backbenchers only, and how important it was to the party's success.

Under the Treaty, every party would have a committee of backbenchers, and simple rules to trigger a confidence vote on 15% of MPs requesting it without their names being disclosed. Whilst in government, electing the new leader/prime minister has to be a task for its MPs only, for two reasons: first, the practical politics of taking such a vote to a party conference with the delays involved render it impossible; second, MPs have been elected by the public (conference members have not) and thus in terms of representation have the remit to make this change.

Funding of Political Parties

State funding for political parties is well established in some countries. Broadly the funding received is based on share of the vote above a certain minimum with a small maximum on any individual or private donations. This is not an immediately popular proposal with many of the public who would of course be footing the bill, not least because of the underperformance of our political parties. But, as we have found, this is the consequence of our inadequate constitutions. Stronger constitutions will produce far better performance, but part of that strengthening is state funding. This is therefore an investment by the taxpayers. Look what it buys you: levelling of the playing field and fair competition between parties unbiased by the money they can raise; supporting parties other than the two major ones and thus strengthening their competition, promoting new entrants, and raising the standards of government; insulation from big business buying decisions for itself and against you; insulation from the preferences of the very rich and their odd requirements of government policy; consequently policies that benefit the public; and an end to cash for honours and to the appointment of people to positions in return for donations.

State funding would be relatively small. In today's world of the Internet, significant sums can be raised through small donations. It is part of competitive democracy for parties to make their case to electors and in so doing to attract donations. Clearly a cap must be placed on these otherwise, as now, large donors can buy influence and distort decisions. This cap would certainly be no more than £50,000.

Four-Year Terms for Governments

All democracies specify terms of office for any government. Typically these are four years. In the UK it is now a fixed five. But under the old 'maximum of five' rules, if a government was doing well then invariably it went for election after four. Only failing governments stay on for five. So that's clear then. The Treaty specifies four. You could argue persuasively for three.

Right to Referendum

From time to time, in competition with the government of the day, we the people will want to take a decision by referendum. The Treaty therefore has to incorporate a means for one to be called by means other than a vote in Parliament. To bring the Treaty into effect will take just such a referendum, but at present we would have to wait until a government decided to allow us this vote. This is clearly absurd. And uncompetitive.

The Treaty therefore includes a provision for a number of signatures proportional to the number of electors to call a referendum on a specific subject. This proportion will be set by looking around the world at practice and adopting which works best. Fairly obviously the proportion should not be so low that votes are being held excessively, nor so high to make any vote impossible.

Referenda serve other purposes too. One of Churchill's' famous quotes is: 'The best argument against democracy is a five-minute conversation with the average voter.' To produce successful government, democracy must be infused with intelligence. The Treaty already contains a number of ways of doing this, from Engagement to Feedback. All of these will help us to learn. A referendum is a further powerful tool, in that we get to live with the consequences of our choice – good *and* bad. The Swiss system for regular referendum on matters small and large, local and national, is designed to bring together and reassure the many peoples forming the federation, but it also means people take much more responsibility for decisions and are party to (sometimes culpable for) wrong decisions.

Having the power, as in Switzerland, to refer back any piece of national or local legislation or decision through collecting signatures and holding a vote is a further expansion of competition and democracy. At present, I think we may have enough to do to get the Treaty to work, and I therefore see this as a later change.

Tamper-Proof Democracy

For this whole new system to work well, and to promote competitive democracy, the rules must be tamper-proof. That means some body on the end of them to patrol and enforce if necessary. As mentioned already, under the Treaty this would be the House of Lords. If you are in a country with a politicised second chamber then this role would have to be carried out by others, most likely a constitutional court. My experience of our judicial system is that it can be really right, but it is also unaware of what it does not know or has not experienced. So, it has not experienced organisation and consequently has made a hash of employment law. It does not know families and all their complexity and so has made a mess of family law. Organisation is the foundation of the Treaty and I would not want the judges getting involved through a constitutional court. The House of Lords may occasionally need the back-up of the courts, but essentially it would be the custodian of the Treaty, the keeper of the keys.

Two other roles are required of the Lords in this section: standards of behaviour, and regulating news-media relationships.

Behaviour and Standards Applicable to Ministers and Others

We are talking here of the behaviour of ministers and all in government and in the wider system. This is another area where the Westminster model is flawed. The way in which ministerial behaviour is regulated in practice amounts to exposure by the news media or flagging by senior civil servants. It is then up to the prime minister as to whether to bow to such pressure and to force an immediate 'resignation', or to refer it to formal independent investigation.

The civil servants who flag incorrect actions are, of course, the very same civil servants who, under the current convention, are accountable to the same minister for all that they do, deliver, policy-ise, etc. Thus either the accountability loses out (it does) or the flagging droops in the wind (it can).

With the present 'the only sin is to be found out' arrangements, the news media has stepped in. Typically the celebratory pugilist interviewers of the BBC perform the essential constitutional role of regulating ministerial standards through investigation, exposure, and challenge. They should not have to (other than in exceptional circumstances) and it does come with significant downside.

Journalists behave like the judiciary in seeking out the guilty, they decide what constitutes sacking behaviour, and act as judge and jury. Quality ministers get killed in the rush to judgement, as well as the more deserving. It serves the psychopathologies of the journalists and acts as some constraint on the psychopathologies of ministers, but is at the end of the day a flaw for a flaw. In reallocating power, the Treaty would subject governments and their decisions to far greater scrutiny. Thus inappropriate behaviour would reduce. However, Parliament needs rigorous means to regulate behaviour.

Under the Treaty this would be a role for the House of Lords, with straightforward referral, fast and incisive investigation, and appropriate disposal. The news media could then spend its time in contributing intelligence to the many complex issues we face without sniffing a scalp at the end of every interchange.

The statutory duties apply equally to ministers. But there are other standards applicable in terms of conflict of interest – for example a lawyer in government making policy affecting lawyers in practice – and whether a decision is being influenced by a personal connection or incentive. Under the Treaty the opportunities for politicians to bend a decision are far fewer, of course. This is not primarily a moral stance (although it is that as well), but any corruption is inefficient and makes for poor government, which will come out in the Resulture.

News–Media Relationship Rules

Again the Treaty provides for a vastly better balance of influence on the decisions of government. But news media will continue to wield power and this should not be permitted to lead to unstated deals. Is there ever any good reason for a prime minister to even meet the chairman or CEO of a media corporation? The editors and journalists, yes but never the top managers.

Any meeting with the senior people in news-media companies would be reported. The de facto open diaries of today are an intrusion on a politician's privacy and an inevitable response to secret deals. The price of being in politics is some transparency. That should include who you are spending time with (as distinct from in bed with) who has influence and/or interests in government. Competition rulings – the main area of interest for deals – are not matters of politics and should be for apolitical competition authorities where ministers are not found. In any event these rulings should exclude any politician who has had contact with media executives, other than in relation to the reference and on the record.

Finally here, two publically listed media companies with heavy news interests have constructed their shareholdings to maintain personal power. Thus while both News Corp and the Daily Mail and General Trust have voting and non-voting shares, most of the voting shares are held by the Murdochs and the Rothermeres and their man Paul Dacre. This is simply poor corporate governance. Any company with poor governance would be prohibited from all contact with ministers. (Although not the subject of this book, newspaper regulation – which has proved to be impossible on a self-regulating basis but which is feared if government-regulated – could be better placed in the largely non-political House of Lords.)

Our new system now has in place effective feedback, the Resulture, policy vetting, new separations of powers, delivery with zero defects, fit people to work in it, and competitive democracy. One last building block remains to be designed: the foundation of fairness.

13

Fair Shares

This very short but vital chapter is about establishing a core of fairness in our system. Fairness does not happen by chance; it has to be built in. These clauses in the Treaty are both to correct the wrongs we experience through cake capture and to state loud and clear that we wish to run our society in a fair way. Fairness can be thought of in two ways: between us all today, and between us and future generations.

Fairness Today

All of those fault lines which benefit one group or segment of society at the expense of another have a common root: massive income inequality, business leaders in effect setting their own remuneration, exclusive franchises awarded by government and maintained by lobbies from the pension-fund oligopoly to the senior Civil Service, and zero personal accountability or penalty for the stunning misuse of other people's money by banks. The provision in the Treaty would be along the lines that one section or group would not act in a manner that rips off another.

The Treaty would include the objective of fair taxation, fair in the sense of everyone and every company paying it at the standard rate. Thus tax would be determined by its outcome and not by the rules for calculating it. If you live in the UK and the tax rate is 33% for an income of £100,000, you would pay 33% regardless of how and where your income is paid or what it is called. For companies, several countries use a set percentage 'effective minimum tax' on turnover. If these rules work, then we should adopt them.

Peter Drucker was right again: 'The fact is,' he wrote in his 1973 book *Management: Tasks, Responsibilities, Practices*, 'that in modern society there is no other leadership group but managers. If the managers of our major institutions, and especially of business, do not take responsibility for the common good, no one else can or will.' Indeed. And mostly, they have not. Long-term shareholders' interests, let alone anyone else's, are smilingly ignored if an action will boost top management's income in the short term. Our Treaty has to include corporate behaviour. Business leaders are not going to be struck by an enlightening lightning bolt on the way to the office tomorrow. This won't happen without something to make it happen. The essential first step is to regulate top management's bonus schemes such that they are aligned – there's that word again – with the interests of a company's shareholders, customers, staff, community, and environment. So, their pay cannot increase whilst their customers get stuffed. Short-term growth schemes designed to produce heroic bonuses but threaten medium-term continuance of the company would be outlawed. With this clause of the Treaty, we can all go to bed at night secure in the knowledge that these industrial and financial matadors are working late in the wider interest, and not solely for their own financial accumulation.

A number of writers have proposed the changes needed, first through the think tank 'Tomorrow's Company' started in the 1990s (essentially a stakeholder approach), and more recently David Sainsbury – former chairman of the supermarket group and minister – in his book *Progressive Capitalism*. These writers have the depth of analysis about corporations that I aim to bring to systems of government. The Treaty would cohere their proposals during the deliberation phase, and incorporate appropriate clauses.

The other aspect of fairness is that between the funders and recipients of welfare. What is fair here, and what would make it *felt* to be fair so we don't follow the zigzag of too little followed by too much? And what are the other objectives of welfare if we applied a systems-thinking test? Some of this is straightforward: this is how the Swiss constitution is phrased: 'The Federation and the Cantons are working towards the goal that every person is insured against the economic consequences of old age, disability, illness, accidents, unemployment, maternity, orphanhood, and widowhood.' In other words, national insurance would cover many of the welfare needs and costs. But then there is the uninsured element and what is fair and motivating, how much is financial and how much other measures, and for how long, and who pays. We would develop a clause through deliberation.

Intergenerational Fairness

What is fair between generations and between people, and how can this be written into the constitution? Except in extenuating circumstances of war, it cannot be right that future generations pay for us. And, as we have found, wishing away the costs of today on to the next generation – which may well be our older selves, of course, and certainly will be any young relatives – is a really bad call. These debts mount up and can cripple in the blink of the unpredicted – like a financial crisis. When that hits then the sub we have received from our kindly government, seeking nothing more than our votes in return for someone else paying, backfires and we pay twice. This is costly and really awful economic management. Governments have to be controlled. The intergenerational provision in the Treaty would be a requirement not to transfer the costs of our lifestyles to future generations: thus we capture government debt, pension funding, faux PFIs, Enron accounting, and climate chaos.

Government debts would be covered by the return of the Golden Rule, only this time enforced. This would allow genuine investment for our and future generations' benefit but would exclude current cost debts. This would also exclude instruments which are about investment but prove to be of very high cost. Thus a PFI for a toll bridge should work well, but PFI for hospitals, train line maintenance, and other woolly outputs do not and would be excluded by this provision. I wonder where and how student debt would fit into this?

For pensions, the Treaty would say that all would be funded in effect by the beneficiaries' earnings and employer contributions; that the pension will be defined by these contributions (and not the salary); that these sums will be invested for long-term best return and risk – that would be a collective scheme or schemes operated from a mutual or public sector body, or an aligned private fund. The pensions duty in the Treaty would be to ensure fair and effective arrangements are in place for everyone (but not to pay for them).

We need also a Golden or perhaps Titanium Rule for climate chaos, as much to discipline ourselves as government. The end game of excess carbon in the atmosphere is unknown but potentially dire. The tricky part is that we will not find out until it is too late and much of the planet could be wrecked for human habitation. Planets are not the sorts of things to run experiments with, despite human arrogance. The tricky part is that you or I might be of the school that says the science is wrong, it's not going to happen, and even if it is there's nothing we can do about it. But what if we are wrong? We'll be extinct, or most of us. The fact that you or I do not believe it does not make any difference to whether it will or will not happen. So, do we sit and wait and watch and hope and possibly then find it is too late for future generations to have the lives we have lived, or do we take the intergenerational view and say it is simply not fair to take this degree of risk with other people's lives? We should not follow the path to self-extinction.

The *Stern Report* estimates the clean-up costs to be relatively small and do not need to be that intrusive on our lifestyles. We just need an imperative to do it, and that imperative would be written into the Treaty. But of all the targets of the Treaty this is the one that will take most deliberation to resolve.

Congress for the Future

These intergenerational and fairness issues will continue as we all live longer. This is a recent phenomenon and nowhere in the structure of the governance of states is this represented. People within government are forced into concentrating on the short term and are constrained by the media and its agenda; financial markets and corporate behaviour are more short than long term. There is nowhere that has the remit and the responsibility to consider the long term and the consequences for the future. We have seen this weakness and its consequences. Somewhere and someone should be looking over the horizon. Imagine the UK with long-term thinking enshrined at the heart of governance, raising awareness, creating political space, and generating action on the biggest issues of our time. This is where the Congress for the Future would stand. Is there anyone who would not want more of the long term to be incorporated into policy and practice?

This part of the Treaty would give adequate space to the long term through the creation of a mechanism that would:

- Be convened probably annually by Parliament (with rights for members of the public to petition Parliament) as an established part of the country's governance to consider and pronounce on one or more critical long-term issues.

- Consider issues needing public (as opposed to media-led) debate and the emergence of a new consensus; in practice these are likely to be areas where either a) the government of the day feels it lacks the political space to take the action it should and would like to take, or b) there is sufficient public concern to provoke a petition and so provoke Parliament to put the matter on the agenda.

- Engage citizens (selected on a random basis) and stakeholders in informed, deliberative debate that works through differences in preferences and opinion to come to an informed view about long-term vision and direction for the UK.

- Ensure its quality by having informed high-end deliberation at its core, going beyond traditional consultation and market research in order to research, debate and resolve contentious issues.

- Generate interest and awareness across the nation through media and web-based activity.

- Influence and help to create a mandate for the policy, outcome targets and delivery.

- Have a secretariat that monitors progress, as part of the Resulture.

If such a mechanism was in place, what would we as a nation be doing about resource shortages, agriculture and its subsidies, company takeovers, funding research and development, unpicking failed monopoly privatisations, or indeed climate chaos? It would act as a counterweight to short-term 'something must be done' quick fixes. It would generate a sense of collective responsibility on issues that cannot be solved by government alone.

Now we have designed a new system for government (a world's first, so far as I am aware). The final task is *doing* it.

14

Making the Treaty Happen: Talk, Vote, Do

Hopefully, you are now convinced by the design and the concept of the Treaty. But you may be wondering if it really will happen. The usual barrage of apparently authoritative spin, mud, and disinformation might undermine our collective will once more. Is it not all too difficult? The Treaty represents bold and extensive change, and some may believe we just cannot do it.

Actually, whether it can be done (and the loud answer is yes) is the wrong question, because it *has* to be done – the present system of government is unsustainable. It only gets worse from here – the rate of problem solution is slower than the rate of problem generation. Despite some good changes, the unsolved problem backlog will only grow. We continue to slide down every league table in the world. Are we going to stick with the mess? In which case, governments will continue to fail to our substantial cost, only minor reforms will happen, and little will improve.

Are we really happy with things as they are? No we are not. Do we really want to live with this much aggravation, this much waste? The alternative really is a good life. The system of government matters to you and to me in terms of taxes, wealth, services, pensions, fairness – and even, according to some recent research, to happiness. Quality of government counts towards the strength and future of our economy. It's a hyper-competitive world out there.

Do we fear the change and fear losing out? We must be mad – we lose out now in a big way. Will it be all too risky? What is there to lose? What is the risk? It's risky not to do it. Will I miss my prejudices? No, they just belittle us. Will this take effort? Yes, a lot, of course, but worthwhile work with a big prize at the end.

Should anyone in power object to this design for successful government, then ask them what their alternative is. The existing semi-shambles is not an option. It is unacceptable simply to seek holes in this Treaty. It is far far better than what we have. So a better Treaty must accompany any objection. Those in power have either to adopt this proposal or produce a better one, quickly.

How do we get from government today to the government of tomorrow? Let's see what we have to do to get the Treaty operational. In practical terms it's Talk, Vote, Do. (To be clear, the Treaty is to be adopted as much for the governments of Wales, Scotland and the EU, as for Westminster.)

Talk

The first step is to talk about it, widely, everyone, and not to do this like the recent fiasco to elect police commissioners. These were introduced to restore a drop of local accountability of police forces. Such direct election of public officials is common in many countries, but not the UK. We have neither history nor understanding through long usage of these mechanisms. Very little went into informing people of this form of governance, how it works, and why it's important for the quality of policing. No deliberation, no understanding, and few people therefore voted in their election. Any major change takes public engagement.

By contrast, we will all need to understand what problems the Treaty is addressing and the solutions it is proposing. This takes proper deliberation, a fancy word for talking and thinking alongside solid information and our own views to get to a good conclusion. This is the opportunity on a very wide scale to learn about, test, prod, discuss, interrogate, discuss again, and propose change to the Treaty. For such a major and extensive change, this would take several bites such that, when everyone has sufficient understanding, the vote on the Treaty can be conducted from a foundation of knowledge.

During deliberation a constitutional convention (see below) would sit both to make choices as to thresholds for future change of each clause – from full two-thirds referendum to parliamentary simple majority – and to avoid 'paralysis of the articles' through requiring unanimous state approval, and translate into constitution-speak that which is needed in the subsequent legislation.

During the period of deliberation its costs would be estimated in accordance with the policy tests of the Treaty. What *will* it cost? At this stage I know for certain it will be far, far less than it will save. The cost is mainly in determination and ambition. Much of it comes in redirecting costs and resources to effective work. The main cost will be in running the Resulture – but even here much of this will come from focusing existing public expenditure.

Also during deliberation, the delivery test will be applied as to how to put the Treaty into action – transition planning, order of implementation, resources. Some parts will not take long; but building the full Resulture will. This will take determination and collective leadership of a high order. Schooling all the policymakers in the new method will take time too. A balance will be needed between accurate vetting and overloading the voters. Building real local government will also take time, but the early results will give momentum to the change. And as we all learn more about what is working from government and what is not, what to reform and what to abandon, so we will feel the benefits. Once those are apparent we can say this: It is an attainable objective in politics that unless the government is world class, they will not be re-elected.

Vote

After full deliberation, other kinds of votes come in – like votes for a new way of running government. Voting is not just about a party for government but about new rules and new disciplines for governments. The Treaty would be voted into effect at a national referendum, and put into constitutional law when passed. Once the house of good government is up and running we can get back to party voting, confident that we are electing politicians to a functioning system.

Right, so when will this happen? Let's have a look at what experience tells us. France is a recent example of successful change. Proposed in Nicolas Sarkozy's manifesto during the presidential election of 2007, a bill to modernise and rebalance its institutions of government was passed by the National Assembly in 2008. The bill set out a two-term limit of five years each for presidents, gave Parliament a veto over some presidential appointments, ended government control over Parliament's committee system, allowed

Parliament to set its own agenda, and ended the president's right of collective pardon. The most contentious part was the plan to allow the president to address Parliament, opening up the possibility of an annual US State of the Union-style address. This had not been permitted since 1875, in an attempt to keep the executive and legislative branches separate.

Thus, the new Sarkozy government arrived, had seen beforehand weaknesses in its organisation, and developed proposals for its manifesto. On election, these went to an expert committee composed primarily of constitutional jurists and political personalities with legal competence, presided over by a former prime minister. Following three months of work, it submitted its report to the president. The changes followed.

The same early action was true of the new British government in 1997 when on its first day in office it gave the Monetary Policy Committee of the Bank of England responsibility to set interest rates, to depoliticise this economic decision. Quickly it also devolved government to Scotland, Wales, and London; established a Human Rights Act (a rather belated update of Magna Carta); and introduced what proved to be a curate's egg of a Freedom of Information Act.

The new coalition government in 2010 reformed the parliamentary committee system (although these are still nowhere near as effective as their US counterparts in the Senate), held a referendum on a new voting system called AV+ (which fell), switched the term of government from a maximum to a fixed five years (as I've said, it should have been four), introduced the Civil Service Redundancy Act, and perhaps, most significantly in the long run, opened up much expenditure data to the public.

The point here is that changes in the deployment of power invariably come from *new* governments. Old governments get used to the existing rules. As power seduces, these folk with high control needs will not give it away willingly – despite improvements to the machinery of government being in their longer-term interests.

So, the Treaty is a day-one issue for a new government.

But here comes the catch-22. Unlike those countries where the public can call a referendum if sufficient numbers sign a petition, we are dependent on the Houses of Parliament to do so, and on the Welsh and Scottish governments. How do we sort this out?

Tricky. How many politicians really want to create and run a world-class government? And how many just want to be in power? Who has the courage to give this its political leadership? Where are our visionary politicians? We are not over-endowed with them, particularly once they taste power. Improving the system of government is the point where ego confronts democracy, where the psychology of the leaders entangles the needs of the people, and where the constitution should mediate between the two. The Treaty addresses all of this – but first it needs to be in place in order to do it.

From time to time throughout history, the people have had to push back against the powerful who dominate decision taking and wealth distribution. Good versus evil is an age-old battle. This is one of those times. We must demand far higher standards of government and we must demand that government does much more for the people and much less for the rich and powerful. Power has to be redistributed, and as a result super-wealth too. This will take much public pressure.

Everyone who wants the Treaty has a role in generating this leadership. Politicians respond to public opinion – this is part of the job description. The more you and I raise our dissatisfaction with the status quo of government and the prospect of the Treaty, the more political parties will respond. Let's get agitating. The call is to revolt – not in the streets but in the paraplegic chambers and offices of government.

The history of change management demonstrates it takes the 'burning platform' to get an organisation's people to shift. Without the licking flames, we all tend to stick where we are rather than risk the unknown. Life is full of power structures reinforcing the existing. 'Things are all right as they are' was fed to the confused AV voters, and they took the bait.

We can expect existing players in the current dysfunctional system whose livelihoods depend on it to raise objections and seek to undermine the Treaty. Not only the established parties and politicians, but some senior civil servants, some public sector managements, some political journalists and presenters, some news-media owners, some think tanks, some academics, lobbyists, and all of those businesses that benefit from or operate in the set-up as it is. But there is a lot of dissatisfaction around to force the referendum. There's the non-voters and the other party voters in the Lib Dems, UKIP, BNP, and the Greens. This may appear an unexpected grouping, but there's a common interest, first to be fairly and properly represented, and second to improve government radically. There are the several pro-democracy NGOs that have campaigned for a decent constitution for decades. There are the online pressure groups like Avaaz and 38 Degrees whose effect is proving to be strong. There's anyone who wants a far better return from their taxes, fairer taxes, or lower taxes. There are all of those who have also followed a different journey in think tanks, philosophical societies, universities, and similar spaces. These different thinkers are found elsewhere too – financial journalists, celebrity chefs, sports coaches, political commentators, and social reformers. There's all of the staff and management in the public sector who have seen waste, wrong decisions, poor services. And there's all of the staff and management in those big companies who have seen them get away with the commercial equivalent of murder. This looks like a majority. And a political movement.

At the end of the day, it is down to us whether we push hard enough, whether we persist, whether we buy sops or not. Raise the Treaty, and keep raising it – with friends, neighbours, MPs, on radio, television, online, in newspapers. Sign every petition. Review this book and the Treaty online. Put it on social media. Heckle. Ask people in government if they are scared of something this good, and if they are up to its demands. Use shame.

At the same time, some of us will have opportunities to light fires along the way. For students and lecturers, constitutional conversations can be very different from those conducted today. Elected councillors can probe local authority decision-makers using the ten tests. That should produce some fun answers. Executive mayors can establish small-scale independent Resultures, and insert some cutting edge into running a city. Local and national journalists can craft with greater incision about some tough-to-solve issues. And I very much look forward to our pugilist interviewers asking the minister sixteen times how his policy of the day is to be put into practice successfully. Prove it. Think tanks can present all of their policy proposals ready-vetted. Select Committees can choose only to accept data on the results of a government programme from wholly independent sources, otherwise it is inadmissible. The

House of Lords can go quite a long way and refuse any further political appointments. But that's unconstitutional, some might say. Ah, but an uncodified constitution cuts both ways – if the Lords decides it has control over appointments, then it does; after all, it is only the Civil Service that has previously claimed the opposite.

All of this is movement in the right direction. Tick. But the whole system has to be changed, and this means a binding referendum. Therefore if the existing parties do not adopt the Treaty in their manifestos, the Treaty Party will have to be formed. The Treaty Party would have as its manifesto putting the Treaty to deliberation, referendum, and to enact it. This would take two years, and thus the party would seek a mandate just for this period. It would propose no reforms or policies other than to run things such as they are as well as can be expected. As the most significant aspect of the day-to-day is the economy, an experienced Chancellor of the Exchequer and advisers would be part of the Treaty Party's government. At the end of the two years, and when the Treaty was starting to operate, a new election would be called – under PR of course, and regular parties would resume power in a system that now functioned. One way or another, the Treaty will happen.

Do

In a sense the Treaty is radical, truly modern and designed for its job – but only by comparison with what exists. In terms of the job it's there to do, it's simply appropriate. We could labour on with the equivalent of my hedge trimmer – old, mechanically weak, poorly designed for the job, but works sometimes, so I cling on to the notion that a new one, fit for purpose, is an extravagance. It's not – it's just good sense. So let's treat ourselves to a quality hedge trimmer, in this case a new system of government. Let's cut the crap, end the bollocks, and breathe life into our body politic.

And, politicians, just imagine how much more enjoyable it will be to work in something that delivers. That you get thanked far more often than blamed – a reverse of the current climate. That you get known for your expertise. That you go to work not dog tired from an endless round of meetings, photo shoots, and late-night red boxes, your main refuge high-class spin to convince yourself as much as the public that something worthwhile has occurred; but with an ambitious step, a clear role, an abiding sense of achievement, and bags of integrity.

To use our earlier analogy, will UK government follow the example of its now extinct car industry, or take the lead? We are at a similar place with government, both in the sense that analysis provides insight and common factors for success, and that the competitive performance of our nation's governments will make a significant difference to the quality of our lives. Those with renaissance government will become more attractive places to live, particularly for the pioneers. Is it a coincidence that Switzerland, with the top current constitution, is also the best place to live (ranked by the Economist Intelligence Unit) while the UK is at number 27?

The analysis in this book has been organisational. Its proposals are constitutional. The changes will be political. Political parties, politics, and politicians in the right places doing the right things are vital, alongside the humility to seek answers from around the world. But, to succeed, they need the right system.

I used to believe in politics and political parties as the answer to our ills. I used to believe government is government, a fixture except at the margin. I used to believe better democracy on its own would sort out most things. With life's experiences come wisdom, disabusement, and self-belief. Having embarked on this analysis of why governments fail and how to make them succeed, I now know what will sort it. But as Roosevelt famously said when the US seemed trapped in an inescapable economic depression, the 'only thing we have to fear is fear itself'. It was a clever way of changing attitudes from resignation to fight. To change our lives will take much, much less than this, and absolutely nothing like the effort we displayed in the Second World War.

We have to open our minds to what is possible. We have to weigh up the pros and cons of doing something. We have to be sufficiently motivated to rouse ourselves into action. We have to see the future and want it. (And not want what we get now.) Surely the time has come. What's stopping us? Only our own inertia.

So let's do it. Let's be the generation that really did make a difference, that got a grip, that produced world-class governments, that the history books record as initiating one of the great turning points. Then let's enjoy the fruits and the renaissance of our country. It's a chance we cannot afford to miss.

Acknowledgements

The first acknowledgement must go to the hundreds of interviewees contributing to this book, all conducted on the anonymous and confidential basis that produce most insight and truth – with ministers, lords, political advisers, MPs, researchers, managers, constitutional experts, political theorists, charity staff, office dwellers, actuaries, journalists, consultants, judges, civil servants, engineers, dentists, doctors, nurses, soldiers, social workers, teachers, radio producers, business executives, gardeners, sound engineers, DJs, farmers, paint sprayers, small-business owners, investors, bankers, pensioners, benefit recipients, facilitators, citizens, consumers, parents and children. Their knowledge, experiences and insights have been invaluable. I can't thank them by name but they know who they are.

Second are the many extraordinary thinkers and writers in the fields of organisation, psychology, democracy, political theory, and constitutional matters. The bibliography lists my main inspirers.

Third is my editor David Milner, without whose grasp of what it was that my original swirling manuscript was trying to say, this digestible book would never have been published. He is a master of his profession.

Fourth are most of my friends who have at one time or another come up with critiques of the book – Tom Parker, Linda Thomas, James Park, Jeremy Monroe – or been advisers on the digital world of blogging, tweeting, infographics, and publishing.

Finally my partner/wife – depending on the acceptability of each term to you. Lindsey has been a constant sounding board, constructive critic, comforter, and expert, and my children – Edison, Odette, Chloe, Adam, and Dan – all keep me young, disabused as to my own powers, and provide much knowledge from their own experiences.

Bibliography

Al-Khalili, Jim (2010) *The Secret Life of Chaos*, BBC Television

Beer, Stafford (1972) *Brain of the Firm*, Allen Lane

Bones, Christopher (2011) *The Cult of the Leader: A Manifesto for More Authentic Business*, John Wiley & Sons

Bridges, Willima (2000) *The Character of Organisations: Using Personality Type In Organisational Development*, Davies-Black Publishing

Church, Clive H. (2004) *The Politics and Government of Switzerland*, Palgrave Macmillan

Collins, Jim (2001) *Good To Great: Why Some Companies Make the Leap … and Others Don't*, Random House Business Books

Crick, Bernard (2002) *Democracy: A Very Short Introduction*, Oxford University Press

Crouch, Colin (2000), *Coping with Post-Democracy*, Fabian Society

de Toqueville, Alexis (1998 edition abridged by Patrick Renshaw, original 1835, 1840) *Democracy In America*, Wordsworth Classics

Dixon, Norman (1976) *On the Psychology of Military Incompetence*, Random House

Dixon, Norman (1982) 'Report on Ministry of Defence rejection of Pilot Testing', *New Statesman*

Drucker, Peter (Number 14, Winter 1969) *The Sickness of Government*, The Public Interest

Drucker, Peter (1973) *Management: Tasks, Responsibilities, Practices* HarperCollins

Fabian Society *Europe's Left In Crisis : How The Next Left Can Respond*

Foresight (2007) 'Tackling Obesities: Future Choices – Obesity Systems Atlas', Government Office for Science

Friedman, Mark (2005) *Trying Hard Is Not Good Enough: How to Produce Measurable Improvements for Customers and Communities*, Fiscal Policy Studies Institute

Galbraith, John Kenneth (1954) *The Great Crash 1929*, Penguin

Galbraith, John Kenneth (2004) *The Economics of Innocent Fraud*, Penguin Books

Gardner, Howard (2006*) Changing Minds – The Art and Science of Changing Our Own and Other People's Minds* Harvard Business School Press

Goldacre, Ben, and Torgeson, David (2012) *Test, Learn, Adapt: Developing Public Policy with Randomised Controlled Trials*, Cabinet Office

Handy, Charles (1990) *Inside Organisations: Twenty-one Ideas For Managers*, Penguin Books

Handy, Charles (1994) *The Empty Raincoat: Making Sense of the Future*, Arrow Business Books

Hayek, F. A. (1960) *The Constitution of Liberty*, Routledge

Hennessy, Peter (2012) *Distilling the Frenzy: Writing The History of One's Own Times*, Biteback Publishing

James, Oliver (2002) *They F*** You Up*, Bloomsbury

Keynes, John Maynard (1936) *The General Theory of Employment, Interest, and Money*, Harcourt Brace

Levitt, Steven D., and Dubner, Stephen J. (2006) *Freakonomics: A Rogue Economist Explores the Hidden Side of Everything*, Allen Lane

Mair, Peter (2013) *Ruling The Void: The Hollowing Of Western Democracy*, Verso

Mosley, Ivo (2013) *In The Name of the People*, Imprint Academic

Murray, H. A. (1938) *Explorations In Personality*, Oxford University Press

Nicholson, Max (1967) *The System – The Misgovernment of Modern Britain*, Hodder & Stoughton

Park, James (2013) *Detoxifying School Accountability: The case for multi-perspective inspection*, Demos

Peck, M. Scott (1978) *The Road Less Travelled*, Random House

Pitt-Watson, David (2010), *Tomorrow's Investor: Building the Consensus for a People's Pension in Britain*, Royal Society for the Arts

Pollitt, Christopher, and Bouckaert, Geert (2011) *Public Management Reform: A Comparative Analysis – New Public Management*, Oxford University Press

Porter, Michael E. (1990) *The Competitive Advantage of Nations*, The Free Press

Romanow, Roy J. (2002) *Building on Values: The Future of Health Care in Canada*, Government of Canada Publications

Rose, Chris (2011) *What Makes People Tick: The Three Hidden Worlds of Settlers, Prospectors And Pioneers*, Matador

Russell, Meg (2013) *The Contemporary House of Lords: Westminster Bicameralism Revived*, Oxford University Press

Schumpeter, Joseph (1976) *Capitalism, Socialism and Democracy*, George Allen and Unwin

Senge, Peter (1990) *The Fifth Discipline: The Art and Practice of the Learning Organization*, Random House

Stoker, Gerry (2006) *Why Politics Matters: Making Democracy Work*, Palgrave Macmillan

Strauss, Norman (2009) http://normanstrauss.wordpress.com/tag/norman-strauss/

Straw, Ed (1998) *Relative Values: Support for Relationships and Parenting*, Demos

Straw, Ed (2004) *The Dead Generalist: Reforming the Civil Service and the Public Services*, Demos

Straw, Ed (ed. Sir Douglas Hague and Marshall Young) (2007) *Templeton Applied*, Oxford Strategic Leadership Programme 1982–2007

Webb, Paul (2000) *The Modern British Party System*, SAGE Publications

Wiegmann, D., and Shappell, S. (2001) *A Human Error Analysis of Commercial Aviation Accidents Using the Human Factors Analysis and Classification System*, US Office of Aviation Medicine

★

Institutes, think tanks, and research organisations: Institute for Government, IPPR, Demos, Reform, National Audit Office, Policy Exchange, Public Services Trust, Progress, Fabian Society, Social Market Foundation, Institute of Fiscal Studies, Smith Institute, World Economic Forum